MIN YŎNG-HWAN

故閔忠正公泳煥節竹
光武十年七月十五日
大韓俱樂部應需
菊田寫真館謹寫

Min Yŏng-hwan in a military uniform of the Taehan period (1897–1910). In the background is the "blood bamboo" that grew in the room where Min's blood-stained clothes were kept. The photograph is dated the 15th day of the 7th month of the 10th year of Kwangmu (1906). Photo courtesy of the Korea University Museum, Seoul.

HAWAI'I STUDIES ON KOREA

MIN YŎNG-HWAN

A Political Biography

MICHAEL FINCH

University of Hawai'i Press, Honolulu
and
Center for Korean Studies, University of Hawai'i

© 2002 University of Hawai'i Press

Printed in the United States of America

07 06 05 04 03 02   6 5 4 3 2 1

Library of Congress Cataloging-in-Publication Data

Finch, Michael.
　　Min Yŏng-hwan : a political biography / Michael Finch.
　　　　p.　cm.—(Hawai'i studies on Korea)
　　Includes bibliographical references and index.
　　ISBN 0-8248-2520-9 (cloth : alk. paper)
　　　1. Min, Yŏng-hwan, 1861–1905.　2. Statesmen—Korea—
Biography.　3. Korea—Politics and government—1864–1910.
I. Title.　II. Series.
DS 915.5.M5 F56　2002
951.9'02'092—dc21
　[B]　　　　　　　　　　　　　　　　　2002018786

 The Center for Korean Studies was established
in 1972 to coordinate and develop resources for
the study of Korea at the University of Hawai'i.
Reflecting the diversity of the academic disciplines
represented by affiliated members of the university
faculty, the Center seeks especially to promote interdisciplinary and
intercultural studies. Hawai'i Studies on Korea, published jointly by
the Center and the University of Hawai'i Press, offers a forum for
research in the social sciences and humanities pertaining to Korea
and its people.

University of Hawai'i Press books are printed on acid-free paper and
meet the guidelines for permanence and durability of the Council
on Library Resources.

Designed by Integrated Composition Systems
Printed by The Maple-Vail Book Manufacturing Group

HAWAI'I STUDIES ON KOREA

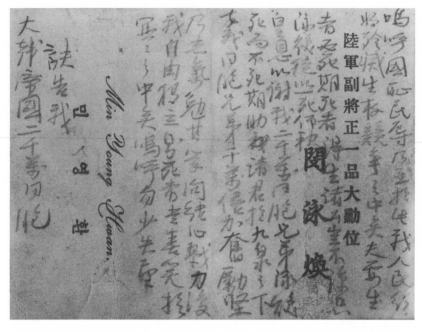

Min Yŏng-hwan's last testament written on his calling card shortly before his death on 30 November 1905. Photo courtesy of the Korea University Museum, Seoul.

Contents

Note on the Romanization Systems Used in This Work

All Korean, Chinese, and Japanese words have been romanized according to the McCune-Reischauer, pinyin, and Hepburn systems respectively. Alternative romanizations for both Korean and Chinese words may be found in many of the quotations, which have been left unaltered. If any of these words are liable to lead to confusion, however, the standard romanization according to the systems mentioned above has been included in square brackets after the word concerned.

伊顏不過一整農西佃由將显修功課黍瓦器

家斡隆啟用清朝埋百工

Min Yŏng-hwan in official Chosŏn court attire. The photograph was taken in St. Petersburg during Min's mission to Russia in 1896. Photo courtesy of the Korea University Museum, Seoul.

Acknowledgments

Upon completion of this biographical study of Min Yŏng-hwan, I would like to express my sincerest appreciation to all those who have assisted me along the way. In particular I would like to thank my former supervisor at the Oriental Instititute at the University of Oxford, Dr. James B. Lewis, for his sound guidance and encouragement throughout the four years that I was a research student there.

At that time I was also fortunate to have received astute criticism and advice from Professor J. A. A. Stockwin, Dr. David Faure, and Dr. Ann Waswo. During a research fellowship in Seoul in 1997, I was also given very timely assistance by Professor Lew Young Ick and Professor Yi T'ae-jin, who generously found time for me in the midst of their busy schedules.

I am most grateful to Professor Martina Deuchler and Dr. James Hoare for their meticulous examination of this work in an earlier version as a doctoral dissertation and to the three anonymous readers at the Center for Korean Studies at the University of Hawai'i for their sound advice and helpful comments. In addition I would like to acknowledge the kind assistance of Professor Choe Kwang Sik, the director of Korea University Museum, and Mr. Kim Woo Lim, its chief curator, in providing the illustrations for this book. I would also like to thank my editors at University of Hawai'i Press, Patricia Crosby and Ann Ludeman, and Joanne Sandstrom, copyeditor, for their care and skill in bringing this book to publication. Any remaining shortcomings that it may have are entirely my own responsibility.

During my time as a research student at Oxford, I was a grateful recipient of a Korea Foundation Scholarship in Korean Studies from 1995 to 1997, an Anglo-Korean Society Bursary in 1995, a three-month Korea Foundation Fellowship for Korean Studies in Seoul in 1997, and from 1997 to 1998, a Daesan Foundation Grant for Korean Studies Overseas. I would like to express my gratitude to these three organisations for their generous support of my work.

Being married with children, however, has meant that I could never have completed the research required for this book without considerable additional support from my parents, for which I would like to thank them from the bottom of my heart.

Finally, I must also thank my wife, Kumbin, and our children, Daniel, Sarah, Edward, and Alastair, for the many ways in which they have encouraged and inspired me during the years that this book has been in the making.

INTRODUCTION

The original motivation behind this biographical study of the late Chosŏn official Min Yŏng-hwan came from an interest in Min's aunt Queen Myŏngsŏng (Queen Min), the consort of King Kojong. Even a casual visitor to Seoul is likely to visit Kyŏngbok Palace and come across the site of her miserable death on 8 October 1895. In the precincts of this royal palace she was brutally murdered by a band of Japanese *sōshi*[1] and their Korean collaborators under the direction of the Japanese minister in Seoul, Miura Gorō. Her violent death under cover of darkness at the hands of a foreign aggressor with the collaboration of her own people remains a potent symbol of Korea's own loss of sovereignty, which occurred just a decade after her death with the signing of the Ŭlsa Treaty of Protection (Ŭlsa poho choyak) in 1905.

Queen Myŏngsŏng, however, has been an ambivalent figure in Korean historiography. Although her contemporaries and subsequent generations of Koreans have expressed outrage at her assassination at the hands of the Japanese, the queen herself has generally been viewed as a reactionary force in the politics of the period. In particular, she has been blamed for obstructing the reform programs of members of the Enlightenment party (Kaehwadang) such as Kim Ok-kyun and Pak Yŏng-hyo. Furthermore, according to her critics, she manipulated her weak husband, King Kojong, ensuring that the reins of power were firmly held by leading members of the Min clan such as Min Yŏng-hwan's paternal uncle Min Sŭng-ho and his own father, Min Kyŏm-ho. The queen was also accused by the contemporary diarist Hwang Hyŏn of being involved in various violent intrigues in the court, including the death of Wanhwagun,

Kojong's son by a concubine, who threatened the position of her own son as crown prince.[2]

The ambivalent attitudes of Korean historians to Queen Myŏngsŏng, therefore, appear to have their origins in the queen's own Machiavellian struggle for survival within the intrigues of the Korean court, which for the first ten years of her husband's reign was dominated by her hostile father-in-law, the Taewŏn'-gun. Such attitudes may also be based on the supposed incompatibility of strong women with Confucian traditions or in the undoubted fact that members of the Min clan who held official posts were viewed by their contemporary critics as being irredeemably corrupt. Furthermore, as a staunch opponent of Japanese policy in Korea until her death, Queen Myŏngsŏng also received biased treatment from Japanese historians who sought to belittle her: for example, by referring to her by the informal term "Min *bi*" rather than by her posthumous title Myŏngsŏng.

Western contemporary observers of the Korean scene who met Queen Myŏngsŏng, however, appear to be in agreement that she was a woman of outstanding intelligence and ability. As women were more freely, although not exclusively, permitted to have interviews with the queen in person, it is to the accounts of Western women in Seoul that we must mainly look for an idea of the impression that she made on the foreign community. The following is an account of the queen by her personal physician, the missionary nurse Annie Ellers Bunker:

> To me the face of the Queen, especially when she smiles, is full of beauty. She is a superior woman and she impressed one as having a strong will and great force of character, with much kindliness of heart. I have always received the kindest words and treatment from her and I have much admiration and respect for her.[3]

This account of the queen is corroborated in every respect by other accounts of personal interviews by Lillias Horton Underwood, the wife of one of the most prominent American missionaries in Seoul, Horace G. Underwood, and Isabella Bird Bishop, an intrepid British travel writer, who made four visits to Korea between 1894 and 1897.[4]

In addition to these accounts by Westerners is an account by a contemporary Korean observer of the political scene in Seoul, Yun Ch'i-ho. Yun, as a fringe member of the reform party, was a severe critic of the Korean court and members of the Min clan in particular, including the queen. Nevertheless, he sympathetically recorded in his diary an account of the queen related to him by her nephew Min Yŏng-hwan himself:

She was a wonderful woman. Mr. Min told me that ever since the violent death
of her brother about twenty years ago, she had not been able to sleep in the night.[5]
When she rose in the morning about eleven, after a rest of a few hours, her hours
were taken up in reading and writing private letters, in examining all state papers, in transacting all the state business, from the appointment of a "seuri" [*sŏri*]
or a clerk to the negotiations of foreign treaties. She could not only read the Chinese classics but knew by heart their principal passages. She was well up in the
Corean and Chinese histories.[6]

The fact remains, however, that in Korean historiography the queen and almost all the members of the Min clan are generally portrayed in a poor light
as conservatives bound to the outmoded forms of Confucianism, subservient
to the Qing, and above all grasping and selfish in office. Some Korean historians, however, have argued that this negative perception of Queen Myŏngsŏng
and the Min clan is largely a result of the distortions imposed on Korean history by Japanese historians during the colonial period. Dalchoong Kim, for example, points to the pre-1945 Japanese historians of Korea such as Kikuchi Kenjō
and Okudaira Takehirō as blaming the failure of Korea to modernize on "the
backward, egocentric, reactionary, and factional nature of Korean political leadership, in particular of the Min clan and their political associates."[7]

Reformers such as Kim Ok-kyun, Pak Yŏng-hyo, and Sŏ Chae-p'il, on the
other hand, have generally received more sympathetic treatment at the hands
of Korean and American historians despite the brutality and political folly of
their coup of 4 December 1884 *(Kapsin chŏngbyŏn)*. This venture, far from fur-
thering the cause of reform in Korea, merely provided the excuse for increased
interference in Korea's domestic and foreign affairs by both China and Japan,
while at the same time presenting an unfavorable image of a politically volatile
Korea to influential Western observers in the Far East. The British minister in
Beijing, Sir Harry Parkes, for example, was personally acquainted with Kim
Ok-kyun and appears to have had a relatively favorable view of him and other
members of the reform party. On hearing news of the coup, however, he commented, "What a bloody villain Kim Ok Kiun [*sic*] must be! . . . He certainly
ought to be brought to the gallows."[8]

The analysis of the late-nineteenth-century political scene by Japanese historians during the colonial period tended to emphasize its polarization into a
pro-Chinese group, the Min clan and its associates, and a progressive group
that drew its inspiration from the example of the Meiji Restoration in Japan.
This group was centered on Kim Ok-kyun, Pak Yŏng-hyo, Sŏ Chae-p'il, and
other members of the Kaehwadang. According to Dalchoong Kim, "The qual-

ity of Korean political leadership was judged simply on whether it was cooperative toward Japan and held political objectives identical with Japan's."[9] One
of the main purposes of this study, therefore, is to correct the distortion of such
a polarized interpretation and to show that the political scene in late Chosŏn
Korea should not be viewed as a simple dichotomy of progressive reformers
pitted against conservative reactionaries.

Regardless of the accuracy of the impression that the royal in-laws were irredeemably tainted by corruption, Min Yŏng-hwan, the subject of this biographical study, appears to have been an exception in that both Koreans and
Westerners alike considered him to be a man of integrity. Furthermore, despite
being a powerful noble with the same vested interests as other members of the
Min clan, he was, nevertheless, deeply concerned about the modernization and
reform of his country. An impartial and unsentimental observer of the late
Chosŏn court, the American adviser William Franklin Sands, testifies to this
view. In *Undiplomatic Memories,* his candid account of his experiences in Korea in the years immediately preceding the Ŭlsa Treaty of Protection, Sands
wrote,

> In addition to my staff there were several men in the palace who were real friends.
> Min Yong Whan [*sic*], Min Sang Ho and their cousin Prince Min Yong Ki all
> members of the late queen's clan, had the interests of Korea very much at heart.
> The two former had lived abroad; all three were powerful nobles at home. . . .
> Min Yong Whan . . . is honoured by Koreans as a great martyr and patriot.[10]

In addition, evidence of Min's integrity in the eyes of his Korean contemporaries is provided by Chŏng Kyo, a leading figure in the Independence Club
(Tongnip hyŏphoe), who memorialized King Kojong to appoint Min to the
post of minister of military affairs *(kunbu taesin)* and chief of police *(kyŏngmusa)* because Min was considered to be the only official in the Chosŏn administration, apart from his political ally Han Kyu-sŏl, whom the Korean people
trusted.[11] Further evidence of the general support that Min received from the
Independence Club, the most important political force outside the Chosŏn
court in the late 1890s, may be seen by the fact that he received the second most
votes after his relative Min Yŏng-jun, considered to be the most powerful member of the Min clan, among the eleven officials, including "progressives" such
as Yun Ch'i-ho and Sŏ Chae-p'il, elected and proposed by the Independence
Club to be Kojong's policy advisers in December 1898.[12]

Min Yŏng-hwan's reputation as an open-minded and honest official also
extended to members of the foreign diplomatic community in Seoul. In a communication with the American secretary of state dated 13 October 1898, Ho-

race N. Allen, the American minister to Seoul, noted with approval the appointment of Min to the Korean cabinet, referring to him as "Min Yung Whan ('The Good Min')."[13] More recently an American historian of Korea, Gregory Henderson, described Min in the following glowing terms: "Prince Min Yŏnghwan, handsome member of the most powerful of private clans, cousin of the king and nephew of the queen, minister, general, well-educated, liberal of mind, uncorruptible, and observer of the West and its ways, lacked none of the class, personal, or official attributes of Korean leadership."[14]

Fortunately, unlike Queen Myŏngsŏng, who left no known written records, Min Yŏng-hwan left behind a collection of writings after his death that provide a unique insight into the politics and diplomacy of the late Chosŏn court. Compiled in a single volume from original manuscripts in the possession of Min's grandson, Min Pyŏng-gi,[15] by the Kuksa p'yŏnch'an wiwŏnhoe (National history compilation committee) under the title *Min Ch'ungjŏnggong yugo* (The posthumous works of Prince Min), the collection comprises five sections *(kwŏn)*. The first four sections are all written in classical Chinese, the written language used almost exclusively by educated Koreans until the end of the nineteenth century.

Several of the works in the final section, however, are written in a mixed script of the native Korean alphabet *(han'gŭl)* and Chinese characters. With the rise of nationalist sentiments in Korea, the use of *han'gŭl* was actively promoted by reformers and gained widespread acceptance as a result of its use in Korea's first popular vernacular newspaper, the *Tongnip sinmun* (Independent). Its editors, Sŏ Chae-p'il and then Yun Ch'i-ho, chose to use *han'gŭl* exclusively in the Korean-language edition of their newspaper as a deliberate expression of Korea's independence from China and its equality of status as a sovereign nation with its other neighbors, Russia and Japan.

The first section of *Min Ch'ungjŏnggong yugo* comprises a collection of memorials, under the heading *Soch'a* (Memorials), that Min Yŏng-hwan presented to the throne from the outset of his official career in 1877 until shortly before his death in 1905. This collection provides important insights into the course of Min's political career and includes several significant memorials, most notably his early indictments of official corruption in the conduct of the civil service examinations *(kwagŏ)* and his last impassioned protests against the Ŭlsa Treaty of Protection. The majority of these memorials, however, are Min's polite refusals to accept official appointments or his repeated requests to be relieved from his official duties, reflecting his cautious approach to the byzantine politics of the late Chosŏn court.

The second section, *Ch'ŏnilch'aek* (One policy in a thousand), an extensive policy essay written circa June 1894, makes many recommendations for social, political, and military reform within a traditional Confucian framework and modeled on the policies of early Chinese dynasties. This essay appears to have been incorrectly dated in Korean historiography and, as will be shown, was written well before Min's experiences of the West in 1896 and 1897. This fact undoubtedly accounts for the conservative character of the essay, which nevertheless clearly shows Min's indignation at the apparent indifference of so many of his fellow officials at the Korean court toward the fate of their nation. It could also be argued that Min's extensive use of Chinese precedents for his reform proposals does not necessarily reflect an innate conservatism, but simply a desire to make the proposals more acceptable to the Chosŏn court, steeped as it was in neo-Confucian ideology and a traditional reverence for China. *Ch'ŏnilch'aek* is an important document in the study of this period both for the light it casts on the problems that the Chosŏn administration faced at home and abroad and also for the insights it provides into the response to such problems of an important figure in the politically dominant Min clan.

The third section, *Haech'ŏn ch'ubŏm* (Sea, sky, autumn voyage), is a daily record of Min's diplomatic mission to Russia in 1896, ostensibly to attend the coronation of Tsar Nicholas II. In fact, this visit was the occasion of critical Russo-Korean negotiations that resulted in the Min-Lobanov Agreement of 1896, which temporarily helped to stem the tide of increasing Japanese influence on the peninsula in the wake of Japan's victory over China in the Sino-Japanese War (1894–1895). The diary also provides a daily record of the mission's journey around the world from Inch'ŏn to Moscow via China, Japan, Canada, the United States, Great Britain, and Europe and from Moscow back to Korea via Siberia. In addition, it contains detailed accounts of the modern institutions and technology that Min and his party encountered on their travels and during their sojourns in Moscow and St. Petersburg. Min's record is also valuable for the unique insights that it provides into the attitude of the Chosŏn administration toward the Korean immigrant community in the Russian Far East, which Min encountered on his return journey. In conclusion, *Haech'ŏn ch'ubŏm* is a seminal document for the study of late Chosŏn's diplomatic relations with Russia and Europe.

On this pioneering diplomatic mission to Russia, Min was also accompanied by the well-known Korean Protestant intellectual Yun Ch'i-ho. Yun's personal record of this journey in the fourth volume of *Yun Ch'i-ho ilgi* (Diary of Yun Ch'i-ho) also provides invaluable, additional information about Min's negotiations with the Russian foreign minister, Prince Alekseii B. Lobanov-Rostovsky, and the minister of finance, Sergei I. Witte. Furthermore, Yun's franker account fills in many details of the daily life of the members of the mission that are absent from the more official record, *Haech'ŏn ch'ubŏm*.

The fourth section of Min's collected works, *Sagu sokch'o* (Additional notes of an envoy to Europe), is a daily record of his second mission to the West to attend the Diamond Jubilee of Queen Victoria's coronation in London in June 1897 and to take up his post as minister plenipotentiary to Chosŏn's six treaty partners in Europe—Russia, Great Britain, France, Germany, Austria, and Italy. As the record of the first official Korean diplomatic mission to the United Kingdom, this diary is of unique importance in the study of the history of Anglo-Korean relations.

For political reasons, however, Min abandoned his post without official permission soon after the jubilee celebrations ended. He never visited the other European capitals to which he was accredited, nor did he take up residence in St. Petersburg as he had been instructed. Instead he went to the United States, where he spent one year in Washington in self-imposed exile, only returning to Korea in 1898 after receiving a special pardon from Emperor Kojong. On his return from abroad to the newly founded Taehan Empire (Taehan cheguk; 1897–1910), Min became increasingly aligned with the progressive, reform movement in Seoul, which at that time was centered on the Independence Club. In government he took charge of the military affairs of the Taehan Empire as president of the Department of Military Affairs (Wŏnsubu), encouraged the emigration of impoverished Koreans to Hawaii as vice president of the Bureau of Emigration (Yuminwŏn), and also founded a modern technical school in Seoul, the Hŭnghwa hakkyo.

The fifth section of *Min Ch'ungjŏnggong yugo* comprises a miscellany of writings about Min Yŏng-hwan, including *Min Ch'ungjŏnggong sillok* (The veritable record of Prince Min), which provides an anonymous, contemporary account of Min's protest against the Treaty of Protection, his suicide, and his funeral. In addition, the miscellany contains other biographical records such as *Min Ch'ungjŏnggong chinch'ungnok* (A record of Prince Min's loyalty unto death), *Haengjŏk* (Biographical record), his posthumous letters *(yusŏ)* to the Korean people and the foreign diplomatic representatives in Seoul, and various articles lamenting his death published in the *Hwangsŏng sinmun* (Capital gazette) and the *Taehan maeil sinbo* (Korea daily news). Together these documents provide a vivid and at times heart-rending account not just of one man's resistance to the Japanese takeover of Korea but also of the grief of a whole nation as it lost its right to self-determination and came under the control of a colonial overlord.

Several monographs have been written on the activities of Western advisers and diplomats in Korea such as Fred Harvey Harrington's *God, Mammon, and the Japanese: Dr. Horace N. Allen and Korean-American Relations, 1884–1905*; Robert R. Swartout Jr.'s *Mandarins, Gunboats, and Power Politics: Owen Nick-*

erson Denny and the International Rivalries in Korea; and Yur-Bok Lee's *West Goes East: Paul Georg von Möllendorff and Great Power Imperialism in Late Yi Korea.* In addition two substantial studies focus on prominent Koreans of the period: Ching Young Choe's *The Rule of the Taewŏn'gun, 1864–1873: Restoration in Yi Korea;* and Harold F. Cook's *Korea's 1884 Incident: Its Background and Kim Ok-kyun's Elusive Dream.*[16]

The remaining works written in English on this period of Korean history, however, come mainly under the heading of "diplomatic history" and have tended to focus on events and institutions rather than personalities.[17] There is, therefore, a necessity for further studies aimed at gaining an understanding of the late Chosŏn political leadership and its efforts to prevent Korea's loss of independence as it was first made a Japanese protectorate in 1905 and then annexed outright in 1910.

This study examines each section of *Min Ch'ungjŏnggong yugo* together with supplementary materials from Korean and Western archival and secondary sources to create a coherent political biography of this late Chosŏn-Taehan official, Min Yŏng-hwan. Special emphasis has been placed on Min's diplomatic activities of 1896 and 1897 in Russia and Great Britain; these activities not only formed an important turning point in his own career, but also marked significant changes in late-Chosŏn foreign policy as it shifted from its traditional orientation toward China first to Russia and then finally to Great Britain and the United States. As will be seen from this study, largely as a result of Min's experiences in the West and his close contact with Western diplomats, advisers, missionaries, and their Korean associates in Seoul such as Yun Ch'i-ho and Sŏ Chae-p'il, Min was able to go beyond his neo-Confucian, conservative background to become the most important ally of modernization and reform at the Korean court.

Although Min's suicide is invariably mentioned in standard Korean histories of this period, ironically perhaps, the efforts that he made during his life for the independence of his nation have been largely overlooked. By providing a substantial portrayal of this important scholar-official, diplomat, and reformer, and the turbulent times in which he lived, this biographical study aims to provide a deeper understanding of the wide range of responses of the late Chosŏn leadership, particularly in the sphere of international diplomacy, to the dual challenges of internal stagnation and external intervention at the end of the nineteenth and beginning of the twentieth century.

1

EARLY LIFE
AND POLITICAL CAREER

The Closing Decades
of the Chosŏn Dynasty (1866–1910)

To understand the course of Min Yŏng-hwan's life, which culminated in his suicide in 1905 at the age of forty-four, it is necessary to be aware of the immense changes that were taking place in Northeast Asia during the fifty-year period from 1860 to 1910. These changes, which have been described by Martina Deuchler, Key-hiuk Kim, M. Frederick Nelson, Han-Kyo Kim, Eugene Kim, and many others, made the opening of Korea to Japan and the Western powers an apparent inevitability and ultimately resulted in Korea's loss of sovereignty and subjection to thirty-five years of Japanese colonial rule.

Until the end of the regency of the Taewŏn'gun (1864–1873), Korea still belonged to the old East Asian world order. According to Nelson, this order was essentially unequal, emphasizing moral rather than legal obligations. This was in contrast to the European view of international relations, based on such concepts as sovereignty, equality, and international law. These characteristics, Nelson argues, derived from Confucian ideology, which saw social and international relations as being extensions of family relations: that is, the essentially hierarchical relations of parents and children, and elder and younger siblings. In his pioneering study, *Korea and the Old Orders in Eastern Asia,* Nelson writes,

> Here is the basic theory of Confucian international relations. The rules which were to govern this Far Eastern family were the same natural rules, the same code

of *li,* that governed the individual family. . . . Since inequality was an essential element in the natural family, these principles were likewise projected into the international sphere.[1]

As neo-Confucian thought was adopted as the state ideology of the Chosŏn dynasty, Korea was easily assimilated into the sinocentric world order as a respectful "vassal state," becoming China's model tributary.[2] Nevertheless, there was also a strategic reality behind both the Korean acceptance of Chinese superiority and China's desire to maintain close relations with its eastern neighbor. That is to say, the politics of power and national self-interest operated within this Confucian framework in the sinic zone just as it did within the nominally Christian framework of the West.

In geopolitical terms Korea has been described as "a shield protecting the eastern flank" of the Chinese empire.[3] Furthermore, the Chinese likened the close relationship between themselves and their diminutive neighbor as being the same as that between "the lips and the teeth."[4] The development of Korean foreign policy, therefore, into one of respectful submission toward its much larger and more populous neighbor was not the policy of political and cultural servility suggested by the popular Korean term *sadaejuŭi* (flunkeyism) but rather an acceptance of geopolitical realities, resulting in a relationship that was mutually beneficial to both parties. This relationship was proven by the successful repulsion of Hideyoshi's armies from the Korean peninsula at the end of the sixteenth century by a combined Ming and Korean force. "Respecting the great" *(sadae),*[5] therefore, became the guiding principle of Chosŏn foreign policy toward China throughout the five hundred years of its existence until it was forced out of that relationship by Japan and the Western powers at the end of the nineteenth century.

According to Key-hiuk Kim, Sino-Korean relations during the Qing dynasty were largely ceremonial and comprised "the exchange of ceremonial envoys, symbolic observances, and an attendant trade between the two countries."[6] Under the conditions of maintaining tributary relations with China, the Korean king was required to seek investiture from the Chinese emperor when he succeeded to the throne, to use the Chinese calendar, and to communicate with the Chinese emperor through the presidents of the Board of Rites, thus acknowledging his inferior status to the "Son of Heaven" in Beijing. In addition to these symbolic practices, Korea also sent one regular embassy to China at the time of the winter solstice each year as well as other special embassies.[7]

The nature of the Sino-Korean tributary relationship was not clear-cut and legalistic, but rather ambiguous and moral. Within the Chinese tributary system, Korea enjoyed autonomy, but only as long as it was perceived as not acting against the interests of China. This relatively precarious position led the Chosŏn leadership to adopt a seclusionist policy in order to avoid any occasion for military conflict with Korea's more powerful continental neighbor, China, on the one hand, and its more populous island neighbor, Japan, on the other. The Chosŏn foreign policy of *sadae* was, therefore, complemented by its policy of maintaining *kyorin* (neighborly relations) with Japan.[8]

Korean-Japanese relations were conducted on the basis of equality between the Korean king and the Tokugawa shogun. The legacy of resentment created by the activities of Japanese raiders *(wakō; waegu)* along the Korean coastline and the Hideyoshi invasion of 1592, combined with Koreans' sense of their own innate cultural superiority, made for complex relations between the two countries, resulting in what Hilary Conroy has aptly described as "a standoffish sort of *modus vivendi.*"[9] The Korean court, for fear of Japanese espionage, permitted trade only between the port of Pusan and the Tokugawa feudatory, Tsushima, which was required to adopt the status of a semitributary of Korea.[10]

As long as nothing upset this balance of relations between China, Korea, and Japan, Chosŏn foreign policy was successful in accomplishing its goal of preventing the intrusion of its neighbors into the Korean peninsula. Confident in the loyalty of Korea to the emperor in Beijing, the Qing dynasty maintained its policy of noninterference in the internal affairs of Korea, while Tokugawa Japan was satisfied to rely on the daimyo of Tsushima to conduct Japanese relations with Chosŏn.

With the arrival of Russia and the Western powers in force in the mid-nineteenth century, however, the traditional sinocentric world order was to undergo a radical shift in the power ratio between the declining Qing dynasty and the vigorous new regime brought into being with the Meiji Restoration in Japan in 1868. This power shift initiated the eventual collapse of Chinese hegemony in Northeast Asia in 1895 with China's defeat at the hands of Japan in the Sino-Japanese War. This defeat ushered in a new era of Russo-Japanese rivalry. In turn this "uneasy condominium" between Russia and Japan ultimately resulted in a new Japanese hegemony ten years later after Russia's ignominious defeat in the Russo-Japanese War in 1905.

Among the many complex events that set this transition of power in motion were the defeat of the Qing forces by the British in the Opium War, resulting in the Treaty of Nanjing in 1842; the Taiping Rebellion (1851–1864); the opening of Japan to the West by Commodore Matthew C. Perry in 1854; and the Qing administration's cession of the Maritime Province to Russia in 1860, which brought the eastern border of the vast Russian empire to Korea's northeastern frontier. Apparently powerless in the face of British and Russian pressure and undermined by internal rebellion, the Qing empire lost face in the sight of its traditional tributaries and with each succeeding crisis betrayed the fact that it was incapable of defending itself, let alone providing a security guarantee for its traditional dependent nations *(shu bang)* such as Korea.[11]

In the case of Japan, which unlike Korea had never fully accepted the sinocentric world order, opening to the West led to the downfall of the Tokugawa shogunate and the successful transition to a regime oriented toward a neo-imperialist model of modernization under the nominal leadership of the restored Meiji emperor, Mutsuhito. Abandoning its traditional closed country *(sakoku)* policy, the new Japanese leadership sought to emulate the West, revise the humiliating unequal treaties that had been forced on it by the Western powers, and reassert Japan's own claim to being the foremost nation in East Asia. This was, of course, a claim that had foundered some three centuries earlier with the failure of the two Hideyoshi Toyotomi expeditions to the Korean peninsula at the end of the sixteenth century during the reign of King Sŏnjo.

Meanwhile, in Korea, from 1864 to 1873 foreign policy was determined by the chauvinistic de facto regent for King Kojong, his father the Taewŏn'gun.[12] In an attempt to avoid suffering the same fate as the Qing at the hands of the Western powers, the Taewŏn'gun strengthened the traditional seclusion policy of Chosŏn and, as a result of a complex chain of events set off by the appearance of the new foreign threat of Russia on Korea's northern border, initiated the suppression of the only significant Western influence in Korea during that period, Roman Catholicism.[13] Ironically, the Taewŏn'gun's zealous execution of French missionaries in 1866 brought Korea into the focus of Western attention.[14]

In response to the Taewŏn'gun's persecution of these missionaries and the wholesale slaughter of thousands of their Korean converts, the French minister to Beijing, Henri de Bellonet, sent an unauthorized punitive expedition under Rear Admiral Pierre Gustav Roze that attacked Kanghwa Island in October 1866. This expedition, known as the Foreign Disturbance of 1866 (Pyŏng'in yang'yo) in Korea, was ultimately repulsed by the Korean troops stationed on Kanghwa Island without having achieved any of its objectives. On the contrary, it gave the Taewŏn'gun and ultraconservative Korean officials a false confidence in their policy of *wijŏng ch'ŏksa* (defend right learning, reject heterodoxy).[15]

Also in 1866, a second incident occurred, in which the *General Sherman,* a British trading ship chartered by an American company, was burned and its entire crew killed after they had ignored the protests of local Korean officials and sailed up the Taedong River with the intention of compelling the Koreans to conduct trade with them in P'yŏngyang.[16] Needless to say, this incident became a bone of contention between the United States and Korea and eventually led to an abortive effort by the former to open Korea to trade by means of the same tactics as those it had used to open Japan more than a decade earlier in 1854.

The American expedition of 1871, known in Korea as the Foreign Distur-bance of 1871 (Sinmi yang'yo), was led by Rear Admiral John Rodgers and the U.S. minister to Beijing, Frederick K. Low. The American expeditionary force inflicted many casualties on the Koreans defending Kanghwa Island but, like the French expedition before it, also failed to attain its objectives and even had the effect of further retarding the possibility of Korea's establishing relations with the West.[17] Regret for the U.S. expedition was expressed by the former secretary of state John W. Foster, who "was of the opinion that the American undertaking 'placed the American Minister and Navy in a false light before the world,' and that it might be regarded 'as the most serious blunder of American diplomacy in the Orient.'"[18]

Where the United States and France had failed in opening Korea to the mod-ern treaty system of the West, however, Japan ultimately succeeded. Emulat-ing the strategy that Perry had used against Japan in 1854, the Japanese sought to create a diplomatic incident that would provide them with the necessary ex-cuse for a show of force that would get Korea to abandon its traditional re-strictive trade relations with Japan through Tsushima and replace them with Western-style treaty relations.

The necessary pretext was provided by the *Unyōkan* incident, in which the Japanese ship *Unyōkan* deliberately sailed provocatively close to the strategi-cally sensitive Kanghwa Island in 1875, was fired upon by a Korean artillery bat-tery, and retaliated. This incident led to a Japanese expedition in the follow-ing year under the leadership of Lieutenant General Kuroda Kiyotaka, who coerced Korea into negotiations that resulted in the Treaty of Kanghwa, con-cluded on 26 February 1876.[19] This treaty was almost a carbon copy of the West-ern unequal treaties that had been forced on China and Japan and, in fact, was even more unfair in that it placed no tariffs whatsoever on Japanese goods im-ported into Korea. The most significant aspect of the treaty, however, was its attempt to extract Korea from its traditional relationship with China, as Nel-son points out:

> The treaty in two instances also endeavoured to affect the relationship between China and Korea: Article I, in the English translation, stated that "Chosen, be-ing an independent State *(tzu chu)*, enjoys the same sovereign rights as does Japan," and the document was dated, not according to the Chinese reign year, but by the Japanese reign year and that of the Li dynasty of Korea.[20]

Nevertheless, neither Korea nor China interpreted the treaty as changing their relationship, as Korea had always enjoyed autonomy, a more correct trans-lation of the term *"tzu chu" (zi zhu; chaju)*, in its relations with Japan. As Martina Deuchler states, "Korea did not attach the same meaning to the first article that the Japanese did. The Koreans considered it a mere reaffirmation of a tradition-sanctioned reality."[21]

It was not until the United States resumed efforts to make a treaty with Korea, however, that the traditional order in East Asia began to show signs of real strain. After first trying without success to approach Korea through Japan, Commodore Robert W. Shufeldt, the U.S. treaty negotiator, made a second approach through the governor-general of Zhili Province and imperial commissioner for the northern ports, the de facto foreign minister of China, Li Hongzhang. Together they drew up a treaty in Tianjin, with the Korean representative Kim Yun-sik firmly in the background. This treaty of friendship and commerce was then signed by Shufeldt and the Korean plenipotentiaries Sin Hŏn and Kim Hong-jip at Chemulp'o (present-day Inch'ŏn) on 22 May 1882.

Underlying the problem of accommodating the Western and East Asian systems of international relations was the question of the status of Korea vis-à-vis China. To overcome the apparent contradiction of Korea as an independent tributary of China, a letter was attached to the treaty from King Kojong to the president of the United States "in which the Korean king acknowledged that Korea was a tributary of China, but independent in regard to both internal administration and foreign affairs."[22]

As this statement was not in the body of the treaty, from which it had been removed at the request of Shufeldt, little attention was paid to it, and Korea was treated for diplomatic purposes as a sovereign nation. As the U.S. secretary of state, Frederick T. Frelinghuysen, wrote: "As far as we are concerned, Corea is an independent sovereign power, with all attendant rights, privileges, duties and responsibilities; in her relations to China we have no desire to interfere unless action should be taken prejudicial to the rights of the United States."[23]

Nevertheless, the very fact that the treaty had been drawn up in Tianjin under the auspices of Li Hongzhang clearly shows that the approach of the United States was purely pragmatic, acknowledging de facto Chinese suzerainty when it suited its purpose, while asserting Korea's de jure independence for the purpose of bringing Korea into the Western treaty system.

That the United States government had no interest in establishing Korea's independence for its own sake, far less guaranteeing it, is clearly shown in the following communication from the secretary of state, Thomas F. Bayard, to the American minister to Korea, Hugh A. Dinsmore, in 1887:

> If, contrary to the expectations of this Government, the progress of Chinese interference at Seoul should result in the destruction of the autonomy of Korea as

a sovereign state with which the United States maintain independent treaty relations, it will be time then to consider whether this government is to look to
that of China to enforce treaty obligations for the protection of the persons and
interests of citizens of the United States, and their commerce, in Korean territory as a dependency of China.[24]

As this letter reveals, after helping Korea to conclude treaty relations with
the United States and the European powers, China subsequently began to increase its influence in Korea. Contrary to its previous policy toward its tributary, the Qing administration began to actively intervene in Korea's internal
affairs while at the same time preventing it from consolidating its diplomatic
relations with its Western treaty partners.

In the wake of the Soldiers' Rebellion of 1882 (Imo kullan), Li Hongzhang
sent two thousand troops to Seoul, had the Taewŏn'gun kidnapped and removed
to exile in China, and appointed advisers, including the German Paul Georg
von Möllendorff, to positions of influence in the Korean government.

In December 1884, a group of young, reform-minded Koreans, generally referred to in Korean historiography as the Enlightenment Party, under the leadership of Kim Ok-kyun carried out the coup d'état of 1884 and seized power
for four days. During the planning of this coup, the conspirators had been encouraged by the Japanese minister to Seoul, Takezoe Shinichirō, but at the very
last moment the Japanese government had withdrawn its tacit support, and the
coup was crushed by the Chinese troops stationed in Seoul under the leadership of Yuan Shikai. Without any significant support among the Korean populace, the conspirators were forced to go into exile in Japan.[25]

This incident provided the pretext for Li Hongzhang to bring the Korean
government and the royal household more firmly under Chinese control by
the appointment of Yuan Shikai in late October 1885 as director-general of diplomatic and consular affairs resident in Korea *(zhu za Zhaoxian zong li jiao she
tong shang shi yi)*."[26] As Young Ick Lew points out, Yuan Shikai himself adopted
the more overtly imperialistic English title "His Imperial Chinese Majesty's Resident in Seoul."[27] For almost a decade the Chinese resident interfered in Korea's domestic and foreign affairs, Lew maintains, as a "modern-day equivalent
of the Mongol royal supervisor appointed to the Koryŏ court in the fourteenth
century."[28]

By acting in this way, the Qing dynasty departed from its traditional
Confucian-based policy toward Korea and competed with the West and Japan
within the framework of the power politics of late-nineteenth-century imperialism. Qing intervention proved detrimental to the development of Korea,
which was effectively prevented from strengthening its diplomatic relations with

the West on the one hand and from carrying out urgent internal reforms on the other. By retarding Korean development throughout this decade, China did nothing to reduce the vulnerability of Korea to the ambitions of Japan. Indeed, Lew goes as far as to state, "Ch'ing China unwittingly contributed to the demise of the Korean kingdom and its eventual subjugation as a Japanese colony in the early twentieth century by blocking the development of the Korean enlightenment movement."[29] The crisis that China had sought to avoid through its own imperialistic policy toward Korea came in 1894, when on the pretext of suppressing the Tonghak Rebellion and restoring internal order both China and Japan sent troops to Korea—the former at the request of the Korean government, the latter on its own initiative under the terms of the Convention of Tianjin (18 April 1885).[30] The outcome of this action was an open clash of arms and the outbreak of the Sino-Japanese War fought on the Korean peninsula and in the seas around it. China was severely defeated by the modernized army and navy of Japan, and with the signing of the Treaty of Shimonoseki on 17 April 1895, the era of Qing hegemony in the region came to an ignominious end, and a new era of Japanese supremacy in Northeast Asia began to emerge.

This supremacy was hindered only by the rival ambitions of Tsarist Russia in the region and the fact that Japan could not yet afford to alienate the United States and the European powers. Working in concert with Germany and France, Russia was successful in negating Japanese gains from its war with China by means of the Triple Intervention of 1895. Bowing reluctantly to the pressure of Russia in combination with the two other European powers, Japan was forced to retrocede the Liaodong Peninsula and "honor her avowed policy of aiding Korea's independence."[31]

Initially, therefore, Japan was prevented from capitalizing on its military success. This failure was later exacerbated by the fact that the Japanese minister in Seoul, Miura Gorō, allegedly at the bidding of the Japanese elder statesman Inoue Kaoru and with the probable knowledge of the Japanese cabinet, instigated the assassination of the Royal consort, Queen Myŏngsŏng, on 8 October 1895.[32] This act of premeditated brutality removed a major obstacle to Japanese influence in Korea but also precipitated the flight of the Korean sovereign to the Russian legation on 11 February 1896, and a decade of rivalry between Japan and Russia for the mastery of the Korean peninsula ensued. As shall be seen, it was during this period that Min Yŏng-hwan came to the fore, both as an envoy to the West in 1896 and 1897 and as a supporter of the Independence Club and advocate of domestic modernization and reform until his death in 1905.

The growing rivalry between Japan and Russia was ultimately decided not by diplomacy but by force of arms, when Japan, confident in its newfound military might, precipitated the Russo-Japanese War with a surprise attack on Port Arthur on 8 February 1904. Japan once again pitted its modernized army and navy against a much larger continental power and emerged victorious. In fact, even before the conclusion of the war under the terms of the Treaty of Portsmouth (5 September 1905), it had begun to tighten its grip on Korea. Through the coerced Ŭlsa Treaty of Protection of 17 November 1905, Korea became a Japanese protectorate, and control of its foreign relations was transferred from Seoul to Tokyo.

The Western powers, far from hindering this process, simply acceded to it. It is an irony of history that Korea, which had opened itself to the West precisely as a countermeasure to Japanese intrusion, should find the leading Western powers, Great Britain and the United States, now apparently bending over backward to smooth the way for Japan to take complete control of the Korean peninsula, even at the expense of both existing and potential British and American interests. In the text of the Anglo-Japanese alliance treaty of 1905, Britain made no mention of Korean sovereignty but simply recognized Japan's "paramount political, military, and economic interests in Corea."[33] This concession was made as a quid pro quo for Japan's recognition of British interests in India and Burma. Also, with the defeat of Russia in the Far East, the architects of British foreign policy had less reason to concern themselves with the fate of Korea.

The United States similarly recognized Japanese predominance in Korea in return for recognition by Japan of American hegemony in the Philippines. This informal agreement was secretly established between the U.S. secretary of war, William Howard Taft, and the Japanese prime minister, Katsura Taro, and enshrined in the so-called Taft-Katsura Memorandum of Agreement, which had the complete approval of President Theodore Roosevelt.[34] Indeed this informal agreement was a direct reflection of Roosevelt's pro-Japanese foreign policy, as Harrington explains:

> Pro-Japanese, the chief executive was most contemptuous of Chosen and was perfectly willing to have the region ruled from Tokyo. "I cannot see any possibility of this government using its influence to 'bolster up the Empire of Korea in its independence,'" said Rockhill in outlining what both he and Roosevelt believed. "I fancy that the Japanese will settle this question when the present war is finished. The annexation of Korea to Japan seems to be absolutely indicated as the one great and final step westward of the extension of the Japanese Empire. I think when this comes about it will be better for the Korean people and also for the peace in the Far East."[35]

When Japan requested the closure of all foreign legations in Seoul in 1905, the United States, Korea's first Western treaty partner and the only one to have included a "good offices" clause in its treaty, was the first to comply.[36] Despite eleventh-hour attempts by the Koreans to preserve their independence, including an abortive mission to the Hague Peace Conference of 1907 by a deputation secretly appointed by Emperor Kojong, the process that led to Korea's annexation by Japan on 22 August 1910 proved irreversible.

The Intellectual Background of Late Chosŏn

Before embarking on an examination of the life and early career of Min Yŏng-hwan, it is also helpful to have an understanding of the background to the intellectual climate into which he was born and how that climate developed during his lifetime. As has been mentioned in the previous section, in the 1860s Korea was still a closed country, resisting the efforts of Japan to open it to Western-style treaty relations until 1876, just two years before Min Yŏng-hwan passed the civil service examination. That does not mean, however, that Korean intellectuals had had no intercourse with Western ideas. It is true that not a single Korean had ever traveled to the West and returned with information about what lay beyond Chosŏn's shores, but a substantial number had met Western Roman Catholic priests in Beijing, and many more had read Western books translated into Chinese under the auspices of the Ming and Qing dynasties.

Historically, the Chinese mainland had always been a major source of cultural, ideological, and technological innovation on the Korean peninsula. Buddhism, which came to the Korean peninsula from India by way of China, was adopted as the state religion of the Three Kingdoms, Koguryŏ, Paekche, and Silla between the fourth and sixth centuries A.D., and Chinese modes of government were also introduced around that time. Buddhism flourished and declined during the Koryŏ period to be replaced by Zhu Xi's neo-Confucianism as the leading ideology throughout the Chosŏn period. It is not surprising, therefore, that Chosŏn's first contact with Western knowledge, including religion, technology, geography, and so on, should have come through the regular tribute missions made by representatives of the Korean court to Beijing. Even during the late Ming period, religious texts such as Matteo Ricci's *True Principles of Catholicism (Ch'ŏnju sirŭi)* had already been introduced to Korea. In fact, as Ki-baek Lee points out, Catholicism initially spread on the Korean peninsula not through Western missionaries but through books brought in from China.[37]

Not only religion but also Western science began to influence the Chosŏn

intelligentsia. Adherents of the Sirhakp'a (School of practical learning) in particular were receptive to the new scientific and technical knowledge coming
from the West through China.[38] As early as 1631, Chŏng Tu-wŏn brought back
a musket, telescope, alarm clock, and world map, as well as books on astronomy and Western culture.[39] Around this time Koreans had substantial contacts
with Westerners such as the Jesuit Adam Schall in Beijing and with Dutch sailors
shipwrecked on the Korean coast such as Jan Janse Weltevree, who lived out
his life in Seoul, assisting the Military Training Command with the manufacture of cannons. Another shipwrecked Dutch sailor, Hendrik Hamel, finally
escaped from Chosŏn Korea to the Dutch enclave at Nagasaki and, after returning to his own country, published the first account of Korea in the West
in 1669.[40]

In the early nineteenth century Chŏng Yag-yong, the "great synthesizer" of
sirhak thought, brought practical learning to the threshold of "enlightenment
thought" *(kaehwa sasang)*. Just as the Western Enlightenment had seen the appearance of the Encyclopedists in France, so the nineteenth century in Korea
also witnessed the emergence of such encyclopedic works as Sŏ Yu-gu's *Imyŏn
simnyuk chi* (Sixteen treatises written in retirement) and Yi Kyu-gyŏng's *Oju
yŏnmun changjŏn san'go* (Random expiations). The latter work in particular examines the whole range of Chosŏn scholarship from astronomy to economics.
These endeavors culminated in 1908 with the compilation of the *Chŭngbo
munhŏn pigo* (Augmented reference compilation of documents on Korea), an
expanded version of the late-eighteenth-century *Tongguk munhŏn pigo* (Reference compilation of documents on Korea).[41]

The previous section touched on the emergence of the Kaehwadang, cen-
tering on such scholars as Pak Kyu-su, who as magistrate of P'yŏngyang had
been responsible for the destruction of the *General Sherman* and yet was later
to advocate the establishment of treaty relations with Japan. After the establishment of diplomatic relations with Japan in 1876, some Korean scholars began to look toward the example of the Meiji Restoration as a model for the
modernization of Korea. These scholars rejected the Qing approach to self-
strengthening, summarized in the expression "Eastern ways, Western machines"
(tongdo sŏgi), to which the Chosŏn administration, dominated by the Min clan
and their supporters, adhered throughout the 1880s.

In 1876 after the conclusion of the Treaty of Kanghwa, Kim Ki-su was sent
to Japan as a special envoy. Kim recorded his observations in *Iltong kiyu* (Record
of a journey to Japan), which was presented to King Kojong on his return to
Seoul. As an intimate of the royal family, Min Yŏng-hwan probably had access
to this and subsequent journals of Korean envoys to Japan and the West. Kim
Ki-su's early assessment of the Japanese model, however, was highly critical.

Four years later, in 1880, Kim Hong-jip, who was later one of the leading figures in the Kabo-Ŭlmi reforms (Kabo kyŏngjang) of 1894–1845, was sent as an envoy to Japan and, unlike his predecessor Kim Ki-su, returned with the conviction that Korea should emulate Japan and embark on an urgent program of modernization and reform. It was during Kim Hong-jip's visit to Japan that he received a copy of Huang Zunxian's *Zhaoxian ce lyue* (A policy for Korea). This work, which among other things advocated the formation of diplomatic relations with the United States, was well known to Min Yŏng-hwan and is discussed favorably in his policy essay, *Ch'ŏnilch'aek,* which will be examined in detail in the following chapter. Another work brought back by Kim, *Yi yan* (Presumptuous views), by the Qing scholar Zheng Guanying, made the important point that the adoption of Western technology alone was insufficient for successful modernization and that Western institutions should also be adopted. As will be seen, on his return from traveling in the West in the late 1890s, Min also came to accept this view and began to align himself with such Independence Club leaders as Sŏ Chae-p'il and Yun Ch'i-ho. Toward the end of his life he was even to become a sponsor of the young nationalist radical Syngman Rhee (Yi Sŭng-man).

In 1881 a far larger group of young Korean officials known as the *sinsa yuramdan* (gentlemen's sightseeing mission) traveled to Japan to study modernization there. This group included among others Cho Chun-yŏng, Pak Chŏng-yang, Ŏ Yun-jung, Hong Yŏng-sik, and Min Chong-muk. Their observations were recorded in individual reports under the title *Sich'algi* (Diary of an inspection tour).[42]

Another member of the 1881 mission, who remained in Japan to study under the Japanese reformer Fukuzawa Yukichi, was Yu Kil-chun. In 1883 Yu also accompanied Min Yŏng-hwan's elder cousin Min Yŏng-ik on the first Korean diplomatic mission to the United States. When Min returned to Korea via Europe, Yu remained in the United States as a student. Finally, Yu also returned to Korea via Europe; he completed writing *Sŏyu kyŏnmun* (Observations on a journey to the West) in 1889, while under house arrest because of his connections with the conspirators of the coup of 1884. In fact, Yu only narrowly avoided execution on his return from the United States because of the intervention of Han Kyu-sŏl, a political ally of Min Yŏng-hwan.[43]

Sŏyu kyŏnmun, which was not published until 1895 in Tokyo, was the most comprehensive examination of Western society by any Korean until that time. It was based not only on firsthand observations but also on extensive study of Western texts and was undoubtedly the most influential Korean treatise on modernization in the closing years of the Chosŏn era. It was also the first book to be printed in a mixed script that used both *han'gŭl* and Chinese characters.

Although Yu later rose to the position of minister of home affairs (*naemu taesin*) during the period of the Kabo-Ŭlmi reforms, he was eventually forced to flee to Japan after Kojong's flight to the Russian legation in 1896 and was unable to return to Korea until he received a special dispensation after the abdication of Kojong in 1907. It is not within the scope of this biography of Min Yŏng-hwan to examine in detail the extent or nature of the Kabo-Ŭlmi reforms, carried out during and after the Sino-Japanese War under the auspices of Inoue Kaoru, Japanese advisers, and Korean progressives such as Pak Yŏng-hyo, Kim Hong-jip, Sŏ Kwang-bŏm, and Yu Kil-chun. Even though the reforms were a significant watershed in the history of this period, the Min clan were excluded from participation in them until just before Kojong's flight to the Russian legation. It is indicative of Min Yŏng-hwan's integrity that even though he was a member of the ousted Min clan, he was a member of Kim Hong-jip's cabinet and was appointed to the post of minister plenipotentiary to the United States in 1895. He was never to take up the post, however, because of the assassination of Queen Myŏngsŏng.[44]

It is clear from Min Yŏng-hwan's own writings that he came from a quite different intellectual background from Yu Kil-chun, or another of his contemporaries, Yun Ch'i-ho, who accompanied him to Russia in 1896 and had a similar background to Yu. Both Yu and Yun had converted to Protestant Christianity, and both had been involved on the fringes of the Kaehwadang. Min, on the other hand, as will be seen, was firmly entrenched in the world of the court. He did not have the freedom of action or thought of such thinkers as Yu and Yun, both of whom had spent a considerable time living and studying abroad in Japan and the United States by the 1890s.

Nevertheless, as a well-connected court official, it is probable that Min Yŏng-hwan, even before traveling abroad himself, had already gained considerable information about Japan and the West both from his own reading and directly from his close relative Min Yŏng-ik, who had initially been viewed as an ally at the court by the leadership of the Kaehwadang. Indeed, in an interview published in the *Independent* on his return from Russia in 1896, Min specifically stated, "Before I went abroad, I had heard a great deal of the wonderful things of Europe and America through those who have travelled in these places."[45]

Furthermore, Min appears to have had good relations with various Western residents in Seoul, as will be seen in later chapters. Consequently, Min Yŏng-hwan, together with other officials such as Pak Chŏng-yang and Han Kyu-sŏl, was able to traverse the gulf that appeared to separate the court and the advocates of reform and made more effort than any other official of his rank and background to draw these two worlds together.

Min's Family Background and Early Life

Min Yŏng-hwan's lifetime, which lasted from 1861 to 1905, almost exactly spans the closing years of the Chosŏn dynasty. Unfortunately, however, although we know much about the times Min lived in from the numerous studies of the period, finding biographical information about Min himself is not such an easy task. Unlike his contemporary, the American-educated, Protestant intellectual Yun Ch'i-ho, Min did not keep a daily record of his life and opinions. There are no publicly available collections of his personal correspondence, and his most substantial biography, *Aegukcha Min Ch'ungjŏnggong*, written by Cho Yong-man and published in 1947, is more an account of the salient historical events that occurred during Min's lifetime than an in-depth study of the man himself.

There are, however, tantalizing Western records concerning Min by those who met him personally such as the American adviser to the Korean government, William Franklin Sands, whose positive opinion of Min and other members of his clan, Min Sang-ho and Min Yŏng-ki, has already been mentioned. Min also had friendly relationships with the American missionary Horace Underwood and his wife, with the Russian chargé d'affaires at Seoul Karl Waeber, and with the British consul-general John Jordan. Even Yun Ch'i-ho, who accompanied Min on the 1896 embassy to the coronation of Tsar Nicholas II and, as will be seen later in this study, was highly critical of his superior, ultimately thought of him as a friend.[46]

As a member of the Yŏhŭng Min clan, which came to dominate the Chosŏn political scene from the downfall of the Taewŏn'gun in 1874 until the Kabo-Ŭlmi reforms of 1894–1895, however, Min Yŏng-hwan was liable to be open to condemnation by association.[47] In fact, the leader of the Tonghak uprising in 1894, Chŏn Pong-jun, specifically mentioned Min Yŏng-hwan along with Min Yŏng-jun and Ko Yŏng-gŭn as being typical of the "self-seeking, covetous officials in the capital."[48] Furthermore, his father, Min Kyŏm-ho, was roundly condemned by his contemporary, the diarist Hwang Hyŏn, who wrote of him,

> Min Kyŏm-ho was an ignorant person who coveted possessions. His mansion and gardens were luxurious, and he revelled in music and women. Not a single day passed that he did not demand a bribe. He sold official posts on behalf of Kojong and was responsible for the administration of serious criminal cases, the collection of bribes, and so on.[49]

Nevertheless, Min Yŏng-hwan himself came to be generally respected by members of the reform group in Korea and thus performed an important role in promoting a cooperative and evolutionary approach to reform that, if it had been more widely practiced, might have enabled Korea to face more effectively the twin challenges of internal reform and the external threat posed to its sovereignty by China, Russia, and Japan. Min's importance in the late Chosŏn political scene lies mainly in the role he played as a bridge between Kojong's inner court and those reform-minded Koreans both inside and outside the administration.

As a scion of the Yŏhŭng Min clan, Min Yŏng-hwan's ancestral line may be traced back to the late Koryŏ official Min Ch'ing-do.[50] The line of descent continues through the early Chosŏn official Min Sim-ŏn and Min Kwang-hun, a governor of Kangwŏn Province in the mid-Chosŏn period and the founder of the so-called *sambang p'a* (three-branch line) of the Yŏhŭng Min clan.[51] The name *sambang p'a* derives from the fact that Min Kwang-hun had three sons: Min Si-jung, Min Chŏng-jung, and Min Yu-jung. It was with Min Yu-jung (1630–1687), Min Kwang-hun's third son, that the Yŏhŭng Min clan came to the fore as one of Chosŏn's politically powerful family groups during a brief period in the latter part of the seventeenth century.[52] Furthermore, as Dalchoong Kim points out, "With a few exceptions, all the Min who emerged as power holders in the later half of the nineteenth century were descendants of Min Yu-jung's branch."[53]

Min Yu-jung, like his father before him, also had three sons: Chin-hu, Chin-wŏn, and Chin-yŏng. The family's rise to prominence, however, was due not to these sons but to Min Yu-jung's daughter, who became the second consort *(kyebi)* of King Sukchong (r. 1674–1720) on the death of his first wife.[54] As the king's new father-in-law *(kukku),* Min Yu-jung subsequently rose in the ranks of the Chosŏn administration and became a prominent figure in the Old Doctrine (Noron) school of the Westerner (Sŏin) faction at the court. Min's daughter, Queen Inhyŏn (Inhyŏn wanghu), however, was unable to bear the king a male heir and was supplanted by a concubine, Lady Chang (Chang hŭibin). This concubine gave birth to a son who later became King Kyŏngjong (r. 1720–1724). Lady Chang succeeded in alienating King Sukchong from Queen Inhyŏn, who was stripped of her rank and dismissed from the palace with grave repercussions for her relatives and supporters, including her father.[55]

Queen Inhyŏn was eventually reinstated as the royal consort, however, and Lady Chang was condemned to take poison *(sayak),* a traditional mode of execution for Chosŏn's nobility, after the discovery that she had brought female shamans *(mudang)* into the palace to perform occult rites intended to bring about the death of the rightful queen. Soon afterward Queen Inhyŏn herself died from illness in 1701, and the Min clan's influence at the court evaporated with King Sukchong's remarriage to the daughter of Kim Chu-sin, a member of the Kyŏngju Kim clan.[56]

Min Yŏng-hwan was descended from the youngest of Min Yu-jung's three sons, Chin-yŏng, through the three generations of Yo-su, Paek-sul, and Tan-hyŏn[57] to Min's paternal grandfather, Min Ch'i-gu (1795–1874). Like Min Yu-jung before him, Min Ch'i-gu also had three sons and a daughter who married into the royal line. Although Min Ch'i-gu's daughter did not marry the king, she became the wife of Yi Ha-ŭng, better known as the Taewŏn'gun, who was to become the de facto regent on the accession to the throne of his son, Yi Myŏng-bok (Yi Hŭi), better known by his posthumously conferred temple name, Kojong (r. 1863–1907).[58]

Min Ch'i-gu's three sons were T'ae-ho,[59] Sŭng-ho, and Kyŏm-ho. Min Yŏng-hwan was the eldest son of Min Kyŏm-ho, but he was later adopted into the line of his father's eldest brother, Min T'ae-ho, who had died childless in 1860. The second brother, Min Sŭng-ho, became the adopted heir of Min Ch'i-rok, the father of Kojong's consort, Queen Myŏngsŏng. Consequently, Min Yŏng-hwan's relationship with the Chosŏn royal family was exceptionally close. He was not only the cousin of King Kojong through his paternal aunt but also a nephew of Queen Myŏngsŏng by virtue of the fact that his paternal uncle, Min Sŭng-ho, was the queen's adopted elder brother.

Min Yŏng-hwan was born in Chŏndong[60] in Seoul on 17 August 1861 (Ch'ŏl-chong 12).[61] His courtesy title was Munyak (In accord with culture), his pen name Kyejŏng (Cassia court),[62] and his posthumous name bestowed on him by Emperor Kojong was Ch'ungjŏng (Loyal righteousness). As has been mentioned, he was the eldest son of one of the most influential and powerful members of the Yŏhŭng Min clan, Min Kyŏm-ho. Min senior held many important posts in the Chosŏn administration, including minister of war. In 1880 he became a director (kyŏngni tangsang) of the newly established Office for the Management of State Affairs (T'ongnigimu amun) and as such was deeply involved in the national self-strengthening program carried out by the Chosŏn administration in response to the new challenges Korea was facing from Japan and the West. Min Kyŏm-ho was also responsible for the creation of the Special Skills Force (Pyŏlgigun), a modern military unit under the command of the Japanese military instructor Horimoto Reizō. Kang Sŏng-jo suggests that the interest that Min Yŏng-hwan himself showed in military affairs throughout his career was a result of his father's influence.[63]

Min Yŏng-hwan's mother was the daughter of an auditor in the Five Military Commands Headquarters (Owi toch'ongbu tosa), Sŏ Kyŏng-sun of the Talsŏng Sŏ clan.[64] Min had one older sister and one younger brother, Min Yŏng-ch'an, who was twelve years his junior.

Little is known about Min's childhood. In Kiro sup'il (Biographical essays), however, Song Sang-do records that after conceiving her eldest son, Min's

mother had an auspicious dream in which she caught three pearls and saw many
senior officials in ceremonial clothes gathering outside her house and kneeling
before her husband. The account goes on to say, perhaps predictably, that as a
child Min was a son of filial piety, who respectfully listened to his elders and
could not tell a lie. Furthermore, he would not join in with the local children's
games and never did anything dishonest.[65]

Min Yŏng-hwan's biographer, Cho Yong-man, describes Min in his childhood in similar terms:

> From his childhood Min Yŏng-hwan showed exceptional filial piety toward his
> parents and affection toward his brother and sister. His character was exceed-
> ingly gentle and kind, and he was quite incapable of hurting others even in the
> slightest. He particularly disliked the killing of living creatures, and it is said that
> he never once killed an insect or a bird and that once when he cut his finger by
> mistake while cutting his fingernails with a knife, he could not bear to look at
> the blood.[66]

Cho goes on to maintain that in counterbalance to this gentleness of character, Min also had a strong sense of righteousness and that once he was con-
vinced of the correctness of a course of action, he would carry it out regardless
of any opposition that he might face. It was this strength of character, Cho concludes, that enabled Min to avoid being sucked into the web of corruption in
which so many of the Min clan were entangled and that also enabled him ultimately to resist the Japanese absorption of Korea with his own life.[67]

Although such accounts as these of Min's early life may seem too close to
hagiography to be trusted as strict historical fact, they are all that remain to us
of his early childhood. Also, from what is known of Min in adult life, the accounts appear to be more or less in character. Whatever his faults, Min's friends
and critics alike seem to have agreed that he was a gentleman.

Although evidence for this assertion may be found throughout this work,
the following anecdote recounted by Lillias Underwood is of interest. After having arrived late for a luncheon being given by "the highest of all the Korean
princes both in actual rank, official position and in royal favor," for "a guest of
extremely high rank, I believe, from Japan," the Underwoods found that their
places had been removed. Nevertheless, Mrs. Underwood continued,

> Before another plate could be laid, the Prince quickly rose, gave Mrs. Under-
> wood his chair and, motioning away the attendant, served her himself. Con-
> sidering oriental ideas of rank and class, this was a very remarkable condescen-
> sion, a special token of friendship for the missionary. The Prince had probably

never before in his life carried a plate or cup to serve any one or even the smallest article for himself.[68]

Although Lillias Underwood provided no name either for the Japanese guest or for the prince, the latter appears, from the description "the highest of all the Korean princes," to have been Min Yŏng-hwan. The anecdote is not dated precisely, but from the context it occurred some time before the Japanese protectorate, in which case the Japanese "guest of extremely high rank" may have been Itō Hirobumi whom Min was responsible for welcoming on his visit to Korea in March 1904.[69]

It is known that Min married twice. His first wife was also born in 1861, the daughter of Minister *(p'ansŏ)* Kim Myŏng-jin of the powerful Andong Kim clan and granddaughter on her father's side of Minister Sim Sŭng-t'aek of the Ch'ŏngsong Sim clan.[70] She bore no children and died at the age of thirty in 1891. She was buried in T'owŏlli, Sujimyŏn, Yongin County.[71]

Min's second wife was the daughter of Pak Yong-hun, a county magistrate *(kunsu)* and member of the Miryang Pak clan. Her maternal grandfather was An T'ae-hyŏng, a member of the Sunhŭng An clan. She gave birth to three sons and two daughters. The eldest son, Min Pŏm-sik, was born in 1898.[72] The second son, Chang-sik, was born in 1904; and the third son, Kwang-sik, was born in June 1905, only a few months before his father's death. According to Kang Sŏng-jo, all of Min's children survived into adulthood but led relatively obscure lives.[73]

Min's Early Political Career (1877–1882)

In 1877, at the age of sixteen, Min Yŏng-hwan was appointed children's education officer *(tongmong kyogwan),* a post that entailed the responsibility for the education of boys at the county level.[74] Kang Sŏng-jo suggests that Min may have been asked in this capacity to tutor the four-year-old crown prince, the future Emperor Sunjong. In the following year, on 17 February 1878, Min passed the final stage of the Erudite Examination (Munkwa) with the highest mark *(changwŏn kŭpche)* and later that same year was appointed to the post of junior librarian *(taegyo)* in the Royal Library (Kyujanggak).[75] He was then appointed to the post of ninth adviser *(chŏngja)* in the Office of Special Advisers (Hongmun'gwan). Both these posts were at the senior ninth rank *(chŏng kup'um).*[76]

The Office of Special Advisers was, as its name suggests, an advisory organ to the king and was staffed mainly by young officials who had recently passed the Erudite Examination. The commencement of Min's career was made all the more promising by the fact that by 1878, the Min clan had already had five years in which to consolidate its power after forcing the resignation of the Taewŏn'gun in 1873.

The extent of the Min clan's increasing influence in the court is also shown by the fact that in the period from 1800 to 1866 only nineteen members of the Min clan passed the high civil service examination. In the twenty years from the installation of Queen Myŏngsŏng as Kojong's consort in 1866 until the Kapsin coup in 1884, however, twenty-five members of the Min clan successfully passed the same examination, and all of them were assigned to important government posts. Deuchler, however, emphasizes that the consolidation of Min power did not begin in earnest until after the Soldiers' Rebellion of 1882.[77]

Min immediately offered his resignation from his appointment as ninth adviser, protesting his lack of talent and general unworthiness for office. Nevertheless, he was ordered to remain at his post.[78] Min's reluctance to accept official posts as revealed by the many memorials of resignation and polite refusal collected in the *Soch'a* section of *Min Ch'ungjŏnggong yugo* should perhaps not be emphasized. As a powerful member of the royal in-law clan his rise through the ranks of the Chosŏn administration was meteoric, particularly when compared with the progress of a political outsider such as Kim Ok-kyun, who never rose above the fifth rank *(op'um)*.

In refusing to accept appointments, Min may have been protecting himself from the jealousies of other officials or simply adhering to a code of Confucian self-effacement. Nevertheless, the overall impression left by his collected memorials is that he was sensitive to fairness in the appointment of officials. Also, in keeping with Confucian tradition, he clearly placed greater importance on his duties as a filial son than his duties as a court official. Finally, it appears that an innate caution, a modest assessment of his own abilities, and also, in the later stages of his career, his poor health made him reluctant to shoulder the burdens of office.[79]

On 25 January 1879 Min was appointed third diarist *(kŏmyŏl)* in the Office of Royal Decrees (Yemun'gwan), a post that entailed working in the presence of the king, keeping the daily records.[80] Min asked once more to be excused from taking up this appointment because of his mother's poor health, but his request was again refused.[81] In fact, he was concurrently appointed to the post of fifth tutor *(sŏlsŏ)* in the Crown Prince Tutorial Office (Seja sigang'wŏn) and as such would have been responsible for lecturing the six-year-old crown prince on the Chinese classics, history, and moral principles.[82] Although this post was only at senior seventh rank *(chŏng ch'ilp'um)*, it most probably placed Min in close proximity not only to the crown prince but also to his mother, Queen Myŏngsŏng.

On 27 February Min was appointed junior librarian in the Royal Library. He again declined the appointment because of the recent promotion of his father-in-law, Kim Myŏng-jin, to the post of sixth royal secretary *(tongbusŭngji)*. Min protested that his own appointment might be considered evidence of favoritism, and in this instance his request was granted.[83]

According to Hwang Hyŏn, Min's father-in-law was an official of considerable integrity, whose death in 1887 was lamented by the general populace.[84] Perhaps as an illustration of the difficulties faced by honest officials in Kojong's court, Hwang provided the following revealing anecdote about Kim Myŏng-jin and his son-in-law, Min Yŏng-hwan:

> On the occasion of the king's birthday it was customary for governors *(kamsa)* and magistrates *(suryŏng)* to offer gifts, which would be sent to the palace by means of a relative of the royal family.
>
> In the seventh month of the year Chŏnghae [1887], when Min Yŏng-so and Min Yŏng-hwan were having an audience with the king, Kim Kyu-hong was appointed the governor of Chŏlla Province and Kim Myŏng-jin the governor of Kyŏngsang Province. At that time Min Yŏng-hwan presented Kim Myŏng-jin's list of presents. The list comprised merely fifty bolts *(p'il)* of Japanese silk and fifty bolts of hemp cloth. Kojong's face reddened, and he threw the list to the floor. Min Yŏng-hwan hurriedly picked it up and put it inside his sleeve. . . . Min Yŏng-hwan immediately went out and bought presents worth twenty thousand yang with his own money and offered them to the king. Min Yŏng-hwan did this because he was Kim Myŏng-jin's son-in-law.[85]

Shortly after his refusal to accept the post of junior librarian, Min tendered his resignation from his original post as third diarist again, pleading with the king to allow him to return home to attend his sick mother. His request was duly refused, and he offered his resignation again one month later, only to meet with the same response.[86]

Despite this apparent reluctance to accept official posts, however, Min progressed steadily through the ranks of the Chosŏn administration. Later in the same year (1879) he was to hold a series of mid-ranking posts in the administration ranging between senior sixth and junior fourth ranks. These posts included those of sixth counsellor *(such'an)* in the Office of Special Advisers, third inspector *(changnyŏng)* in the Office of the Inspector General (Sahŏnbu), junior fourth adviser *(puŭnggyo)* in the Office of Special Advisers, legal secretary *(kŏmsang)* in the State Council (Ŭijŏngbu), and junior fifth adviser *(pu'gyori)* in the Office of Special Advisers.[87]

On 3 June 1880 Min became third tutor *(munhak)* in the Crown Prince Tutorial Office and in the following month was appointed concurrently to the post of fourth adviser *(ŭnggyo)* in the Office of Special Advisers.[88] These two posts were ranked senior fifth and senior fourth respectively. At the age of nineteen, therefore, Min had already attained the upper levels of the lower ranks of the Chosŏn administration.

On 28 July of the same year, Min was the chief signatory to a memorial urging the strict enforcement of the regulations for the Augmented Examination (Chŭng kwangsi) and the necessity of banishing certain officials who had been involved in irregularities. Min emphasized the importance of the integrity of the examination system and the danger of a loss of public confidence in it as a consequence of the lenient treatment of those who had abused the system. The memorial met a cool response, as did a second memorial presented on the following day. Min and his junior colleagues were simply informed that the necessary action had already been taken and that they should not be so troublesome.[89]

The issue came to a head on 22 October 1880, when Min was once again at the head of an even longer list of signatories from the Office of Special Advisers requesting vehemently that no leniency be shown to those officials who had been banished as a result of their involvement in the examination irregularities earlier in the year.[90] This time the memorial mentioned the officials by name, the most prominent being Pak Chŏng-yang. Pak was later to become a member of the gentlemen's sightseeing mission that visited Japan in 1881 and was also sent to Washington as Chosŏn's first minister to the United States in 1887. At the time of Min's departure for Russia as minister plenipotentiary and envoy extraordinary in 1896, Pak was acting prime minister and minister of home affairs, and at the time of the Min's visit to Queen Victoria's Diamond Jubilee in 1897, Pak held the rank of *ch'anjŏng* in the State Council.[91]

At this time, however, Min and his colleagues demanded that the edict that had been issued by the king pardoning Pak and the other banished officials be rescinded immediately. A second memorial was submitted two days later, after the king rejected the first, but to no avail.[92] The pardon was never rescinded, and, as has been mentioned, Pak Chŏng-yang himself went on to become a high-ranking official at Kojong's court, serving until his death in 1904. Ironically, he was to prove supportive of those officials, such as Min, who were on the side of modernization and reform.

Shortly afterward the king was admonished by another memorial, jointly signed by Min and seven other advisers in the Office of Special Advisers. This memorial appears to have been a parting shot on the issue of the pardoning of the corrupt officials. Min drew the attention of the king to the recent inauspicious portents of thunder and lightning around the capital. He urged the king to examine his moral character and to rectify himself through fervent study and righteous actions.[93] Min appears to have been implying that Kojong's action in pardoning the convicted officials had brought about the displeasure of Heaven.

This idea of the existence of a relationship between the sovereign's conduct and natural phenomena was basic to the East Asian worldview. As John K. Fairbank explains, "Misgovernment on the part of the ruler might produce natural catastrophe; and so a meteor, an eclipse, an earthquake, or a flood could all be regarded as nature's commentary on the ruler's performance."[94]

Nevertheless, Kojong apparently ignored the implication and in his response blandly requested that Min and his colleagues discover the reason for the portents. Probably deciding that discretion was the better part of valor, Min appears to have taken the matter no further.

On 18 March 1881, even before he had reached his twentieth birthday, Min was appointed to the post of sixth royal secretary *(sŭngji)* in the Royal Secretariat (Sŭngjŏng'wŏn tongbu). As one of six such secretaries, he was responsible for dealing with the affairs of the Board of Works (Kongjo).[95] Also, as a consequence of this promotion to a post at the senior third rank *(chŏng samp'um)*, Min entered the threshold of the ranks of the higher-level officials, the so-called *tangsang gwan,* of the Chosŏn administration. As Kang Sŏng-jo points out, such rapid promotion in just four years in government was exceptional.[96]

It was possibly the consciousness of this fact that caused Min to offer his resignation—that and the appointment of his elder cousin Min Yŏng-ik to the position of first royal secretary *(tosŭngji),* another senior third-rank post. Min appears again to have been concerned with avoiding any appearance of receiving preferential treatment.[97] He may also have wished to avoid becoming the object of jealousy among his fellow officials. Inasmuch as many other members of the Min clan were also rising rapidly through the ranks of the administration, it is not difficult to see why they may have been resented by members of the Kaehwadang and also the supporters of the Taewŏn'gun, who were effectively excluded from real political power.

The Soldiers' Rebellion of 1882

The year 1882 was a disastrous one both for Korea and for Min's own family in particular. The year began relatively auspiciously for Min himself, however, when on 7 April he was appointed to the prestigious position of headmaster *(taesasŏng)* of the National Confucian Academy (Sŏnggyun'gwan).[98] This post was also a senior third-rank *tangsang* appointment attained when Min was merely twenty-one years old. It is not surprising, therefore, that Min initially declined the post, claiming that he was too young and inexperienced. His father, he argued in his memorial of 10 April, had warned him not to be too zealous for promotion and run the risk of incurring public ridicule should he prove inadequate for the tasks required of him. He went on, in the self-deprecatory style that is the common feature of all his memorials, to say that to ask him to become the headmaster of the National Confucian Academy was like asking "a pygmy to carry a weight of a thousand *kŭn.*"[99]

Needless to say, his resignation was not accepted, and he was subsequently appointed to the concurrent post of first tutor *(podŏk)* in the Crown Prince Tutorial Office and then first royal secretary in the Royal Secretariat.[100] Both these latter third-rank appointments show that despite his youth, Min clearly enjoyed the confidence of both King Kojong and the crown prince's mother, Queen Myŏngsŏng.

On 22 May 1882, the Chosŏn administration made a significant step in broadening its foreign relations with the signing of the Korean-American Treaty of Amity and Commerce. This was Chosŏn's first treaty with a Western power and was swiftly followed by further treaties with the European powers, Great Britain and Germany. As has already been mentioned, it was by means of these treaties that King Kojong and his administration hoped to offset the undue and unwelcome influence of Japan on the peninsula. It is also important to remember, as Dalchoong Kim emphasizes, that this move toward modernization and the many other reforms of the 1880s were undertaken by an administration dominated by the Min clan, not members of the Enlightenment party.[101]

In July of the same year, however, the Chosŏn capital was shaken by the revolt of the Muwi Regiment (Palace Guards Garrison) in the Soldiers' Rebellion of 1882. The immediate cause of this revolt was that the regiment had received no wages for approximately thirteen months. This neglect was in stark contrast to the preferential treatment given to the Special Skills Force, which had been established by Min's father as an élite detachment in the previous year under the direction of the Japanese military adviser Horimoto Reizō. When the Muwi Regiment was eventually paid in July, the soldiers received barely one month's allowance of rice, half the weight of which was made up with sand and chaff. The soldiers rioted in anger and assaulted the clerks involved in the distribution of the grain.[102]

The government department responsible for the payment of the soldiers' wages, inappropriately named the Agency to Bestow Blessings (Sŏnhyech'ŏng), was headed by Min Yŏng-hwan's father, Min Kyŏm-ho, who, as has been mentioned previously, had a reputation for receiving bribes and living in luxury.[103] Min senior, rather than taking a conciliatory approach, had the ringleaders rounded up and ordered their execution. This action further enraged the soldiers of the regiment, who responded by destroying Min Kyŏm-ho's luxurious home. They then sought the leadership of the Taewŏn'gun and under his guidance attacked the Japanese legation and the royal palace itself. In the latter attack Queen Myŏngsŏng barely escaped with her life, while Min Kyŏm-ho and two others—Yi Ch'oe-ŭng, a key ally of the Min clan who was president of the Office of Royal Kinsmen and the elder brother of the Taewŏn'gun, and Kim Po-hyŏn, the governor of Kyŏnggi Province—were murdered.

Hwang Hyŏn, the author of an unofficial record of the events of this period, *Maech'ŏn yarok,* provides the following account of the death of Min Yŏng-hwan's father, which, if it is accurate, clearly demonstrates the intense resentment and vindictiveness felt by the Taewŏn'gun toward Min Kyŏm-ho despite the fact that he was his own brother-in-law:

> Min Kyŏm-ho urgently embraced the Taewŏn'gun, burying his head in the latter's ceremonial robes. At the same time he cried out desperately, "Your Excellency, please save me!" At which the Taewŏn'gun replied with an icy sneer, "How can I save Your Excellency?"
>
> Before he had even finished speaking these words, the rioting soldiers kicked Min down into the courtyard below, shooting at him with guns and stabbing him with their swords until he was reduced to a mound of flesh.[104]

As a result of his father's brutal death at the age of forty-three, Min Yŏng-hwan resigned from all his official posts and went into mourning. He remained out of office for more than two years until 24 October 1884, when he was appointed third minister *(ch'amŭi)* in the Board of Personnel (Ijo).[105] Min vehemently declined this appointment because he was still in mourning for his father, which according to Confucian tradition should last for a nominal period of three years.[106] His objections were rejected, however, and Min submitted two further memorials, humbly pleading with the king to understand his and his family's grief at the loss of his father and to continue to permit him to be excused from holding office so that he could take care of his desolate mother. The king, however, was adamant that he put public duty before his own private affairs and accept the appointment.[107] As a consequence, Min reluctantly took up the burdens and responsibilities of office once more on the very eve of the outbreak of the second serious catastrophe to strike at the heart of the Chosŏn court in the early 1880s, the Kapsin coup of 1884.

Min's Career from 1884 until the Sino-Japanese War

On 21 January 1885, Min declined to accept the position of first royal secretary. In his memorial he repented for having been so involved in his own grief over the loss of his father that he had not been able to foresee the coup of 1884[108] or warn the king. Nevertheless, he went on to request that the king relieve him of his duties because he did not have the necessary skills and experience to deal with China and the other foreign powers in the wake of the coup. As on previous occasions, he was simply ordered to attend to his duties.[109]

The 1884 coup had resulted in the assassination of two of Min Yŏng-hwan's relatives, Min T'ae-ho, who was the father of Min Yŏng-ik and of the crown prince's consort, and Min Yŏng-mok, as well as the severe injury of his influential cousin, Min Yŏng-ik, under the direction of Kim Ok-kyun and his fellow conspirators. Just how Min was affected while he was still in his early twenties by the violent deaths of so many of his relatives, including his own father, during this turbulent period is impossible to assess. But it is clear from his memorials that he was reluctant to accept the burdens of office holding throughout his career. The loss of so many influential figures from Min Yŏng-hwan's father's generation also meant that the burdens of responsibility for maintaining the prestige and influence of the clan inevitably fell upon the younger shoulders of another royal relative, Min Yŏng-ik and, of course, Min Yŏng-hwan himself.

According to Kang Sŏng-jo, it was at this time, when Min held the influential post of first royal secretary, that he became one of the king's closest and most indispensable political advisers. In evidence of how greatly Kojong valued Min as an adviser, Kang cites Kojong's proclamation after Min's death in 1905, in which he lamented, "This chief minister was of a gentle disposition with an upright will and spirit. We received many benefits from his loyal service when he was in our court. His long-standing dedicated service for the nation was exceptional, and he was a person We turned to on our left and our right for support."[110] Furthermore, according to Sands, at least by the 1900s, Min Yŏng-hwan along with Min Yŏng-gi and Min Sang-ho "had access to the palace when they pleased."[111]

From the end of 1884 through the first six months of 1885, Min was appointed in rapid succession to a bewildering variety of high-ranking posts in the administration, ranging between senior third and junior second rank. These included third minister in the Board of Personnel, second minister *(ch'amp'an)* in the Board of Works, second magistrate *(chisa)* in the State Tribunal (Ŭigŭmbu), first royal secretary in the Royal Secretariat, first adviser *(pujehak)* in the Office of Special Advisers, second deputy director *(tongjisa)* in the Office of Royal Lecturers (Kyŏng'yŏn), and second deputy director *(chikchehak)* in the Royal Library.[112] Such brief periods of office holding, however, appear to have been relatively normal for late-Chosŏn officials. Nevertheless, in this case, the extreme rapidity of appointments was probably the result of the confusion into which the government had been thrown as a consequence of the 1884 coup, which in a single night had eliminated so many key figures from the upper echelons of the Chosŏn court. It is possible that Min benefited from such a broad experience of the various aspects of government at a young age, but it is clear that during this period of crisis, the Chosŏn administration was incapable of either devising or executing consistent policies.

In the second half of 1885 Min was appointed once again as *kyŏm podŏk,* a concurrent post as first tutor in the Crown Prince Tutorial Office and second minister in the Board of Personnel; commandant *(yusu)* of the Kaesŏng Magistracy (Kaesŏngbu); and director *(ch'ongp'an)* of the Mint (Chŏnhwan'guk). The mint was Chosŏn's first permanent mint and had been established two years earlier under the auspices of Min T'ae-ho as part of the administration's self-strengthening efforts in response to the opening of the ports to Japan and the West.[113]

On 7 March 1886, Min was transferred from his post as Kaesŏng commandant to that of coastal defense commander *(haebang yŏngsa).*[114] Given the dilapidated state of the military at the end of the Chosŏn era, it is not surprising that Min found his task overwhelming and promptly offered his resignation after barely a month in the post. In his memorial he claimed that for him to undertake the duties required of the position was "like a mosquito carrying a mountain on its back or like trying to measure the sea with a calabash." Nevertheless, he took the opportunity to emphasize the importance of coastal defense, especially after the opening of the ports, and made several recommendations to improve the defenses along the coast and rivers. He went on to argue, however, that the responsibility for carrying out such an important task should be given to someone with the appropriate talent and experience rather than to him.[115]

Min's resignation was not accepted, however, and in a second memorial three months later he reiterated his unsuitability for the appointment. In addition he argued that as his elder cousin Min Yŏng-ik held the position of right division commander *(uyŏngsa),* it might appear that he was receiving preferential treatment. His arguments fell on deaf ears, however, and he was not granted permission to stand down.[116] Min went on to offer three more memorials of resignation from this post, with the last memorial being submitted on 3 July 1887. In the end his request was finally granted.[117]

During 1886 Min also held the high-ranking appointments of second minister in the Board of Works, commander of the capital coastal defense *(ch'in'-gunyŏn haebang yŏngsa)*, third magistrate *(uyun)* of Seoul (Hansŏng), director of the Arsenal (Kigiguk), and once again deputy director of the Royal Library.[118] That this last post appears to have become something of a sinecure for members of the Min clan and their supporters during King Kojong's reign is indicated by Kim Ok-kyun's singling out the Royal Library for abolition in his reform program of 1884.[119]

On 21 March 1887[120] Min and Han Kyu-sŏl were appointed directors of the Department of Trade (Sangniguk). Han Kyu-sŏl (1856–1930), who appears to have been a political ally of Min throughout his career, held the post of prime minister in November 1905 and, as will be seen in the final chapter of this study, was the sole cabinet minister to successfully resist signing the Ŭlsa Treaty of Protection.

Shortly after his appointment to the Department of Trade, Min was appointed commander *(chŏnyŏngsa)* of the Capital Guards (Ch'in'gun) and minister in the Board of Rites (Yejo); after another short spell as first tutor *(podŏk)* in the Crown Prince Tutorial Office, he became minister in the Board of Punishments (Hyŏngjo) and two days later minister in the Board of Rites for a second time.[121] By this time Min's appointments were consistently at the level of the second rank *(ip'um)*. In this year Min was also awarded the title of *chahŏn taebu*.[122] According to Kang, it was at this stage in his career, at the age of twenty-seven, that Min had already attained sufficient rank to participate directly in the policy making and decision taking of the Chosŏn court.[123]

On 26 May 1888, after a brief three-day spell as deputy director *(chehak)* in the Office of Special Advisers (Hongmun'gwan), Min became minister in the Board of War (Pyŏngjo) for the first time.[124] He soon offered his resignation, but he was ordered to remain in the post. In the following month he presented a memorial requesting punishment for a mistake he had made concerning the supervision of the Capital Garrison Cavalry (Kŭmwiyŏng kisa), one of the five garrisons in Seoul. This memorial may have been a genuine expression of contrition, but it appears to have been a more indirect way of requesting to be relieved of office. Whatever Min's motive, his resignation was not accepted.[125] In addition he was appointed to the posts of deputy director in the Office of Royal Decrees and fourth mentor *(ububin'gaek)* in the Crown Prince Tutorial Office.[126]

From about this time, however, Min appears to have begun to suffer quite seriously from bad health as this became one of the major reasons he cited for his unsuitability for office. Further circumstantial evidence of Min's poor health is also provided by Yun Ch'i-ho, who recorded in his diary that Min was a heavy smoker and on his trip to Russia in 1896 had carried with him a large supply of Chinese traditional medicines. In his diary entry of 11 April 1896, Yun wrote caustically, "Tobacco is a part of this too fine a gentleman. His stock of cigars, cigarettes, and of cut tobacco may easily enable him to set up a tobacco store in Russia. The medical stuffs which he has provided against any sickness might make him immortal, if medicines Corean could do so by their quantity."[127]

In the following two years Min received fewer appointments, probably because he was retained in his onerous post as minister in the Board of War. In 1889 Min received only two additional appointments, to the posts of deputy director in the Royal Library and second mentor in the Crown Prince Tutorial Office, while in 1890 he was simply reappointed to his old position as minister in the Board of War on 19 December.[128] Min's memorials of resignation from his position as minister in the Board of War, had continued from the end of 1888 through to 1890. In each case, however, the resignations were refused and Min was ordered to continue at his post.[129]

On 5 October 1890 Min was a cosignatory of a petition presented by Kim Hong-jip requesting that the king desist from visiting the royal mountain tombs. The king requested his ministers' understanding, and no further memorials were submitted.[130] In the same year Min offered a memorial of apology for a mistake concerning a sedan chair in a welcoming ceremony for the king.[131] The trivial nature of the offense might imply again that Min was simply seeking an indirect way of being relieved of his post. Presumably such self-accusatory memorials were also a way of preempting criticism from political enemies at court.

Min subsequently presented five memorials in succession requesting to be relieved of his post as minister in the Board of War. Each time his requests were rebuffed, the king arguing that he could not be spared.[132] Finally on 5 April 1891 Min submitted a memorial impeaching himself for neglecting his duties and asking to be demoted. As before, the king rejected his reasons for impeachment and ordered him to continue in his post.[133] In this same year, however, Min's first wife died, and Min once again retired from office and went into mourning for one year as required by Confucian tradition. Min's real reason for so urgently requesting his own dismissal might have been his wife's probable lengthy illness before her death.

It was not until 5 December 1893 that Min was recalled to office as second deputy director in the Royal House Administration (Tollyŏngbu) and soon afterward was appointed minister in the Board of Punishments, deputy director in the Office of Special Advisers, chief magistrate (puyun) of Seoul, sixth councillor (chwach'amch'an) in the State Council, and president (tokp'an) of the Ministry of Home Affairs[134] (Naemubusa).[135] This sudden increase in Min's appointments, all at senior second rank, seems to reflect the growing sense of crisis in the capital with the onset of the Tonghak Rebellion around this time.

In the first half of 1894 Min was appointed minister in the Board of Personnel, minister in the Board of Punishments, and once again third mentor in the Crown Prince Tutorial Office.[136] It was at the end of this period in the early 1890s, probably when Min held the post of third mentor, that he wrote and presented *Chŏnilch'aek,* a policy essay that encapsulated his thoughts on reform and self-strengthening for his beleaguered country.

Conclusion

Before examining Min's policy essay *Ch'ŏnilch'aek,* however, it is worth reflecting back over his early career as outlined in this chapter. In this early phase of his career, there is no evidence that Min played any significant role in the modernization efforts of the Chosŏn court. Nevertheless, it is highly probable that he, as an important member of the Min clan, supported the efforts of the young king and his consort together with the senior Min leadership to bring about domestic reform and to establish Chosŏn as a member of the international community of independent nations.

It is a pity that Min's memorials do not cast more light on his early career. They provide little significant information about what Min may actually have done in any of the posts mentioned in this chapter. Indeed, from the long list of rapidly changing appointments, it is hard to believe that Min would have been able to accomplish anything. Many of the posts seem hopelessly anachronistic in relation to the problems faced by Chosŏn in the years leading up to the Sino-Japanese War.

Nevertheless, during this period significant decisions were taken, including the momentous decision to open commercial and diplomatic relations with Japan and the West in 1876 and 1882 respectively. In fact, the whole period was a time of significant firsts for the Chosŏn administration. The first modern armed force and the first modern mint were established; the first Western adviser, Paul Georg von Möllendorff, was employed; the first Koreans visited the United States, completing the first circumnavigation of the globe by Koreans on their return journey; the first modern weaponry was purchased; and the first students went to study in Japan and the West. If Chosŏn's domestic and international position had been more secure, it would have been an exciting time to be a young, well-connected Korean.

As it was, during this period Min Yŏng-hwan was also witness to several crises that shook the venerable kingdom to its very foundations, one of which resulted in the violent death of his own father and the presumed death of Queen Myŏngsŏng herself, the linchpin of Min influence and power. By the early 1890s

Korea was under threat from China, Japan, and Russia abroad, and from the Tonghak at home. It was in the midst of these circumstances that Min composed his major essay on reform, *Ch'ŏnilch'aek*.

This policy essay marked the culminating point of Min's early career. Its urgent appeal for reform was made all the more poignant by the fact that it was written at the time of the upheavals of the Tonghak Rebellion and on the eve of the outbreak of the Sino-Japanese War. The following chapter will examine this essay, which clearly reveals both the strengths and weaknesses of Min's political thought before he visited the West and gained direct experience of the modern technology, culture, and institutions of the United States, Russia, and Europe.

2

PROPOSALS FOR REFORM

The Date of Composition of *Ch'ŏnilch'aek*

To understand the full significance of Min Yŏng-hwan's major extant essay on reform, *Ch'ŏnilch'aek*,[1] it is first necessary to solve the problem of when it was actually composed. The original text itself is undated, and no mention is made of its date of composition by the compilers of *Min Ch'ung jŏnggong yugo*. As the second section of the compilation, however, *Ch'ŏnilch'aek* precedes *Haech'ŏn ch'ubŏm* (1896) and *Sagu sokch'o* (1897), which form the third and fourth sections. Nevertheless, the Korean historian Kang Sŏng-jo surmises that *Ch'ŏnilch'aek* was written around the time of Min's two journeys to the West as Chosŏn's minister plenipotentiary and envoy extraordinary in 1896 and 1897.[2] As internal evidence for this assertion he notes that in the first section of *Ch'ŏnilch'aek*, "Siseji cheil wal" (First statement on the current state of affairs), Min mentioned that the Trans-Siberian Railway had not yet been completed. This means that the essay must have been written before 1898. In addition Kang maintains that in "Piŏji chesip wal" (Tenth proposal for preparation and defense) Min claimed that Korea had thoroughly divested itself of its subordinate relationship to China and also recommended that China, Japan, and Russia should be played off against each other. Kang argues that this also indicates that the essay must have been written around 1896–1897, after China's defeat in the Sino-Japanese War.

Although Kang is correct in his claim that *Ch'ŏnilch'aek* could not have been written after 1898, his argument is less convincing in setting an earliest date for the work. In the first case, contrary to Kang's assertion, Min did not argue that Korea should play off China, Russia, and Japan against each other in the "Piŏji

chesip wal," which also has the explanatory heading "Kyorin'guk" (Relations
with neighboring countries).[3] Min argued, in fact, that Korea should maintain
its traditional close relationship with China to defend itself from the dual threat
posed by Russia and Japan, as the following passage clearly shows:

> Our country must always keep its long friendship of reliance, just like that be-
> tween the lips and the teeth, with China. If the Japanese want to invade, then
> we must unite with China and secretly ask Russia to take advantage of the in-
> ternal weakness of the Japanese. If the Russians want to invade, then we must
> unite with China and secretly ask the Germans to take advantage of Russia's weak-
> ness. Therefore, although we are surrounded by China, Russia, and Japan, China
> is of one household with us.[4]

This is just one of several passages in the essay in which Min advocated the
traditional policy of *sadae* toward China. For this reason it is hard to believe
that the essay was written, as Kang suggests, after the Sino-Japanese War, in
which China had suffered a humiliating defeat at the hands of the Japanese and
proved itself to be incapable of acting as Korea's protector.

Nevertheless, it could still be argued that Min's views may have been so conservative that he simply refused to recognize the changed state of affairs in East
Asia resulting from the outcome of the Sino-Japanese War. This argument is
belied by the general intelligence of the essay as a whole; in addition, further
internal evidence in the text itself proves conclusively that *Ch'ŏnilch'aek* was written just before the outbreak of the war between China and Japan in July 1894.

In the section titled "Siseji chesam wal" (Third statement on the current
state of affairs), Min mentioned that Li Hongzhang was more than seventy years
old. According to both the Korean and Chinese systems of reckoning a person's age, a child is one year old at birth. As Li was born in 1822, this would set
the earliest date that the essay could have been written as 1893. In the same section Min also mentioned the prevalent rumor that Yuan Shikai would soon
leave Korea to return to China.[5] As Yuan only finally left Korea in the summer
of 1894 around the time of the outbreak of the Sino-Japanese War, the essay
must have been written before that time.

Further textual evidence is provided by Min's reference to "five hundred years
of civil government in Chosŏn."[6] As Chosŏn was founded in 1392, this would
again date the time of writing as being after 1892. In addition, in "Piŏ chegu
wal" (Ninth proposal for preparation and defense), Min praised Kojong for
having established the Yŏnmu kongwŏn (Royal military academy) and the
Yug'yŏng kongwŏn (Royal English academy).[7] Min then went on to suggest
how the selection procedure for these two academies could be improved, indi-

cating that they were both in existence at the time that *Ch'ŏnilch'aek* was written. As these institutions were abolished in 1894 and 1895 respectively during the Kabo-Ŭlmi reform period, the essay must have been written sometime before their abolition.

Additional evidence pointing to the date of composition as being before the Sino-Japanese War is provided by the section titled "Siseji chesa wal" (Fourth statement on the current state of affairs). In this section Min discussed the problem of the Tonghak movement in such a way that it is clear that the full-scale rebellion that broke out in the summer of 1894 and the subsequent intervention by China and Japan had not yet occurred:

> People all say that these rebels have no wise strategy and that they are all lower-class people with fish heads and ghost faces. They gather like day flies and scatter like day flies, and they have no weapons, so how can they stand against the troops from the capital? They are absolutely incompetent and not worth worrying about.[8]

If the Tonghak Rebellion had already broken out in full force and the government's élite troops from the capital had already been defeated by the rebels, as they were at Changsŏng in 1894, Min would not have been referring to the kind of complacency mentioned in the passage above.

Even more specific evidence, however, is provided by Min's reference to the dispatch of a *sŏnmusa* (an official sent to pacify the people) in the year before the essay was written.[9] According to Yi Kwang-nin, this official, Ŏ Yun-jung, was appointed in May 1893.[10] Min then went on to refer to the dispatch of a *ch'ot'osa* (an official sent to suppress rebellion) in the same year the essay was written.[11] Again according to Yi Kwang-nin, this official, Hong Kye-hun, was appointed on 6 May 1894.[12] All of this evidence indicates that the essay must have been written in the early summer months of 1894, sometime after the dispatch of the *ch'ot'osa* Hong Kye-hun in May but before the intervention of China and Japan in July of the same year.

Finally, Min referred directly to the years 1894–1895 in the following passage at the close of the "siseji chesam wal," concerning Korea's relationship with China:

> Kyerim[13] and Beijing are just like the two ends of a winnowing basket. If they are separated, therefore, both countries will have crises. Many writers have said that events in each country frequently resemble each other and that in the years of Kabo-Ŭlmi, China will have a crisis and consequently our country will have a crisis, too. Although we may not believe this, we have only to see what is happening now to know that it is partly true.[14]

That the essay was written before the intervention of Japan is shown by the following passage:

> [The Japanese] want to obtain their desire, but they dare not suddenly and reck-
> lessly invade us because they have to consider the fact that China will protect us.
> But if China has some problem and is not free to consider affairs beyond its bor-
> ders, then we must realize that a terrible disaster will definitely happen.[15]

When all the evidence outlined above is considered, one has to conclude that *Ch'ŏnilch'aek* was almost certainly composed during the early summer of 1894, just before the outbreak of the Sino-Japanese War and the initiation of the Kabo-Ŭlmi reforms and long before Min's visits to Russia, Europe, and the United States in 1896 and 1897. The essay, therefore, should be seen as the cul-mination of Min's political thought at the close of the early phase of his career, when he was still in his early thirties, rather than, as Kang argues, a statement of his mature ideas on reform, which were later to become the basis for the re-forms undertaken during the Taehan Empire period.[16]

Min's Assessment
of Chosŏn's Relations with Russia,
Japan, and China, and of the Tonghak Problem

Ch'ŏnilch'aek is divided into fourteen sections. The first four sections come un-der the title "Sise" (The current state of affairs) and the last ten under the title "Piŏ" (Preparation and defense). In Korean historiography the latter are gen-erally referred to as "Piŏ sipch'aek" (Ten policies for preparation and defense). In his short prologue to the main text, Min lamented the unwillingness of his fellow officials in the Chosŏn administration to speak up about the urgency of the national situation, either because they did not wish to exceed their official duty and incur the jealousy of others, or because they believed discussion to be useless and already too late. "Truly," Min concluded, "there is a lack of loyal indignation in these anxious times."[17]

The Perceived Russian Threat

Ironically, perhaps, as Min was later to be sent as Chosŏn's first minister pleni-potentiary and envoy extraordinary to Russia in 1896, the first section of

Ch'ŏnilch'aek, "Siseji cheil wal," deals with the threat that Min perceived Russia posed to the Korean peninsula.[18] Russian military power, Min claimed, was "without equal throughout the whole world,"[19] and as a result of Peter the Great's philosophy that a nation's wealth and strength were increased by plundering other nations, Russia had subsequently "destroyed Poland, invaded Turkey, plundered Central Asia, and interfered in the affairs of all the European nations."[20] Russia, Min concluded, had become a "modern-day, powerful Qin."[21]

Min likened the Russian naval squadron based at Vladivostok and the railway running between that city and the Amur River to the left wing of a hawk, the predatory insignia of the Romanovs. With the completion of the Siberian railway, the right wing of the hawk would also be complete, bringing "all the nations of East Asia under its beak."[22] Because Korea was on the route of any potential conflict in the Far East, Min added, it was bound to be the first to experience Russian aggression.

Min did not rule out the possibility that Korea might have been able to receive assistance from abroad. As will be seen, in later sections of the essay it is clear that he still viewed China as a reliable ally. Nevertheless, he stressed the case for urgent, internal reform to counter the external threat posed in the first instance by Russia.

The accuracy of Min's perception of the threat posed by Russia, which he held in common with many of his contemporaries in the Chosŏn administration, is borne out by the frank assessment of Tsar Nicholas II's policy in East Asia given by the Russian Finance Minister Sergei I. Witte, who wrote in his memoirs, "Emperor Nicholas . . . was anxious to spread Russian influence in the Far East. Not that he had a definite program of conquest. He was merely possessed by an unreasoned desire to seize Far-Eastern lands."[23]

Modern historians, however, have differed widely in their analyses of the supposed Russian threat to the countries of East Asia in the late nineteenth century. In his two-volume work, *Balance of Intrigue,* George A. Lensen concludes that Britain, the United States, and Japan greatly exaggerated this threat to provide a justification for the vigorous pursuit of their own interests in the region.[24] This opinion is also supported in an article by Mikhail N. Pak and Wayne Patterson, who argue,

> An objective historical study of Russo-Korean relations has been prevented, to a great extent, by the myth of the "Russian threat," invented by such masters of political provocation as Lord Curzon. Created in the nineteenth century and widely spread by the English and Japanese press, it was a pretext for Great Britain and Japan to carry out their aggressive policy in East Asia.[25]

Andrew Nahm, however, points to the activities and pronouncements of such Russian "expansionists" as Count Nikolai Muraviev, Vice Admiral Evfimii Putiatin, and General Nikolai Ignatiev and the three treaties extracted from the Qing administration by Russia between 1858 and 1860 as evidence of Russia's expansionist intentions in the region.[26]

Doubtless, the debate as to the true nature of Russian intentions in the Far East at the end of the nineteenth century will continue. Nevertheless, it is worth noting that Min Yŏng-hwan's perception of the threat posed by Russia to Korean sovereignty, which was undoubtedly based on the Qing experience outlined above as well as Chosŏn's own experience of Russia on its northern border, was far closer to that of his contemporary Witte and the modern historian Nahm than to the assessments of Pak, Patterson, and Lensen.

The Perceived Japanese Threat

The "Siseji chei wal" deals with the threat allegedly posed by Japan, a nation that Min described as follows:

> Among the sixty-nine nations in all the world, Japan is ranked eighteenth. It has 25,000 leagues of territory and is extremely densely populated. Its people's physique is undersized, and their will is fierce and cruel. It is their custom, both great and small, to fear the law and to be able to die for their superiors. Their sovereign has also revitalized government policy and renewed all the official laws. Their trade in merchandise and manufacture of machines all imitate foreign systems. On every level they are far in advance of our country.[27]

Min went on to point out what he considered to be the two most important factors in assessing the potential threat from Japan: namely its fear of Russia and its overpopulation. Consequently, he argued, Japan was continually trying to acquire small nations in order to strengthen its own position in the world. Min would presumably have based this assessment of Japanese intentions in the region on its punitive expedition to Taiwan in 1874, its use of military threats to open Korea in 1876, and its annexation of the Liuqiu Islands in 1879. According to Min, however, all the small islands in the Pacific had already been claimed by the European powers, so the Japanese had no further space to expand there. As a consequence, he wrote, "day and night their minds are filled with an overwhelming desire for our country."[28]

Min then went on to summarize why he believed that Japan had a particular interest in annexing Korea. The two countries had many complementary and similar features in their geography, produce, and circumstances. If they were combined, Min argued, "it would be like Japan's teeth and horns being perfected, and it would be a strong country in the world."[29] Furthermore, the Japanese leadership had already developed the so-called *sei-Kan-ron* (argument for attacking Korea),[30] and the conditions for its execution were now ripe. Japanese merchants and craftsmen were spying out the land and, Min wrote, "When they see our country's lax and confused administration, civil disturbances arising on all four sides, and the daily gatherings of the Tonghak, they surely know the situation of our country and are secretly dancing for joy."[31]

Min added that the only consideration preventing Japan from invading was that China would protect Korea, but if China were to be occupied with some other problem, "a terrible disaster will surely happen."[32] Min may have been thinking here of the precedent of the Annam crisis between China and France, which had allegedly encouraged Kim Ok-kyun to carry out the Kapsin coup of 1884.

Min continued his assessment of Korea's vulnerability to the aggressive intentions of its neighbor by painting a bleak picture of the ease with which Japan could invade at Inch'ŏn and Pup'yŏng in the capital region, Pusan in the south, and Ullŭng Island in the east, as well as at P'yŏng'an and Hwanghae provinces in the northwest. In his final paragraph on Japan Min issued a stern but, as he himself was only too well aware, belated admonition:

> We do not build a house when the dark rain clouds have already gathered. We do not read military texts when the enemy is already coming. Among all the innumerable affairs of this world, there is nothing more important than being prepared in advance, and among the things which we must immediately prepare, there is no priority higher than defense.[33]

Min's traditionalist assessment of the threat from Japan was in obvious contrast to the sanguine perception of the leadership of the Kaehwadang, who, ten years earlier, under the spell of the Meiji reformer Fukuzawa Yukichi, had initiated the Kapsin coup, believing that they could seize political power in Korea with Japanese backing.[34] It also clearly shows that whatever the truth of Hilary Conroy's assertion that the Meiji leadership had no long-term plan to annex Korea, that was certainly not the perception of at least one member of Korea's leadership élite as early as 1894.[35]

Furthermore, the perception that Japan was aggressively pushing for annexation was not restricted to Koreans alone. A mere six years later Japanese intentions to annex its mainland neighbor were clear even to a relative newcomer on the Korean scene, William Franklin Sands. Sands first arrived in Korea in the late 1890s as secretary of the American legation. On 24 February 1900 he was appointed as an adviser (*komungwan*) to the Korean government and remained in that post until the outbreak of the Russo-Japanese War in February 1904. Concerning the Japanese minister to Seoul in the years leading up to the protectorate treaty of 1905, Sands wrote,

> Hayashi Gonsuke . . . was aggressive and provocative, not haphazard, but each move marked out in advance and intentional. He was either the most impersonally perfect public servant and party man that ever was, or he was what I think he was: a convinced annexationist himself, hardening a party sentiment at home to a definite war policy. . . . This picture of him grew to be a conviction in the five years during which I faced him. In no other way could I explain the consistent opposition to every reform I attempted. Reform raised an obstacle in the way of annexation.[36]

This passage also suggests that Japan was making every effort to hinder Korean reform, as a reformed Korea would be less susceptible to a takeover and would attract a greater degree of interest from the West. In addition Sands also claims that Hayashi made every effort to prevent the development of Western interests in Korea because an active interest by the United States or European nations would also have caused complications in Japanese plans to seize control of Korea.[37]

Chosŏn's Relationship with China

In the "Siseji chesam wal," Min discussed the relationship between Chosŏn and China. Perhaps in a way that is disappointing to a modern Korean historian such as Kang Sŏng-jo, who appears to have deliberately misinterpreted this section of the essay in his biographical article "Kyejŏng Min Yŏng-hwan yŏn'gu,"[38] Min clearly argued for the traditional Chosŏn policy of *sadae* toward China. He did not, however, argue for blind reliance. On the contrary, Min insisted that the only way for his country to secure the reliable support of China was to undertake internal reform and a program of self-strengthening. He strongly criticized those officials who had a defeatist attitude to the modernization of Chosŏn and simply advocated a policy of total dependence on China. He then provided a stark description of his country's predicament:

> No doctor will give medicine to a corpse, and parents will not share their wealth with a profligate son. If we cannot strengthen ourselves and only depend on China, will not China look upon our country as being like a corpse or a profligate son? In this way we will become isolated from China.[39]

Min then cited Huang Zunxian's work *Zhaoxian ce lyue* (A policy for Chosŏn), which had been circulated in the Chosŏn court more than ten years earlier, circa 1880.[40] In this work Huang had argued, among other things, that Chosŏn's difficulties could be solved only with Chinese assistance. In counterbalance to this Min also cited Li Hongzhang, who, he claimed, had stated that it was impossible for China to reform Chosŏn. Min went on to warn that Li was now over seventy and was preoccupied with China's own internal difficulties. Unless the Chosŏn court, therefore, made its own efforts, assistance from China would not be forthcoming.

Min also mentioned the rumor that Yuan Shikai would soon leave Chosŏn and return to China. For many Korean historians, Yuan has been a bête noir, responsible for stifling nascent Korean reforms while selfishly promoting Chinese commercial and political interests in Korea. The Korean scholar Young Ick Lew, for example, is particularly scathing about the baleful influence of Yuan, the Min clan, and their "hangers-on."[41] Min, however, viewed both Li and Yuan in a rather different light. "These two people," he wrote, "did their best to care for our country and protect it. If other people take over from these two, then how can we guarantee that they will do as well as Li and Yuan?"[42] Just how strongly Min was endorsing Li and Yuan is not entirely clear. He might simply have been arguing, "Better the devil you know."

Min continued by pointing out that Russia and Japan were attempting to take advantage of the Chosŏn court's ambivalent attitude to China and that this in turn was alienating China from Chosŏn. In conclusion he reasserted the inextricable nature of Chosŏn's relationship with China and their mutual importance to each other, and advocated "sincere respect in serving the great" while pursuing vigorous policies in internal reform, defense, and self-strengthening.[43]

Min's advocacy of continued reliance on China was in accord with the attitude of the Min leadership toward China throughout the 1880s but was anathema to progressives such as Pak Yŏng-hyo, Sŏ Chae-p'il, and Yun Ch'i-ho, who saw China as a backward and oppressive influence on Korea. This negative assessment of late-nineteenth-century China and its influence on Korean affairs has also been shared by most modern Korean historians, who blame China for departing from its traditional policy of noninterference in favor of an overtly imperialist one that mimicked the high-handed actions of the West in East Asia.

It is impossible to deny the evidence of Chinese interference and obstruction in Korea's internal and external affairs throughout the period from 1882 until 1894. Nevertheless, given the geopolitical realities of the previous five centuries, it should not be too surprising that the Min leadership viewed the maintenance of a close relationship with China as being among the most feasible of the policy options available to them.[44]

In the first instance, Korea's other continental neighbor, Russia, was very much an unknown quantity. Its acquisition of the territory to the east of the Amur River from the Qing and the antipathy its eastern expansion had aroused in Japan must have caused the Korean court to view its recently acquired neighboring state with considerable trepidation. Although the Chosŏn administration eventually opted to approach Russia for protection, this decision was made under extreme duress after the murder of the Korean queen and the effective imprisonment of the king in his own palace. It must have been bitterly ironic to such officials as Min Yŏng-hwan that to escape the clutches of Japan after the defeat of China in the Sino-Japanese War, Kojong was forced to throw himself at the feet of another threatening power. Similarly, the rhetoric and actions of the Japanese had been generally aggressive toward their weaker neighbor since the *Unyōkan* incident in 1875 and were underpinned by a long history of harassment by coastal raiders as well as the outright Japanese invasions of the late sixteenth century.

In line with Huang Zunxian's recommendations, the Chosŏn leadership had attempted to enlist the interest and protection of the United States. Nevertheless, by 1894 it must have been increasingly clear to Min and his colleagues that the interest demonstrated in Seoul by the American missionaries and even the diplomatic representatives themselves for the independence and modernization of Korea had little resonance in the U.S. State Department and Congress.[45]

Finally, although the option of an international guarantee of neutrality had been mooted at various times and by various powers for the Korean peninsula, the international cooperation, particularly between Great Britain and the United States, required to make it a reality simply did not exist.[46] It is hardly surprising, therefore, that Min did not even mention neutrality as an option in *Ch'ŏnilch'aek.*

Before the Sino-Japanese War there must have been few political analysts who would have predicted that Japan could defeat the vast continental empire of the Qing. Even though it was well known that Japan had superior military forces, contemporary military analysts thought that China's weight of numbers would always tip the balance in its favor. This view was clearly expressed by a contemporary Western observer of the situation in the Far East, the Canadian journalist for the British newspaper the *Daily Mail,* Frederick A. McKenzie, who wrote,

> The great majority of European experts and of European and American residents
> in the Far East were convinced that if it came to an actual contest, Japan would
> stand no chance. She might score some initial victories, but in the end the greater

weight, numbers and staying power of her monster opponent must overwhelm her.[47]

This view had after all been demonstrated on a small scale ten years before the outbreak of the Sino-Japanese War, when two thousand Chinese troops in Seoul had routed two hundred well-armed Japanese legation guards during the coup of 1884. The only other historical precedent was, of course, the Hideyoshi expeditions at the end of the sixteenth century, which had failed in the face of combined Ming and Chosŏn resistance.

When all these factors are taken into account, Min's suggested policy of maintaining an unambiguous alliance with China while pursuing a program of self-strengthening and reform may well have appeared the best option available to the Korean administration before the outbreak of the Sino-Japanese War. Kim Ok-kyun's reliance on Japan in his coup of 1884 had proved to be a disastrous miscalculation that had advanced the cause of both China and Japan on the Korean peninsula while seriously weakening the Chosŏn leadership and damaging its image in the eyes of its Western treaty partners.

Min recognized that Korean ambivalence in foreign relations with these three powerful neighbors would be destabilizing. His recommendation of a frank alliance with China to prevent the further realization of Russian and Japanese ambitions on the peninsula would at least have provided other powers such as the United States and Great Britain with a more consistent image of the power ratio in the region.

It is known that before the Sino-Japanese War, Britain and even the United States accepted that Korea belonged to the sinic zone of influence. Britain, at least, viewed this state of affairs as being necessary to prevent any potential Russian expansion in Northeast Asia.[48] The opinion of the Qing administration itself on this matter was clearly spelled out in a letter by its employee, Sir Robert Hart, written on 29 May 1888 to the American head of Korean customs, Henry F. Merrill:

> In all that concerns Korea, the one point to start from is that Korea is China's tributary, and that China will not only fight anybody rather than give up her suzerainty, but will be forced to absorb Korea if troublesome scheming goes on there. It is useless for America to say "assert your independence!" It is useless for Japan to say "come to my arms!" . . . The backing that your people [the Americans] are giving to the King and the temptations the Japanese are putting in his paths are alike pitfalls. . . . If Korea "flirts" she will lose all her lovers after falling prey to the monetary power of one of them.[49]

Hart's unsentimental assessment of Korea's situation was ultimately proved to be fairly accurate. He was wrong, however, in failing to recognize that Japan would have the capability to remove Korea from China's sphere of influence by force of arms.

After the defeat of China in the Sino-Japanese War, the pragmatic nature of British policy in the region was demonstrated by the British rapprochement with the victor. The British government's new acceptance of Japan as a major player in the Far East overrode all the misgivings expressed by missionaries and other observers on the ground, who recognized the growing ambitions of the island empire behind the façade of reasonableness of the Meiji leadership and its propagandists. This rapprochement eventually resulted in the first and second Anglo-Japanese alliances of 1902 and 1905, which helped pave the way for Japan to make Korea its protectorate and then annex it outright.

Min's advocacy of maintaining Chosŏn's traditional relationship with China is open to criticism because the Qing policy toward Chosŏn, especially as carried out by the arrogant "minister resident" Yuan Shikai, was detrimental to its efforts to modernize and reform itself and establish stable diplomatic relationships with the United States and other Western powers. In the face of pressure from Russia and Japan, however, continued Qing interference may well have appeared the lesser evil. Another serious flaw in Min's policy, of course, was his overestimation of the relative strengths of China and Japan. But if, as has been shown above, *Chŏnilch'aek* was written before the outbreak of the Sino-Japanese War, his assessment would have been shared by most other analysts of the time. In addition, Min's interpretation of *sadae* was of a mutual alliance having its origin in the geostrategic conditions of the two countries; he did not argue for the adoption of a servile attitude to China.

The Tonghak Problem

"Sise chesa wal" deals with the domestic problem of the Tonghak uprisings in the south and civil unrest in the north of the Korean peninsula. Min considered these problems as even more serious than the external threats posed by Russia and Japan and the breakdown of Korea's traditional relationship of alliance with China. He identified three major causes for the unrest: the dishonesty of the majority of local magistrates, the decline of education, and the instability of agricultural production.

Min warned against complacency in the face of such unrest, reminding those who believed that the Tonghak rebels were a mere rabble that just such rabble had overthrown both the Qin and Han dynasties. "From ancient times," he wrote, "when administration was neglected and controls were slack, then finally rebellious people overthrew the dynasty. The precedents are very clear."[50] He went on to point out that Japan would quickly take advantage of any internal unrest in Korea and might even have a hand in the uprisings. China, on the other hand, he argued, would have no other choice but to abandon Korea to its fate.

Min criticized the administration's policy toward the rebels, which entailed sending an official to pacify them in 1893, another official to suppress them the following year. The former had provided the rebels with favors, but those favors had been insufficient to provide them with a livelihood; the latter had vigorously suppressed them, naturally creating resentment.

When troops from the capital were sent down to the southern provinces, the rebels had scattered, but when the troops returned to the capital, the same rebels regrouped. In the meantime the nation's wealth was diminishing daily. Min provided a graphic description of the government's self-defeating policy: "Is this not the same as taking out a sword to strike a horsefly? The horsefly flies off and the ox is beheaded. Or is it not like burning out scorpions? The scorpions may die, but the house is burnt down as well."[51]

Min then put forward a different policy for dealing with the unrest, placing priority on sending officials who could secure the people's livelihood. He advised that the ringleaders of the rebels be arrested. If the local leaders seemed to be protecting the rebels, Min advised sending troops from the capital. In addition, rewards should be offered for the arrest of ringleaders, on the one hand, while an amnesty should be held out to all those who had been coerced into taking part. Otherwise, Min argued, the rebels would have nothing to lose in fighting to the death, and their suppression would be that much more difficult. It is possible that Min's advocacy of leniency for the rebels was a result of his memories of the Soldiers' Rebellion of 1882, which had in large part been sparked by his own father's intransigence toward the rioting soldiers. Finally, Min warned that if the rebellion should spread to the northern provinces, the fierce and stubborn character of the local people there would result in rebellions far more serious than those of the southern Tonghak.

In modern Korean historiography, the Tonghak Rebellion has been cast in a romantic light. Marxists have seen them as manifestations of an incipient class struggle, whereas nationalists have viewed them as assertions of "people power" in the face of corrupt government, feudal oppression, and foreign imperialist intrusion.[52] Whatever the nature and causes of the Tonghak rebellions, however, by providing China and Japan with an excuse to intervene in the Korean peninsula, they did more to further the cause of Japanese imperialism in the region than any other previous incident.

Min did not blame the rebellions on the impoverished Korean peasantry but on the corrupt magistrates and the Tonghak demagogues. Consequently, he advocated a dual approach to the problem of rooting out local oppression and suppressing the leaders of the rebellion, while providing an amnesty to those who were simply caught up in the tide of uprisings. If the rebellions had been swiftly and competently dealt with along the lines recommended by Min, the Sino-Japanese War, although it might not have been ultimately prevented, might have been delayed and, more important, might not have been fought on the Korean peninsula. Although such assertions may be dismissed as mere speculation, it is important to recognize that the Tonghak Rebellion, for all its ostensibly righteous and patriotic motives, did nothing but harm to the cause of Korean independence.

Min's Ten Proposals for Preparation and Defense

Employing Talented People

After presenting his analysis of Chosŏn's international and domestic predicament, Min put forward ten proposals for preparation and defense. The first is concerned with the employment of talented people. The Chosŏn court, Min argued, "does not inquire about people's talent but only esteems their status (pŏl)."[53] According to his analysis, because those with a high social status comprised only about a tenth of the nation's population, the policy of esteeming status disadvantaged the majority of the population. As a consequence of this discriminatory system, people had given up cultivating their talents because those of high status would be selected for office regardless of their ability, while those of low status would have no chance of attaining office no matter how hard they tried to improve themselves.

Min then emphasized the importance of the state examinations as a means of selecting suitable officials who would care for the people under them.[54] As Min outlined in his analysis of the causes of the Tonghak uprising, the selection of unsuitable people as magistrates inevitably led to unrest among those whom they governed. Min accused the officials in charge of the examinations of selling offices to those wealthy enough to buy them. As "most talented people are those who reject the desire for profit and esteem integrity" and "most wealthy people are those who have a desire for profit and have lost their integrity,"[55] Min argued, unsuitable persons were inevitably selected for office. Min concluded by asking the following rhetorical question: "How can we know that those people who are swept up in greed for profit and have lost their integrity will love the people with the compassion one would have for a naked infant or serve their lord with the loyalty one would have for one's parents?"[56]

Min then went on to criticize the inadequacy of officials' salaries. He cited the system under China's three founding sovereigns," Fu Xi, Shen Nong, and Huang Di, in which even the salaries of the lower-ranking officials were equal to the salaries of the three highest ranks of officials in the Chosŏn administration. As a result of such low salaries, Min argued, few people were willing to devote themselves wholeheartedly in the service of the king.

Min then put forward three proposals for selecting suitable people for the administration. In the first place he advocated abolishing examinations based on Chinese verse composition because such examinations were irrelevant to the problems of government. Instead Min argued for exams that tested for "a clear understanding of policy and *The Classics*."[57] In the study of policy, emphasis should be placed on economics, while the study of *The Classics* should stress the principles of righteousness. According to Min's recommendation, the content of the examinations should imitate the content used under the Han system, while the method of examination should imitate the Tang system of oral and written exams—the purpose of the former being to "demonstrate understanding," of the latter, to "ascertain truthfulness and practicality."[58]

In addition to the examination system, Min suggested that the government invite virtuous and principled people living in retirement in the countryside, the so-called *sallim*, to participate in the administration. To add force to this proposal, he cited the Chinese precedents of Prince Tang and Zhao Lie (Liu Bei). Prince Tang overthrew the tyrant Jie of Xia and established the Shang dynasty and is said to have invited a peasant farmer to be his chief minister three times. Similarly Liu Bei, in *San guo ji* (Romance of the Three Kingdoms), also offered three invitations to Kong Ming, who was living in retirement, to be his chief adviser.

Finally, Min suggested a third way of recruiting talented people: advertising for them and allowing them to recommend themselves for posts. This time he cited the precedent of Han Gaodi, the first emperor of the Han dynasty, who established the *Zhao xian guan* (Hall for recruiting the virtuous).

In this section on employing talented people, then, Min identified three problems: esteeming status and ignoring ability (a problem exacerbated by the sale of offices to the wealthy), paying officials inadequately, and maintaining an inappropriate examination system. He then gave three recommendations to rectify these faults: selecting officials by impartial examination, remunerating officials adequately, and basing the exam system on practical government and moral probity.

Both his analysis of the problems and his proposals for their rectification remained within the domain of Confucian orthodoxy and relied on precedents taken from Chinese history. Nevertheless, it should be recognized that Min was constrained to work within the frames of reference of the Chosŏn court. His essay was intended for a readership that shared a common education in the Chinese classics, and he consequently put forward his proposals in terms that could be understood by his readers. By using Chinese precedents in his arguments for reform, he was also protecting himself from any criticism that might come either from conservatives or from Qing observers of the court such as Yuan Shikai. It is clear, however, that Min at this stage in his career was by no means a radical reformer and might be best classed as a conscientious conservative who looked toward the Chinese rather than the Japanese model as the way for Chosŏn to reform.

Restoring the Fundamental Principles of Government

In his second policy recommendation, Min introduced the topic of restoring the fundamental principles of government by apologizing that at first sight it did not appear to be relevant to the issues of military preparation and defense. He went on to argue, however, that these very principles were at the root of the success or failure of a nation:

> Because if the fundamental principles of government are restored then both high and low will unite together firmly and fulfill their duties. If the people are called upon to take up arms, then they will be to their leaders like hands and feet guarding the head and eyes. Everyone will labor at the cost of their lives and never run away. We can call this disciplining the people so that they can attack the impregnable armor and sharp weapons of Qin and Chu.[59]

Unity between the ruler and the ruled, Min argued, was fundamental to the security of a nation.[60] But that was precisely what had been lost in Chosŏn. Internal disunity, not Japan or Russia, was the nation's greatest enemy. Min went on to attack the endemic corruption in the administrative system. Corruption had become so bad that "by means of bribery, even people who have been condemned to death can still live" and "without bribery even those people who deserve to live are put to death."[61] At the heart of this corruption were the powerful *yangban* families, too many of whom conducted their own reigns of terror in the rural towns, and the local magistrates, too many of whom abused their positions to increase their own wealth. "If this problem is not solved," Min concluded, "then greed will become the fashion, and integrity and shame will be lost."[62]

Min described a vicious cycle of corruption prevalent in Chosŏn society, whereby wrongdoers bribed officials to secure their release from prison, then extorted money from the ordinary people to recoup their losses. Robbery was so prevalent that it was "difficult to travel even along major highways."[63] The officials were too cowardly to arrest such robbers because of the trouble that might ensue from their followers.

Min lamented that those who upheld traditional values and committed suicide on the death of their spouse or sovereign were now considered to be fanatics and were no longer respected. Furthermore, even though humility and self-effacement had always been considered virtues, "if a person rejects an appointment in order to preserve his integrity," as Min himself did many times throughout his career, "he is considered to be a fraud."[64]

Min considered that such corruption had come about "because punishments are not absolute and rewards are not honored."[65] He went on to propose the following Draconian remedies: those who gave bribes and those who accepted them should be punished equally; nobles who broke the law should be barred from holding office for life and should return to farming; greedy and cruel magistrates should be boiled to death; unjust judges should be imprisoned; and "wicked and cunning officials should be exiled for minor offenses, but for major crimes their heads should be gibbeted on the streets of the capital."[66] Min advocated the death penalty for anyone guilty of a crime deserving more than ten years in prison and for anyone on the register of robbers. In conclusion, Min pointed out that enacting such a policy would cost the government nothing, but that without such a moral revival in the administration of the country, all efforts to carry out a policy of preparation and defense were bound to fail.

According to Min's analysis, there was a general breakdown of law and order in late Chosŏn. The state at this time appears to have been particularly plagued by bribery and corruption throughout officialdom. This state of affairs was succinctly described by the American adviser Sands, who wrote, "Administrative office was secured by nepotism and heavy payment, which, in turn, carried the necessity of recovering from the people the money expended to get it under the guise of taxation and arbitrary taxation was the source of most of our internal disorders."[67]

Min's Draconian remedies, however, belonged to an earlier era and were impossible to carry out without a strong centralized authority. The Chosŏn monarchy had clearly lost its grip on the nation under King Kojong and in a sense the Chosŏn state was being held together simply by an innate loyalty to the royal house, which still retained a remnant of symbolic power in the eyes of the general Korean populace. It is interesting to note that the Tonghak rebels never criticized their sovereign but only the "wicked officials" surrounding him. The traditional administrative system itself, however, appears to have been almost completely discredited in the eyes of the people, foreign observers, and even, as has been seen in this section, by conscientious Chosŏn officials such as Min Yŏng-hwan.

Reform of the Military System

Min, who held both civil and military posts during his political career, began by characterizing the relationship between the civil and military officials in government as being the same as the interdependent relationship between vitality (*ki*) and the body. He advocated establishing a military academy based on the Song dynasty's system to prevent those "without wisdom, bravery, or knowledge of military strategy" from continuing to gain military posts by illicit means. Officials without any post, he argued, should be allowed to enroll in the academy and be permitted to study ancient and modern military texts, a practice that had been forbidden during the Chosŏn dynasty.

According to Min's proposals, those students who became proficient in martial arts and had an extensive knowledge of history and biography would be given a qualifying examination at the end of three years. Those who passed would be promoted and given posts; those who failed would be permitted to continue studying. Min advocated the Tang system of selecting people "with an imposing physique who are able to speak clearly, are brave and skillful, and are able to command."[68] In other words, Min emphasized practical ability over a classical literary education.

Concerning the selection of ordinary soldiers, Min criticized the fact that many of those serving in the Chosŏn army had been forced to join simply because they had no parents or relatives to care for them. In addition, there was no physical standard or uniformity among the soldiers. "They are tall and short, strong and feeble, old and young,"[69] Min complained. In place of the costly and inefficient method that had produced a small and incompetent standing army, Min suggested universal conscription whereby all male commoners would serve five years in the standing army, after which they would serve in the reserve army. "This would be economical but provide many soldiers," he wrote; "the expense would be small, but the manpower would be plentiful. This is truly the best possible system."[70] This recommendation shows that Min was familiar with the concept of universal conscription, which was introduced in Europe in the nineteenth century. In fact, there had been a system of universal conscription in early Chosŏn times, but this system had rapidly deteriorated. Min's detailed accounts of the Russian and German systems of conscription may be found in *Haech'ŏn chubŏm* and *Sagu sokch'o*, respectively, which are examined in detail in the third and fourth chapters of this study.

Concerning the problem of the regional militias, Min criticized the chaotic state of the militia registers. The lack of organization of these registers, he argued, was the main reason that the local militias were no more than disorderly mobs that ran away at the first sign of trouble. To rectify this situation, Min cited the policy of Guan Zhong, a prime minister during the Warring States period, who had abolished corvée labor and armed every man in three with a bow and arrows. In addition, Min advocated adopting the policy of Li Baozhen of the Tang dynasty, who had created separate registers of military officers in each district, and that of Chong Shiheng of the Song dynasty, who had instituted a *li min* tax (poll tax) in silver to provide for the officers' salaries.

The expenditure of foreign countries on military provisions, Min continued, was far in excess of what the Chosŏn administration could afford. Because foreign soldiers were well provided for, they were "happy to be soldiers and to die for their king."[71] As such extravagance, however, was beyond the means of the Korean government, Min simply recommended that those soldiers who were old or weak be dismissed and their provisions given to the young and strong.

Min then criticized those officers who merely inspected troops in imitation of Western methods but did not participate in any of the training themselves. Although Min encouraged the adoption of foreign training methods such as "exercising, marching, shooting, and bayoneting,"[72] he also pointed out that there was much more to foreign military training than this. Rather than simply slavishly following the methods of foreign instructors, Min argued that it would be better to retain and improve what was valuable in Korea's own traditional systems.

As an example of such mistaken imitation of foreign methods, Min wrote,

Concerning the procedure for giving orders by means of signals, we are already using the system of another country. The signals and orders are also in the language of the other country. Usually we consider it a good thing in the army if we know the meaning of our signals and commands and the enemy does not. But in this case the people of another country all know the meaning of the orders while even the leading officers of our country do not. This fact is extremely shameful. Regardless of whether the training system we adopt is from another country or our own, we must exclusively use our own language for giving orders.[73]

In addition Min criticized the use of bugles in place of the traditional gongs, drums, and flags, arguing that signals using the traditional methods could be learned in a day, whereas it took seven or eight months of practice to learn how to use a bugle, adding "even then will there not still be people who do not understand it?"[74] In conclusion he advocated a return to the Korean way of giving orders and commands.[75]

Min then emphasized the necessity of improving marksmanship and again referred to episodes in Chinese history to make his point: "With one arrow all of Chu was recovered. With three arrows Xie Rengui occupied Tiansan."[76] Surprisingly, however, he made no mention here of the Koryŏ Buddhist monk Kim Yun-hu, who killed the Mongol leader Sartaq with an arrow in 1232, leading to a temporary withdrawal of the Mongol forces. Min went on to recommend regular target practice for all soldiers with liberal rewards for those who hit the target and severe punishment for those who did not.

The loyalty of the troops stationed in the capital was another problem Min identified, referring to the rebellion of 1882, in which his own father had been assassinated. Min suggested the adoption of a system modeled on that of Western Han in which troops were selected from the provinces and stationed in the capital in yearly rotation.

Min then turned his attention to naval defense. He identified the main obstacles to the establishment of a navy as Chosŏn's lack of finances and the fact that the majority of the Korean people were from inland and knew nothing about seafaring. The second obstacle seems to be a strange thing to say about a nation surrounded on three sides by water. It should be remembered, however, that the Chosŏn administration had always restricted coastal settlement in order to limit any contact with the outside world and also to remove any incentive for coastal raiders to visit Korean shores.

To overcome these obstacles, Min advocated the establishment of a register in all the coastal towns, recording the names of everyone engaged in seagoing trade, fishing, and salt making. Again he advocated that they be made to practice with bows and guns with a yearly test. To encourage them to practice sincerely, Min recommended that those who hit the target be given tax exemption for three years.

Finally, Min urged the reestablishment of the system of beacon fires around the coastline; but recognizing the overwhelming power of the modern navies of foreign states, he also advocated relying on the Chinese navy for assistance in naval defense. Soon after this policy was proposed, however, the *Kowshing* was sunk in Asan Bay, and the Chinese navy, which must at that time have appeared far in excess of anything that could be afforded by the impoverished Chosŏn administration, was proven to be incapable of protecting either China or Korea from the naval power of Japan.

Although Min was keenly aware of the unprepared state of Chosŏn's military defenses, he himself obviously lacked sufficient knowledge and training to bring Chosŏn's antiquated military up to date. It is, of course, easy to criticize

Min's naïvety in military matters shown in this section and elsewhere in *Ch'ŏnilch'aek*, but in Min's defense, it has to be added that had his recommendations been implemented, they would have been better than nothing. As will be seen, although Min was advocating archery training as late as 1894, he was not unaware of the necessity of acquiring modern weaponry and ammunition. He must simply have known that the Chosŏn government could not afford to modernize its army at that time. Min's recommendations appear more reasonable when viewed as interim measures designed to raise the general morale of the nation and its army rather than as an absolute blueprint for Chosŏn's modernization.

Adequate Storage of Materials

By means of introduction to the section highlighting the dire inadequacy of food reserves in late Chosŏn, Min referred to the *Book of Rites (Li ji)*, which stated that "less than nine years of reserve supplies in a nation is insufficient, less than six years' supplies constitutes an emergency, and a nation with less than three years supplies is not a nation."[77] According to these criteria, Min maintained, "Our country has not been a nation for a long time already."[78] Min estimated both public and private reserve supplies as insufficient to provide food for even one year, and even if every granary were ransacked, there would not be enough provisions to support ten thousand soldiers for three or four months. "When I think and speak about this," Min wrote, "my blood runs cold."[79]

Min blamed corruption and unemployment (the ratio of unemployed Koreans to those engaged in farming was three to two) for the general failure of agricultural production. To remedy this situation Min recommended that all the unemployed be put to work on rice production. Min also blamed the government's corvée system, which placed a heavy additional burden on the shoulders of the farming populace and interrupted the agricultural seasons. Min asked how the farmers could be expected to produce grain when they were forced to "toil all year round at the whim of their landlords and ruling officials."[80] To make matters even more unfair to the farmers, Min pointed out, the merchant class was exempt from such compulsory labor.

Despite the general shortage of food, Chosŏn was still exporting almost 10,000 *sŏk*[81] (sacks) of grain each year, according to Min's estimate, mainly to Japan. To remedy this, Min argued for the strict enforcement of treaty regulations that had been drawn up to prevent the purchase of grain by foreign countries in famine years. The relevant article in the Regulations for the Conduct of Trade by Japanese Subjects in Corea of 1883 reads as follows:

Should the Corean Government desire to prohibit the export of rice for a time under the apprehension of a scarcity of food occurring owing to floods, drought, or war, the Corean local authorities shall give notice to the Japanese Consuls one month beforehand. In such case [the Japanese Consuls] shall notify Japanese merchants residing in the trading ports of Corea of the date of prohibition, and cause it to be observed.[82]

Despite the treaty provision, grain continued to be exported during famine years because Japanese merchants gave Korean farmers loans that were to be repaid by the grain they harvested in the following year. Any attempt by the Korean government to prevent the export of grain and thus prevent the repayment of the loan was bound to meet strong protests from the Japanese merchants and consuls. Consequently, it was difficult for bans on grain exports to be adequately enforced.[83]

To remedy the chronic shortage of grain, Min argued here, as elsewhere in his essay, for a return to the past. He recommended the "ever-normal granary" (chang ping cang) system proposed by Geng Shouchang in the Han dynasty, whereby the government would buy grain when it was plentiful and cheap to raise its price and thus support the farming populace. When grain was scarce and expensive, on the other hand, the government could sell off the stored grain to lower the price of grain and thus benefit the general population.[84]

Min then cited the "righteous granary" (yi cang) system proposed by Chang Sunping in the Sui dynasty, whereby every family, rich and poor alike, would donate one sack of barley mixed with millet to the village association in the autumn. This grain would then be kept for distribution in a famine year. "This," wrote Min, "is truly a beautiful system from ancient times."[85]

In addition, Min recommended the adoption of the "village granary" (she cang) method of Zhu Xi and more especially the "military-camp-field" (tun tian) system of Zhao Chongguo. The latter method involved planting areas of uncultivated land in strategic areas under the supervision of military officials. To summarize, Min argued for the establishment of ever-normal granaries in the capital and other major cities, righteous granaries in every town, and village granaries in every village and hamlet.[86]

As a way of further increasing grain reserves, Min also recommended the payment of fines in grain rather than silver, as proposed in the Zhou dynasty work Lyu-xing. In addition he cited Zhao Cho of the Han dynasty, who sold titles and granted amnesties in return for grain supplies for the army, and Zhu Xi, who encouraged grain donations for the drought-stricken provinces of Hunan and Jiangxi. Concerning the sale of titles for grain, however, Min counseled caution: "even if the titles sold are unimportant, we should be careful. Indeed, how can the responsibility of governing the people, and the selection of great and talented people, be exchanged for millet?"[87]

The Repair of Weapons

In the section on repair of weapons, Min first tackled the problem of the army's rifles, of which there were two kinds: "Western guns," which appear to have been some form of antiquated muskets, possibly dating back to the Hideyoshi invasions, and modern rifles. According to Min, the former were practically useless and beyond repair; as for the latter, there were not enough of them—no more than a few thousand for, potentially, an army of ten thousand. In addition, they had been bought with only five hundred bullets per rifle. Min insisted, therefore, that despite all the difficulties, including insufficient resources and a lack of skilled artisans, the government should develop, as a matter of the utmost urgency, the capacity to produce rifles and bullets inside the country.[88]

On the other hand, Min believed modern artillery pieces to be beyond the capabilities of the Chosŏn armorers to manufacture, but because of their utility in strategic defense, he advocated that they be imported from abroad. Min also recommended the use of the Chinese *qian bu chang* (lit., "one-thousand-paces gun"). This gun could apparently be supported on the shoulder of one soldier, while being fired by another. According to Min's description, the *qian bu chang* was loaded with twenty to thirty bullets and one to two *kŭn*[89] of gunpowder. It had an effective range of eight or nine hundred paces and was capable of hitting more than thirty people. Such capabilities led Min to give it his strong recommendation: "In terms of hitting the most people from a long distance, therefore, it is ten times better than foreign guns. In terms of lightness and convenience for transport, it is ten times better than cannons. Also, our country can manufacture it by itself."[90]

Min concluded his comments on guns and cannons by criticizing the government's Kigiguk[91] as being an arsenal in name but not in reality. Consequently, he proposed that talented craftsmen be recruited from all over the country and not just the capital, that they be provided with generous salaries, and that they be given instruction by Western specialist artisans.

In the second half of this section on armaments, Min turned his attention to traditional Korean weaponry. He considered the Korean bow and arrow to be "outstanding in the world" and refused to believe that it had been made obsolete by the development of the rifle. "How can we omit our strong points and just adopt the strong points of others?" he demanded and then made his case for their continued use:

> Battles take place at long and close range, so there are long- and short-range weapons. At long range we use cannons. When they have been used up and the range is closer, we can use rifles. When their bullets have all been used up, and the range is even closer, we can use bows and arrows. When the arrows have all been used up and both sides are engaged in close combat, we can use spears and swords in the mêlée. How then can we dispense with any of these methods?[92]

Given the decrepit state of the Chosŏn army and the scarcity of modern weaponry, Min probably felt that using any weaponry available made sense. To that effect, he also recommended the repair of the hopelessly outmoded single-shot fowling pieces and even the use of slingshots and stones. Stones, after all, he argued, had the advantage over bullets in that they were in inexhaustible supply. Although this suggestion that stones be used in modern warfare does appear somewhat far-fetched, they had, in fact, been put to just such a use in the defense of Kanghwa Island against the American expedition of 1871. According to Hwang Hyŏn, Ŏ Chae-yŏn, the Korean commanding officer, had fought off the American troops by throwing spent bullets at them after his sword had been broken.[93] Robert T. Oliver provides the following account of the defense of Kanghwa: "The Korean garrison fought till their ammunition and arrows were exhausted, and then threw gravel in the faces of the attackers. None surrendered, and at last the defenders were all killed."[94] In addition, because stone fights were a popular custom between rival villages, the Korean peasantry were well versed in the use of the slingshot.[95]

Min then went on to advocate the purchase of breastplates and cuirasses to enable the troops to keep marching forward "when bullets fall like rain, and arrows fly like locusts."[96] Although Min held the office of minister of war several times in his official career, this statement seems to indicate that his experience of actual warfare was theoretical rather than actual.

As far as the building of warships was concerned, Min admitted that it was far beyond the financial capacity of the Chosŏn administration. Once again he accepted that Chosŏn had no choice but to rely on China for naval assistance.

Finally, Min criticized the use of sedan chairs. Because of the popularity of the chairs, he argued, horses were no longer raised in Korea and people no longer knew how to ride. To encourage the raising of horses, Min recommended heavily fining anyone (apart from "civil officials, magistrates, old, infirm, or sick people, and women") using a sedan chair.[97] In conclusion, he countered those who argued that Korea's geographical features made it unsuitable for cavalry by pointing out the necessity of horses for scouts and rapid-attack forces.

The Defense of Strategic Points

Given Chosŏn's limited number of troops, Min emphasized the importance of concentrating troops at strategic points. The first point to protect, he argued, was the capital:

> It is the root and foundation of the whole country and is connected to the minds of the people in all eight provinces. If there is a crisis, and the capital is abandoned, then the power of those who govern will be like that of a dragon out of water, and those who are governed will be like a flock of chicks in an overturned nest. The security of the capital, therefore, should be double that of any other place.[98]

Min continued by advocating strengthening Seoul's defenses in the north around Mt. Pukhan.

Min then pointed out how modern artillery had changed defensive methods. In ancient times, he explained, defense depended on deep ditches, high battlements, strong walls, and clear fields. But modern defense depended on building earthworks and setting up artillery at high strategic points. He therefore recommended placing artillery at "Puak in the north, Mongmyŏk in the south, Pua in the east, Anhyŏn in the west,"[99] and also on Mt. Kwanak near Kwach'ŏn to the south of Seoul.

As the terrain of the Pukhan region was inhospitable, Min calculated that any enemy would be unlikely to launch an attack from that region, whereas the west of Seoul with its weak West Gate invited attack. Consequently, he suggested setting up artillery at high vantage points inside the capital to protect this area.

For general defense around the country, Min advocated the establishment of torpedo launchers at coastal towns and any other points where steamships might anchor. In addition, he urged that supplies and weapons be stored in the old mountain fortresses, which should also be protected by artillery. As all the trees along the major routes to the capital had been cut down, removing all cover for troops lying in ambush, Min advocated the implementation of the prohibition against tree cutting, which had been in force in China during the Five Dynasties[100] period.

Finally, Min pointed out the importance of selecting the right commanders in strategic regions, citing for the first time past examples of outstanding

Korean (rather than Chinese) commanders such as Yi Mok, who had held the
northern border against the Xiongnu, and Ch'ung Se-hyŏng, who had held off
the Jin barbarians around Hwanju.[101]

Relieving the People's Suffering

Min opened the section concerning the common people's welfare by citing the
Kang gao's[102] (The announcement of Wu Wang to Kang) likening of the ruler's
care of the people to parents' care of infants:

> Because infants are without knowledge and cannot speak, their parents must sin-
> cerely concern themselves about them in order to understand their feelings and
> nurture them. The people, however, have knowledge and are able to speak, so if
> their rulers sincerely concern themselves about them, how can it be difficult to
> understand their suffering and relieve them? If those who rule over the people
> were like parents to a naked infant, then would not all the world's problems be
> solved?[103]

Min once again condemned the oppression of the ordinary people, which
had become commonplace in late Chosŏn times. In the first place, he stated,
many innocent people were being imprisoned and even executed or tortured
as a result of the perversion of the laws by bribery. Furthermore, even marriage
required large bribes; consequently, the poor were unable to marry, while the
wealthy, even those with commoner backgrounds, had many concubines. Min
recommended appointing judges to investigate those imprisoned on false
charges and enacting strict laws to prevent the "custom of marriage bribes" and
the keeping of concubines by commoners.[104]

In the medical field, Min criticized his country for having permitted foreign doctors to enter the country and establish hospitals. He pointed out that
it was extremely shameful that the Chosŏn government was unable to provide
care for the sick so that the people were forced to rely on foreign hospitals. He
advocated the establishment of a health care system in the capital and in major cities.[105]

Min then cited historical precedents from China concerning the welfare of
the people:

> Among the subjects of King Wen there were no cold or hungry old people. At
> the time of Emperor Wu of the Han dynasty, rice and silk were given to the eld-
> erly. This is the beautiful policy of caring for old people. In Han times there were
> statutory relief granaries. In Song times a milk bureau was established. This was

a good policy for caring for the young with compassion. We should follow these examples and put them into practice.[106]

Concerning the problem of migrants who had left the land as a result of two years of bad harvests, Min suggested that the government adopt the policy of Western Han, which had lent public fields and seeds to returning migrants, and also that of Northern Qi, which had transferred poor people without land to pioneer uncultivated areas.[107]

With the controversial closure of private academies *(sŏwŏn)*, which took place during the rule of the Taewŏn'gun, the shrines erected to loyal and meritorious subjects had also been destroyed.[108] Min argued that this act had not only angered those subjects' spirits and caused them to resent the sovereign but had also discouraged loyalty and meritorious deeds. He therefore advocated the reestablishment of all such shrines.[109]

Further social problems that Min identified were those of elopement, adultery, and the exploitation of peasant farmers by usurers, who loaned grain at exorbitant interest rates. Concerning interest rates, Min advocated that anyone charging more than 30 percent be heavily fined. In addition, he emphasized the need to carry out all the recommendations made in the section "Restoring the Fundamental Principles of Government."

Managing Wealth and Expenditure

Under this heading Min tackled the problem of lost tax revenues. Without stemming the loss of revenue, Min argued, it would be impossible to rearm the country. According to the ancient system of taxation, he explained, every field was taxed, and every person was liable for corvée labor. In addition, every home and all goods were also taxed. By Kojong's reign, however, many people were managing to avoid taxation and consequently, wrote Min, "Our wealth is being secretly lost."[110]

Min recommended levying a tax of one-tenth of all rice produced *(kyŏlchŏn)*. In addition, as in the time of the Three Dynasties,[111] men and women above the age of twenty and under sixty should be taxed two *yang* and children one *yang*.[112] Also, as in foreign countries, one *yang* should be levied for each thatched cottage and two *yang* for each tiled house. A charge should also be made for official licenses and certificates. Min condemned ineffective tax laws that "just fatten the wicked and sly without contributing to the national budget."[113]

Because of the low estimation of the military under the Chosŏn dynasty, Min argued, the military budget had been cut continuously, so that the nation had become increasingly dependent on the Chinese army. This situation had been exacerbated by the flight of manpower from the rural areas. To counteract this, Min recommended the establishment of military fields *(kunjŏn)* for grain production for the army. Those who had no land to donate to this system were to give cash or grain instead.[114]

Min went on to ask why the taxable land area in Chosŏn had declined from two million to one million *kyŏl* even though more and more land was being reclaimed each year.[115] Fraudulent reporting of landholding explained the decline, he maintained, and he recommended that the records of taxable land be accurately verified.[116] Concerning tax on iron and salt, Min cited the example of Lyu An in the Tang dynasty, who had increased the iron and salt tax over a three-year period from four million to ten million *min,*[117] thus proving the importance of selecting officials with ability and integrity to oversee tax collection.[118]

Min then advocated a reduction in the number of officials serving in the counties and districts, arguing,

> Before the time of Imjin [1592], when our national strength had still not declined to this extent, Master Yulgok[119] nevertheless sent a memorial to the king advising that superfluous officials in the counties and districts be dismissed. At present our national strength is far worse than at that time. If we were to carry out such a policy now, we could immediately save not less than one million wŏn for our emergency expenditure.[120]

In his conclusion, Min argued that the government regain control of ginseng production from private monopolies, issue paper currency as in Japan, and select tax officials with integrity to oversee the collection of taxes on gold, mountain ginseng, and sable. Finally, although he advocated a ban on luxurious items, he urged the government to encourage farmers to grow mulberry trees for sericulture.[121]

Promotion of Schools

In his penultimate proposal, Min tackled the problem of the decline of education in Chosŏn society. "If education declines," he argued, "then the upper classes do not obey the Way, and the lower classes do not receive kindness."[122] Furthermore, he continued, if people did not receive education, they would be easily misled by demagogues into rebelling. Min again cited the system of the Three Dynasties, in which all children attended a first school at the age of eight. Outstanding students were then selected for a secondary school at the age of fifteen. This simple system, Min maintained, was sufficient to "provide security for the nation and peace for the people for ten million years."[123]

If poor people simply studied filial piety from the age of eight to fourteen, Min continued, and the virtuous studied the arts of government from fifteen to forty, then, "all the people in the countryside will be filial and loyal, and all office-holding gentlemen will be talented people of virtue and goodness. Enemy countries will cease to desire to invade us, and all manner of things will improve each day."[124]

Min pointed out that Korea already had village schools and academies in place, but that the contents of the educational system itself had become outmoded. He advocated that "good gentlemen" at national, town, and village level be appointed to be teachers at each level. In addition, there should be compulsory primary school education for all children, regardless of their class, from the age of eight. Anyone not sending their children to school should be fined as should any village that had not established its own school.[125]

Min then recommended a system of selection whereby the best students from the village schools would be provided with places in the town schools and also with food. In the town schools the students should learn *The Classics* as their Eastern education, on the one hand, and government affairs as their Western education on the other. There should be examinations according to the rules of Hu Anding: namely, the students in the town schools should be examined every spring. The tests should focus on "the students' integrity and capacity to govern."[126] Successful candidates could then proceed to university study while the unsuccessful would return to school.

Once at university the students would be examined again with successful candidates being given official posts. Those who failed could continue to study and take a later exam. If they did not pass by the age of forty, however, they should return home. Once again, Min claimed that he had modeled his system on the one in place under the Three Dynasties.

Min also recommended a system whereby well-known scholars would be invited to take up government posts without taking an examination, just as he had outlined earlier in his section on recruiting talented people. In this way, Min argued, people would come to see that "not only is study the way to become a person of virtue, but that also wealth and honor may be attained by studying."[127] Furthermore, he concluded, if people studied hard they would not be deceived by demagogues and there would be no more Tonghak and no more Sŏhak.[128]

Min then went on to introduce various aspects of Western educational principles. In the West, Min recounted, all children, regardless of their class, entered a village school at the age of seven or eight. From there they went on to a county school, then a government school, and then a university. They studied subjects under four headings: classics, law, science, and medicine. According to Min, the study of classics was concerned with education, the study of law with "ancient and modern administrative affairs, welfare systems, diplomacy, and commerce."[129] Science covered such areas as the principles of nature, human nature, natural laws, and the languages and alphabets of all countries. Finally, medicine covered the origins of diseases and medicines.

Min then described technical schools dealing with subjects such as steam engines, telegraphy, textiles, assaying, and so on. Next, he went through the gamut of different types of academies in the West, including those for military and naval officers, art, music, business, and so on. In addition, he mentioned institutions for orphans, the sick and disabled, and young offenders.[130]

Min praised the Western system for focusing on practical results. "This is truly the best method," he argued, "except that those foreigners do not understand the saintly and virtuous teachings of *The Classics*."[131] Min also attempted to put the Western educational system into the framework of the classical Confucian tradition by maintaining that it was similar to the promotion and selection system of *xiu shi, zao shi,* and *jun shi* of the Three Dynasties and that law, science, medicine, mathematics, and chemistry were all part of "the study of the principles of government."[132]

In concluding this section, Min praised Kojong for having established the Royal Military Academy and the Royal English Academy based on the technical colleges of Western countries. Nevertheless, he added that it was necessary to recruit talented students for these academies from all over the country and not just from the capital; otherwise the academies would become ineffective and burdens on the national budget.[133]

Relations with Neighboring Countries

Min began his final section by citing Mencius, who stated that "in relations with small countries it is virtuous for the small to serve the great as one would fear heaven,"[134] as the authority for Chosŏn's traditional policy of serving the great in its relations with China. Min pointed out that even in the past when nations had little communication with one another, the principle of serving the great existed. Now that nations all over the world had relations with each other, and there was a prevalent attitude of the strong occupying the weak and attacking the ignorant, it was even more important for Chosŏn to be cautious in its dealings with its three neighbors, China, Russia, and Japan. "There is no other way to treat them," Min maintained, "than to proclaim virtue, emphasize teaching, and make those neighboring countries happy by sincerely serving them and restoring them to civilization."[135] Min's use of the phrase "restoring them to civilization" clearly shows that members of the Chosŏn leadership still maintained a sense of moral superiority despite their nation's weaknesses. Countries with imperialist and militaristic policies were considered to have lapsed into a form of barbarism from which they needed to be restored by Chosŏn's peaceful example.

Min offered some practical recommendations for dealing with Chosŏn's neighbors. First, national defenses should be strong to prevent those countries from acting arrogantly toward Chosŏn. Second, strict treaties should be drawn up and observed meticulously. Third, envoys should be carefully selected from those men capable of upholding the nation's dignity. Envoys from abroad should be treated well so that they would be well disposed toward Chosŏn. In particular, Min recommended the careful selection of loyal and honest interpreters. Fourth, there should be strict regulations concerning commerce. Merchants should be prevented from cheating and putting exorbitant prices on their goods. All foreign debtors should be charged under the law, and anyone not involved in commerce should not be permitted to enter the country. Fifth, Min maintained that just as one should be careful in choosing one's friends, a nation should also be careful in choosing with which nations to establish close relations.[136]

Min pointed out some were arguing for a policy of balancing China and Russia against each other. He then went on to vehemently criticize this attitude and to reaffirm traditional Chosŏn foreign relations:

> Some say that Russia is more powerful than China so we should cling to Russia to avoid their reproach. If we are invaded by Russia, then we should rely on China to defend ourselves, and so on. My reply to this is that the mutual support between China and Chosŏn is far greater and has already existed from ancient times. Concerning China's border, we are only one stretch of water away. Concerning its people, we are of the same race. Concerning its kindness, we are like brothers. Concerning our relationship of reliance, it is no different from that of the lips and the teeth. As for Russia, its border is far away. Its people are completely different. There is no previous friendship. What is there to rely on? To discard a friendship of several thousand years of mutual reliance and take up a new relationship based on the acquaintance of a morning and an evening is not in accord with righteousness. To turn one's back on a brother's affection in order to join a pack of wolves will result in harm.[137]

Min concluded his argument in favor of maintaining traditional relations with China by asserting that "Russia has the intention of swallowing the whole world,"[138] whereas China had an interest in supporting Chosŏn, which acted as its eastern bulwark against Russia and Japan. This view on Sino-Korean relations is remarkably similar to the assertions of Yuan Shikai in *Yu yan si tiao*

(Four points of verbal order) and *Zhaoxian da ju lun* (Views on Korea's public interests).[139] This is somewhat surprising as Min has been considered to have been supportive of Kojong's pro-Russian policy in 1884 and 1886.[140] Min Yŏng-ik, on the other hand, opposed Kojong's policy and kept Yuan informed of it. From the evidence of *Ch'ŏnilch'aek,* however, it would appear that Min Yŏng-hwan was also opposed to any pro-Russian policy at court and was aligned with his elder cousin Min Yŏng-ik.

Min advised against Chosŏn's entering into closer relations even to the point of "uniting" with Japan as it would be bound to lose its sovereignty. Nevertheless, he did not agree that Chosŏn should have no relationship with either Japan or Russia:

> I say that we can have a relationship with Japan, but we cannot unite with it. We can have a relationship with Russia, but we cannot serve it. But with China, we can not only have a relationship, but we can also serve it. Not only should we serve, but also we must respect China with perfect sincerity so that there is no gap between our people.[141]

Min advocated a basic strategy in Chosŏn foreign relations of playing off Russia and Japan against each other while maintaining close relations with China. In addition, in line with Huang Zunxian's recommendations in *Zhaoxian ce lyue,* he recommended that Chosŏn form closer relations with those nations that China had also courted to protect itself from Russia—namely, Germany and the United States.

Min concluded his essay by reiterating the necessity for the implementation of laws and the development of technology to be underpinned by the increase of virtue in those who ruled and the cultivation of a sense of duty in those who served. In addition, the sovereign should rectify himself, and for one last time Min appealed to the authority of the Confucian tradition:

> Mencius said, "Rectify the sovereign's mind." Dongzi[142] said, "Regulate the sovereign's mind," because the sovereign's mind is the great root of the whole country. If the great root is rectified then the whole country will be governed.[143]

Conclusion

Min's reform proposals show that before the outbreak of the full-scale Tong-hak Rebellion, the Sino-Japanese War, and the initiation of the Kabo reforms, Min was basically advocating the same conservative approach toward reform as that taken by such Qing leaders as Prince Kong and Li Hongzhang—namely, "Eastern ways and Western machines." Nevertheless, throughout Min's proposals it is possible to see an attempt at finding a compromise between tradition and innovation as well as a heartfelt concern for the welfare of the ordinary people and the continued survival of his beleaguered nation.

Certain proposals appear naïve, particularly those dealing with weaponry and military strategy. The constant references to the golden age of Chinese civilization also seem outmoded in the context of the problems faced by Korea at the end of the nineteenth century. Min had at this stage clearly not had the same exposure to Western ideas as members of the Enlightenment party such as Sŏ Chae-p'il, Sŏ Kwang-bŏm, and Pak Yŏng-hyo, all of whom were at this time in exile in Japan or the United States.

Ch'ŏnilch'aek reflects Min's ideas on reform before the shock of China's defeat in the Sino-Japanese War, before the Kabo reforms, and also before his visits to the West, where he gained firsthand experience of Western technology, particularly military technology, in Russia, Britain, and the United States. The following two chapters will examine those visits abroad and show how Min's outlook changed as a result of his experiences in the West.

3

MISSION TO RUSSIA

Brief History of Russo-Korean Relations

Before examining Min Yŏng-hwan's mission to Russia in 1896, it is worth taking a cursory view of the evolution of Russo-Korean relations during the preceding decades. Since 1864, twenty years before the signing of the first Russian-Korean treaty on 7 July 1884, Russia had made numerous unsuccessful efforts to establish trade relations with Korea across the latter's northern border.[1] As a result of the 1884 treaty, Russians were permitted to trade at Korea's open ports, although the northern border remained closed to overland trade because of Chinese opposition. It was not until 3 October 1885, however, that Karl Waeber arrived in Seoul to exchange ratifications and to take up his post as Russian chargé d'affaires.[2] Waeber appears to have been a good choice for the post as he carried out his diplomatic responsibilities with such tact that he won the approval of both the Korean court and the other foreign representatives in Seoul.

In the wake of the failed Kapsin coup, Russia became caught up in the political rivalry between Japan and China for the control of the Korean peninsula. Although King Kojong is known to have wanted the United States to assume the role of Korea's protector vis-à-vis its larger neighbors, the indifference of the State Department propelled certain members of the Korean court, most notably the German adviser to Kojong and vice-minister of foreign affairs Paul Georg von Möllendorff, to look to Russia as a counterbalance to Japanese and Chinese interference in Korea's domestic and foreign affairs.

At the end of 1884 Möllendorff and King Kojong's envoy, Sŏ Sang-u, visited Japan and entered into negotiations for Russian assistance with the secretary of the Russian legation in Tokyo, Alexis de Speyer. In addition, another agent, Kim Yong-wŏn, was sent to Vladivostok for the same purpose. Neither mission was carried out with the knowledge or sanction of the Korean administration. The agreement reached between Speyer and Möllendorff was approved by Tsar Alexander II, and Speyer subsequently traveled to Seoul in June 1885 to ratify the agreement. In Seoul, however, he discovered that the agreement had been made without the consent or approval of the Korean ministers and that it was vehemently opposed by the Korean foreign minister, Kim Yun-sik. As a consequence, Speyer abandoned his mission, and Möllendorff was dismissed from his posts in the Korean government and recalled to China.[3]

Events were further complicated around this time by the occupation of Kŏmundo (Port Hamilton) by the British navy in May 1885 as a precaution against a possible conflict with Russia that was brewing on the border of Afghanistan. This occupation of Korean territory inevitably became a bone of contention between Great Britain and Russia, not to mention Korea, China, and Japan. The matter was eventually resolved in February 1887, however, when the British finally withdrew from Kŏmundo. This was not done out of any consideration for the territorial integrity of Korea, however. The reasons for the British withdrawal were characteristically pragmatic. In the first case the crisis in Afghanistan had subsided, and the Russians had given a commitment not to occupy any Korean territory themselves. Furthermore, the British Admiralty considered Kŏmundo to be too expensive to fortify and maintain as a viable outpost of British naval power in the Far East.[4]

Although King Kojong and Queen Myŏngsŏng maintained good relations with Waeber and his wife throughout this period until the outbreak of the Sino-Japanese War in 1894, Russo-Korean relations were continuously hampered by the interference and intrigue of the Chinese resident in Seoul, Yuan Shikai. As a consequence, Waeber was able to achieve few concrete results other than the opening of Kyŏnghŭng in Hamgyŏng Province to overland trade in August 1888.[5] With the outbreak of the Sino-Japanese War and the departure of Yuan from Seoul, leading to the effective end of Chinese influence in Korea, new opportunities for Russian intervention began to emerge, as will be seen in the following section.

The Background and Purpose of Min's 1896 Mission to Russia

At the beginning of 1896 the Chosŏn court was in a severe crisis after a series of catastrophic events on the Korean peninsula. Two years earlier the Tonghak

Rebellion had broken out in the southern provinces, and China and Japan had intervened militarily. This intervention in turn had led in July 1894 to the outbreak of the Sino-Japanese War, which had been fought primarily on the Korean peninsula and the seas around it. Because of Japan's rapid dispatch of troops to Seoul, it had gained control of the Korean court even before the outbreak of the war. As a consequence Japan, together with such "progressive" Korean officials as Pak Yŏng-hyo and Kim Hong-jip, who were willing to work in concert with their Japanese advisers, was able to initiate the Kabo reforms. The Japanese were effectively opposed, however, by King Kojong's consort, Queen Myŏngsŏng, and those officials at the court such as Yi Pŏm-jin, Yi Wan-yong, and Yi Yun-yong, who looked to Russia and the United States for protection from Japan.[6]

Consequently, the newly appointed Japanese minister to Seoul, Miura Gorō, instigated the assassination of Queen Myŏngsŏng on 8 October 1895. Although there is only circumstantial evidence that Miura did not act in isolation, Yi Min-wŏn argues convincingly that this assassination was most probably carried out at the behest of Miura's superior, Inoue Kaoru, and also with the knowledge of the Japanese cabinet.[7]

Subsequently, the royal palace again came under the control of the Japanese faction at the court. There was a failed coup by anti-Japanese royalist elements on 27 November of the same year. Finally, Kojong and the crown prince managed to escape from the palace in a closed sedan chair and took refuge in the Russian legation on 11 February 1896. The political situation in Seoul underwent a complete reversal as King Kojong appointed a new pro-Russian cabinet and purged those officials who had cooperated with the Japanese.

The decision to send a mission to Russia to participate in the coronation ceremony of Tsar Nicholas II was taken while Kojong was residing in the Russian legation under the protection of the Russian chargé d'affaires, Karl Waeber. Tsar Alexander II had been assassinated on 1 November 1894, and the Chosŏn court had been informed of the fact by Waeber one week later, on 8 November. The court sent its condolences on the same day. On 3 December 1894, Waeber notified the Chosŏn court of the accession of Tsar Nicholas II, and two days later the newly appointed minister of foreign affairs, Kim Yun-sik, conveyed a message of congratulations. The precise date on which the Chosŏn court received an invitation to participate in the coronation at Moscow, however, is not known. It is probably correct to assume, however, that given the series of crises through which the court had been passing, participation in a foreign coronation had not been a priority for Kojong and his officials.[8]

Kojong's flight to the Russian legation was undoubtedly the decisive factor in making Min's mission to Russia a possibility. The appointment of Min Yŏng-hwan as minister plenipotentiary and envoy extraordinary was made on 10 March 1896, about one month after Kojong had taken up residence at the Russian legation and scarcely more than two months before the coronation itself was due to take place.[9] As Ko Pyŏng-ik points out, given the difficulties of travel at that time and the inexperience of the Korean envoy and his party, the decision was undoubtedly made at extremely short notice.[10]

During the Kabo reform period, which saw leading members of the Min clan such as Min Yŏng-jun and Min Hyŏng-sik purged from the government, Min Yŏng-hwan had also been relatively sidelined in the administration. In 1895 he had been appointed to posts in the Privy Council and Department of the Royal Household. On 28 September he had been appointed to the post of minister plenipotentiary and envoy extraordinary to the United States but had not been able take up the post because of the crisis precipitated by the assassination of his aunt, Queen Myŏngsŏng, just ten days later, on 8 October 1895.[11] According to Yun Ch'i-ho, who was to be Min's adjutant on the mission to Russia, the appointment of Min was made with the knowledge and approval, if not the actual recommendation, of Waeber.[12] Min was an ideal appointment in that he had close connections to the Korean royal family and does not appear to have belonged to either the Japanese or Russian parties at the Korean court. Nevertheless, just before the departure of the mission, Min informed Yun that he intended to resign—because, according to Yun's account, Min had heard that a secret mission comprising Sŏng Ki-un, Chu Sŏng-myŏn, and Min Kyŏng-sik would also be going to Russia to keep an eye on his activities. Yun informed Waeber of Min's sudden change of mind, and between them they managed to persuade him not to resign his post, "on the condition," Yun wrote in his diary, "that Mr. Waeber would promise to protect him from any false accusation to His Majesty and that he should be allowed to travel in Europe at least a year."[13]

It appears that the Russian government wished to use the coronation of the Tsar as an opportunity to further several of its goals in East Asia by using it as a pretext for conducting simultaneous negotiations with China, Japan, and Korea without attracting too much international attention. The Russian minister in Beijing, Count Artur P. Cassini, managed to persuade the Qing court to replace its original envoy, Wang Jichun, with Li Hongzhang, who had the rank and experience to act as a plenipotentiary in negotiations with the Russian minister of foreign affairs, Prince Aleksei Lobanov-Rostovsky, and the minister of finance, Sergei I. Witte. Concerning their relative capacity to deal with East Asian affairs, Witte wrote frankly in his memoirs about Lobanov,

In those years [circa 1895] very few statesmen in Russia had a clear notion about Korea, Japan, and, especially, China and their mutual relations. Prince Lobanov-

Rostovski, Foreign Minister, knew no more about the Far East than the average schoolboy. Inasmuch as I was in charge of the construction of the Trans-Siberian Railway, I gave a good deal of attention to Far-Eastern affairs. In fact, I was the only Russian statesman familiar with the economic and political situation in the region.[14]

These negotiations were primarily concerned with a secret treaty of defensive alliance against Japan between Russia and China. As a result of this treaty China received a Franco-Russian loan on favorable terms to pay off the indemnity it had incurred as a result of its defeat in the Sino-Japanese War; in return China granted Russia permission to construct a section of the trans-Siberian railway through Manchurian territory, with the stipulation that the Chinese would have the right to buy the railway thirty-six years after its completion. The line was to run from Chita to the Russian South Ussuri Railroad and was to be constructed and operated by the Chinese Eastern Railroad Company established by the Russo-Chinese Bank.[15]

Soviet historian B. A. Romanov has revealed that three million rubles were set aside as a bribe to ensure the cooperation of Li Hongzhang over the construction of the Manchurian line.[16] Li, in fact, received only one million rubles, and as Lensen points out, it is unlikely that the bribe had much influence on Li's decision making. The fact was that the Chinese wanted the line built but lacked the funds to build it. As a result of the agreement with Russia, the line could be built at Russian expense and then be purchased later by the Chinese.

At the same time Marshal Yamagata Aritomo joined the Japanese mission to Russia to conduct negotiations concerning the balance of Russian and Japanese influence on the Korean peninsula, a balance that had been upset by the flight of the Korean king to the Russian legation. The result of the negotiations between Yamagata and the Russian foreign minister Lobanov was the Yamagata-Lobanov Protocol signed in St. Petersburg on 9 June 1896. The essence of this agreement was that both countries would help Korea's financial reforms with loans, while leaving military reform to Korea itself. In addition, there was a secret article in which Russia and Japan agreed to define areas of occupation in Korea with a buffer zone to prevent mutual conflict if they should ever send troops to Korea.[17] As a consequence of this agreement, the negotiations for which were concluded several months earlier than those between Min and Lobanov, the Russian minister of foreign affairs was hindered from responding more positively to the requests of King Kojong's envoy.

From the Russian point of view, although Korea was a key element in Russia's negotiations with China and Japan, through which it sought to consolidate its position in East Asia, growing Russian interest in Manchuria meant that Lobanov was willing to sacrifice his country's interests in Korea to avoid antagonizing the Japanese. This trend in Russian Far Eastern policy, which inter alia ultimately saw Russia's abandonment of aims to lease Wǒnsan (Port Lazareff) as a warm-water port on the east coast of Korea in order to focus on developing Port Arthur and Dalian and connect them by rail to the Manchurian leg of the trans-Siberian railway, has been termed the "Port Arthur orientation" by Andrew Malozemoff.[18]

Waeber, nevertheless, exerted himself to ensure that the Russian Ministry of Foreign Affairs was also in a position to conduct secret negotiations with a Korean plenipotentiary under the pretext of his participation in the coronation celebrations of the Tsar. Although no mention of any such negotiations is made in the text of *Haech'ŏn ch'ubŏm* itself, the fact that Min was instructed to conduct negotiations with the Russian government is clear from his credentials (*kuksŏ*) and the set of injunctions (*hunyu*) that he received from the court.[19] In the former of these two documents his mission was clearly set out as follows:

> You must strengthen the friendship of our close neighborly relations with that country [Russia]. If there are any important issues concerning our country, you must negotiate about them. I expect you to obtain a satisfactory compromise. It is also necessary that you form close relationships with the envoys and other officials of each friendly nation. It is my hope that you will provide a detailed report on all of these activities.[20]

Min's rank as minister plenipotentiary, of course, also implied that he had been granted the authority to enter into negotiations with the Russians.

The Chosŏn mission to Russia, which was also the first official Chosŏn diplomatic mission to Europe,[21] comprised Min Yŏng-hwan, special entry officer in the Department of the Royal Household, who was appointed envoy extraordinary and minister plenipotentiary; Vice-Minister of Education Yun Ch'i-ho, who was appointed official assistant to the envoy *(suwŏn);* third-grade official Kim Tŭng-nyŏn, who was appointed second-rank mission secretary; and clerk *(chusa)* in the Ministry of Foreign Affairs Kim To-il, who was appointed third-rank mission secretary.[22] Min also took his personal valet Son Hŭi-yŏng with him. In addition, the mission was accompanied by the Russian legation dragoman Evgenii Stein (Sa Tŏg-in), who assisted the Korean party in all aspects of its journey and activities in Moscow and St. Petersburg.[23]

The Authorship of *Haech'ŏn ch'ubŏm*

The complete daily record of Min Yŏng-hwan's mission to Russia in 1896, titled *Haech'ŏn ch'ubŏm*, forms the third section of *Min Ch'ungjŏnggong yugo*. It holds a unique place in Korean historical literature in being the first account of a round-the-world journey by a group of Koreans. It is also the first record of an official Korean diplomatic mission to Europe.

In his article "Nohwang taegwansike ŭi sahaenggwa hanno kyosŏp" (The Russo-Korean negotiations on the occasion of the coronation of Nicholas II in 1896),[24] however, Ko Pyŏng-ik fairly conclusively demonstrates that the primary author of *Haech'ŏn ch'ubŏm* was not Min Yŏng-hwan himself but his mission secretary, Kim Tŭng-nyŏn. Ko's argument is based on the fact that there are three other extant records concerned with the Chosŏn mission to Russia in 1896 in addition to *Haech'ŏn ch'ubŏm*.[25] These records are all held in the Ko-dosŏ (Old books) collection in the central library of Seoul National University under the heading "Nohwangje taegwansik ch'amnyŏl kwangye munsŏ" (Documents relating to participation at the coronation of the Russian Tsar). The catalogue titles for the three works are as follows:

> *Pua kijŏng pu Min Ch'ungjŏnggong ponjŏn* (Record of a journey to Russia appended to Prince Min's biography)
>
> *Hwan'gu ilgi* (Hwan'gu[26] journal) *Chosŏn Kim Tŭng-nyŏn chŏja p'ilsabon 102 chŏng* (Kim Tŭng-nyŏn's manuscript, Chosŏn era, 102 *chŏng*)
>
> *Hwan'gu kŭmch'o* (Hwan'gu sketches) *Chosŏn Kim Tŭng-nyŏn (Yun'gu) chŏja p'ilbon 38 chŏng* (Kim Tŭng-nyŏn's [Yun'gu] manuscript, Chosŏn era, 38 *chŏng*)

Pua kijŏng has no author attributed to it and is a simple record of places visited by Min and his party and the people they met. It appears to have been an aide memoire for the main mission diary. According to Ko, the texts of *Haech'ŏn ch'ubŏm* and *Hwan'gu ilgi*, however, are almost identical. Where *Haech'ŏn ch'ubŏm* refers to "I" and "Kim Tŭng-nyŏn," the respective terms in *Hwan'gu ilgi* are "the envoy" and "I." In *Haech'ŏn ch'ubŏm* Min was met by his relatives on his return to Inch'ŏn, whereas in *Hwan'gu ilgi* Kim was met by his relatives. From a perusal of the texts, Ko maintains that it is clear that one formed the original text and that the other was simply based upon it with such minor modifications as have just been mentioned. The question is, Which text was the original one?

We know that Kojong expected a report of the mission on Min's return from Russia from the final sentence of the latter's official instructions, which read, "It is my hope that you will provide a detailed report on all these activities."[27]

Kim Tŭng-nyŏn was the official secretary of the mission, Kim To-il's function being that of Russian interpreter. It is most likely, therefore, that the task of keeping the mission diary fell to Kim Tŭng-nyŏn.

Fortunately, Min Yŏng-hwan's adjutant Yun Ch'i-ho also kept a diary of the mission's journey and its activities in Moscow and St. Petersburg.[28] Yun's entry for 7 August 1896 provides additional evidence that corroborates Ko's assertion that Kim was the original author for both *Haech'ŏn ch'ubŏm* and *Hwan'gu ilgi:*

> By the way Fish [Kim Tŭng-nyŏn][29] is most worthy of his bread here. He has worked and is working hardest of us all. Ever since we came to Petersburg he has been at work to get up-to-date the journal of the mission. He copies much from certain Chinese diaries of a similar nature. Yet it is work to write pages on pages day after day.[30]

As Ko suggests in his article, it is most likely that Kim and Min discussed how to keep the record of the mission before setting out and came to an arrangement whereby Min would be able to provide a daily record in his own name to Kojong. The third work in the Kodosŏ, *Hwan'gu kŭmch'o,* a collection of poems written by Kim during the mission to Russia, was published independently in Tokyo in 1897.

As the leader of the mission to Russia, it was Min Yŏng-hwan's responsibility to present Kojong with a written record of its activities. As secretary of the mission it would have been Kim's responsibility to support his superior and enable him to be able to present such a record. Min and Kim were also old friends, and Min expressed his sense of debt to Kim in the introduction to a poem that he dedicated to him in his own poetry collection appended to *Haech'ŏn ch'ubŏm:* "Secretary Kim Tŭng-nyŏn and I have known each other over ten years and understand what is in each other's heart. Moreover, our families are old friends, which is why he did not forsake this foolish, sickly fellow."[31] It should also be noted that Min makes no claim to authorship in the text, unlike in the case of *Sagu sokch'o,* the account of Min's mission to Europe in 1897, which is preceded by Min's own preface.

In references to the text of *Haech'ŏn ch'ubŏm* throughout this chapter, however, expressions of thoughts, feelings, and opinions have been attributed to Min Yŏng-hwan rather than Kim Tŭng-nyŏn on the basis that even if Min did simply revise the text of *Hwan'gu kŭmch'o* for presentation to the king as *Haech'ŏn ch'ubŏm,* the action implies that he concurred with the thoughts and opinions expressed in the original text. Furthermore, Min was the central figure for the activities of the mission even though these activities may have actually been recorded by Kim. It is also probable that Min dictated portions of the diary to Kim—for example, the accounts of audiences with the Tsar, at which Kim himself was not present.

The Journey to Russia

Min and his entourage departed from Tonŭi Gate[32] on 1 April 1896 and arrived at Inch'ŏn on the same day. Here they hurriedly boarded the Russian warship *Gremiashchii,* which was to take them on the first leg of their journey to Shanghai. The use of the warship had been arranged by Waeber and is another indication of the active involvement of the Russian chargé d'affaires behind the scenes in ensuring Korean participation at the coronation and opening the way for secret, direct negotiations between representatives of the two countries.

Before leaving Inch'ŏn, Min received 40,000 silver yen from the Customs House at Inch'ŏn for the expenses of the mission. This money was later deposited in a bank at Shanghai, and a banker's draft was used for the remainder of the journey. An itemized account of the mission's expenditure was kept separately from the diary to be presented to the Ministry of Foreign Affairs on the mission's return to Seoul.[33]

After arriving in Shanghai, Min and his party stayed at the Hotel de Colonie in the French quarter. During his stay there Min met various officials who had an interest in Korean affairs, including von Möllendorff (Mok In-dŏk), who had advocated a pro-Russian policy when he had held the post of vice-minister of foreign affairs in the Chosŏn court from 1882 to 1884;[34] the director of the Russo-Chinese Bank in Shanghai, Dmitrii D. Pokotilov;[35] and the Russian consul, I. A. Reding.[36] Min also met two of his influential relatives—Min Yŏng-ik, who had just arrived from Hong Kong, and Min Yŏng-gi, who had just come from Seoul.[37] Unfortunately, as is the case throughout *Haech'ŏn ch'ubŏm,* nothing is recounted of the conversations that Min must have had at such meetings.[38] According to Yun Ch'i-ho, however, Min received the sum of $20,000 from his cousin Min Yŏng-ik, acting on the instructions of King Kojong, as a personal contingency fund. He also received a further $1,000 from another Korean in Shanghai, Kwak Ch'am-bong.[39]

In Shanghai the mission faced its first obstacle on its journey to Russia. It had been planned that the party would take the southern route via Hong Kong, Port Said, and Odessa on a French commercial steamer. As it happened, the steamer had no available berths, and the next steamer would arrive too late to enable the party to arrive in Moscow in time for the coronation. Fortunately, the Russian assistant Stein was able to book a passage on a British steamer, the *Empress of China,* going to Vancouver via Nagasaki and Yokohama. By taking this eastern route, Min and his party would be able to arrive in Moscow two days before the scheduled presentation of foreign envoys to Tsar Nicholas II. The lack of organization shown by this sudden change of plan reveals the extent of the inexperience of the Korean mission and also underlines the fact that Min and his party had left Korea at very short notice to conduct secret negotiations with a "great power" with little previous experience to build on.

Although there had been previous diplomatic missions abroad, most notably the so-called gentlemen's sightseeing group's fact-finding tour of Japan in 1881 and Min Yŏng-ik and Sŏ Kwang-bŏm's official visit to the United States in 1883, these missions abroad were made while the threat of foreign intervention on the Korean peninsula, particularly by Japan and China, was just becoming immediate. By 1896 when Min and his party left for Russia, the crisis in Korea had worsened considerably. The suppression of the Tonghak uprising of 1894 had precipitated the Sino-Japanese War, which Korea's traditional ally or suzerain, China, had lost; the reforms of 1894–1895 sponsored by the victorious Japanese had foundered after alienating the Korean people over such issues as the cutting of the traditional Korean topknot; the Korean queen had been murdered, and the king had taken up residence in a foreign legation for his own protection. The difficult circumstances surrounding Min's mission should not be underestimated, therefore, as Min and his colleagues struggled to play their part in the preservation of Korea's sovereignty and independence under increasingly adverse conditions both at home and abroad.

Despite the burden of responsibility on the shoulders of Min and his party and the anxieties caused by the last-minute change of their travel arrangements, they appear to have enjoyed the sights and sounds of Shanghai in the spring. They visited the Zhangyuan park several times, toured the city's business district, and even took a group portrait at a photography studio. But the vibrant scenes of Shanghai at night seem to have left the most enduring impression:

At nightfall we rode a rickshaw along the streets and looked all around the main streets. Electric lights and gas lamps crisscrossed this way and that and all the shops were still doing business at night. The lamps and candles were shining brightly so that it was just like broad daylight. Everywhere upper-story tearooms were crowded with beautiful women, and the sounds of wind and stringed instruments all mingled together. People came and went in noisy crowds competing with each other to enjoy themselves. Businessmen, who had been doing business all day long, relaxed and spent time enjoying cheerful conversation. They say that it is like this every day. It was as though everything was bathed in a hazy moonlight that cast its spell for ten leagues all around. The melodious sound of flutes warbles throughout the four seasons.[40]

Arriving in Nagasaki on 12 April, Min first met the commander of the Russian Squadron in the Pacific, Admiral Evgenii Alexeev,[41] and the Russian consul, Vasilii Kostylev.[42] From Nagasaki the party traveled to Yokohama, where they were met by the Russian consul, A. G. Lobanov-Rostovskii, a nephew of the Russian minister of foreign affairs, with whom Min was soon to be negotiating. Min and Yun took this opportunity to visit Prince Ŭihwa[43] in Tokyo, but according to Yun, they were met with a cool reception. While in Tokyo they stayed at the Korean legation and also had dinner with the Russian chargé d'affaires, Alexis de Speyer (Sa P'a-a).

Speyer had served as chargé d'affaires in Seoul from 13 January 1896 and had reputedly masterminded Kojong's flight to the Russian legation before being temporarily posted to Tokyo. He was later to replace the more cautious Waeber in Seoul, and during his term of office he aggressively promoted Russia's interests in Korea. In so doing, he alienated the other foreign representatives as well as Korean popular opinion. He was ultimately to preside over the decline of Russian influence on the Korean peninsula as Manchurian affairs began to dominate the policy making of his superiors.

During the mission's stay at the Korean legation in Tokyo, the staff notified Min of the financial hardships of the more than 150 Korean students attending Keiō Gijyuku, a progressive college founded by Fukuzawa Yukichi. Apparently an agreement drawn up between Fukuzawa and the Korean Ministry of Education precluded their return to Korea. "Such a disgrace," wrote Min, "is difficult to endure."[44] Nevertheless, all he could do was leave instructions for the new minister, Yi Ha-yŏng, who was on his way to Tokyo from Nagasaki, to address the problem.

Min and his party were obviously impressed by the evidence of modernization that they witnessed in Japan. On the day of the mission's departure from Yokohama, Min commented on the orderliness and beauty of the harbor and went on to praise the accomplishments of the Japanese, perhaps implicitly criticizing the Korean administration for its excessive dependence on foreign advisers:

The beauty of the mountains and rivers, the solid construction of the harbor front, the height of the buildings, the orderliness of the main roads, and the incessant twinkling of the gas and electric lamps suddenly enlighten one's mental outlook.

In Tokyo, moreover, everything is set up in an exquisite way, improving and becoming more and more refined every day. This enlightenment is the result of the diligent study of Western methods by all the Japanese people, and not because they have borrowed the assistance of others.[45]

The journey across the Pacific was not an easy one. Yun Ch'i-ho was suffering from an injury to his knee, sustained when he fell down a coal hole while their ship was docked in Nagasaki, and Stein was confined to his cabin with seasickness. Min, however, appears to have been able to keep his sense of humor through it all and wrote in his diary entry for 19 April, "The ship is rolling as before. I tried to get up and go from cabin to cabin. Standing up was extremely difficult, and I could not help laughing at myself as I staggered about like a drunken person."[46]

Eventually, however, the weather improved and both Stein and Yun recovered. On board ship Min learned of the Western custom of donating to charitable institutions and contributed 20 yen to a collection for an orphanage. He also witnessed the inoculation of Chinese and Japanese youths on board ship, although the youths' explanation that "by receiving the injection often, they would not contract smallpox and that by drawing out the hot *ki* [*qi*], they could avoid an epidemic"[47] might be described as an intuitive rather than scientific description of immunization. Min also appears to have been unaware that an early form of immunization against smallpox had already been introduced to Korea from China by Yi Ki-yang at the end of the eighteenth century and been taken up by the *sirhak* scholars Pak Che-ga and Chŏng Yag-yong.[48]

On 28 April the *Empress of China* docked at Victoria and early the next day arrived at its final destination, Vancouver. The party stayed at the Vancouver Hotel, where the Koreans had their first experience of an electrically powered elevator, concerning which Min wrote, "As climbing the stairs might be considered inconvenient, there is one room on the ground floor which goes up and down by means of electricity according to one's wish. This is a good idea."[49]

The next day the Korean party set out across Canada by steam train en route to New York. After the rigors of the sea voyage Min was clearly impressed by the comforts afforded by train travel, recording his impressions in his diary entry of 1 May as follows:

The train travels throughout the day and night, rocking slightly. This is a very comfortable "ship." The train runs like wind and lightning along iron rails laid over arduous terrain, bridging mountains and waters. We can see everything flashing by almost like things seen in a dream so that we cannot remember all those sights.[50]

After a life spent mainly in the confines of the Chosŏn court in Seoul, which is itself encircled by mountains, Min was also clearly impressed by the vastness of the Canadian prairies as well as the diligence of the British pioneers in bringing them under cultivation.[51]

During the long train journey, however, Min and his party heard the news of the assassination of the king of Persia. The entry for this day contains one of the few unfavorable judgments in the diary on Britain and Russia, while intimating that the situation in Persia paralleled that of Korea. The analogies made are to Chinese historical precedents and show how Min, and no doubt the majority of his colleagues at court, analyzed contemporary foreign affairs within the framework of a traditional education based on the Chinese classics:

> I heard a Western person saying that the king of Persia has been assassinated. This happened because of factional strife inside that country, which had been stirred up by the mutual rivalry of Britain and Russia. Neither of these countries have an enlightened or appropriate policy, so this rebellion took place. . . . That country is as if it were between the states of Qi and Chu,[52] without the means to improve its situation. Because it is unsettled by internal rebellion, it may be swallowed up by the watching tigers. It is a very lamentable situation.[53]

The Koreans were impressed by the extent of Canada's territory, noting that it was governed autonomously with its own prime minister *(kunjang)* and parliament *(ŭiwŏn)* even though it was part of the British Empire. The train halted at Winnipeg before passing by Lake Superior, which evoked Min's admiring response:

> There is a lake called Lake Superior. It is twice as big as England. I do not know how many thousands of leagues its actual size is. The surface of the lake is as smooth as a river, and islands are scattered across it like chess pieces on linen. Its color is indigo, and its water is fresh. This lake is the biggest in all the five continents. All day we traveled along the lakeside. This made us feel cheerful and washed away our worldly cares.[54]

After an overnight stay at the Windsor Hotel in Montreal, Min and his party continued on their transcontinental journey, arriving in New York at 10:00 P.M. on 6 May. Here they stayed at the luxurious, ten-story Waldorf Hotel. During their stay in New York the Koreans were looked after by the Russian consul-general, Silorevsky,[55] who made all their onward travel arrangements. Min sent a telegram to the Korean minister at Washington, Sŏ Kwang-bŏm, calling him to New York. Sŏ, a former conspirator in the Kapsin coup, had been rehabilitated during the Kabo reforms. In fact, Min himself had originally been appointed to Sŏ's post in 1895 but had resigned because of the death of his aunt Queen Myŏngsŏng, and Sŏ had been appointed as his replacement. No mention is made in *Haech'ŏn ch'ubŏm* of how Min felt toward Sŏ, who had participated in the murder of several of his relatives during the 1884 coup, but Yun Ch'i-ho, who was acquainted with the conspirators and had himself been forced into exile as a result of the coup's failure, wrote in his diary of his happiness at meeting Sŏ again. Characteristically, Yun could not resist making a critical observation as well: "Was happy to see Mr. Soh K. P., the Corean representative at Washington. He wears the European costume and is as dudish as ever. He changed his shoes and clothes almost every hour."[56]

In New York the party had time to visit Central Park with Silorevsky and his wife, where they were most impressed by a four-thousand-year-old monument from Egypt. They also saw a twenty-five-story building, a bridge constructed on three levels for trains, horses, and boats, and an electricity exposition. This exposition appears to have made a great impression on Min, who expressed his struggle to comprehend the marvel of wire broadcasting in his diary entry for 8 May:

> Not only were there telegraphs and lights but also a thousand different everyday things, all powered by electricity. It is difficult to record everything. There was also a strange thing there. Five hundred leagues away there is a huge waterfall, the sound of which is extremely loud. This noise of water tumbling and crashing is conveyed along a cable by electricity so that one can hear it. Its sound makes people frightened. One can also hear the sound of music in this way, and it sounds no different from real music. . . . Everything was so unusual that I could hardly understand it. They say that people are now conducting research into how to power ships and carriages by electricity.[57]

After what must have been a whirlwind of new impressions for the party, Min summed up New York in the following way:

> The population is nearly three million, and it is so crowded that people rub shoulders and wheels clash. There is no difference between day and night. Musical instruments play all year around without pausing for breath. It is like a perpetual spring garden without any cares or a city without any night, a paradise.[58]

On 9 May the party boarded the British liner *Lucania*, heading for Liverpool. Six days later they arrived at Queenstown on the southern coast of Ireland, a country that, according to Min, "had freely united with Britain several hundred years ago."[59] The following day they arrived in Liverpool, the largest port in the world at that time. From there they went directly to London by train and rested at the Royal Hotel.

In London Min was impressed not only by the size, prosperity, and splendor of the British capital but also by its quietness and orderliness. "The people traveling along the streets are not noisy," he wrote; "you can only hear the sound of hooves and wheels. We can see that this country has very strict laws."[60] Praising Queen Victoria for acquiring territory and wealth and for strengthening her nation, Min expressed his regret at not having had the time to visit the Crystal Palace, museums, schools, and historical sights of the British capital.

At 6.00 P.M. on the same day the Korean party set off to Queenborough at the mouth of the Thames and caught a ship to Flushing in Holland. From there they traveled to Berlin. In his account of traveling across Germany to Alexandrof, Min poured lavish praise on the accomplishments of Germany in the nineteenth century:

> This country's wealth and strength increases every day. Nobody can compete with the excellence of its schools or the strength of its army. Its expertise in medicine and music is also the best in the world. Even though the students of all the other nations may have already graduated, only after receiving further education in this country are they free to practice their skills anywhere in the world.[61]

At Alexandrof, Min and his party were met by a Russian military attaché. They then crossed over former Polish territory to Warsaw, where they were welcomed by a high-ranking official from the Russian Ministry of Foreign Affairs. The party stayed at the Grand Hotel d'Europe.[62] In the diary entry for this day, Min commented on the partition of Poland, drawing an analogy with the political situation in his own country:

> I heard that this country [Poland] used to be the most enlightened and independent of nations, but more than a hundred years ago, it gradually became politically weakened. The officials and nobles mistreated the people, and there were frequent rebellions. These could not be suppressed, and finally Russia, Austria, and France divided the land between them. Perhaps this is a warning to the people who are governing our country.[63]

In Warsaw, Min's party was joined by two Russian officials, Planson and Paskov, who accompanied them throughout their time in Moscow and St. Petersburg. From Warsaw they traveled to Moscow in a government train and were "treated with exceptional politeness."[64] After a journey through the green barley fields of western Russia, Min's party finally arrived at its destination at 3:00 P.M. on 20 May 1896.[65]

Through this journey across two continents, Min Yŏng-hwan had moved from the preindustrial to the industrial world. He had had his first experience of travel by steamship and steam train. For the first time in his life he had seen buildings in excess of two or three stories, tar macadamized roads, gas and electric lighting, and wire transmission. He had glimpsed societies that had derived their wealth and power from trade rather than agriculture and that were ruled by democratically elected bodies in cooperation with elected presidents, prime ministers, and constitutional monarchs. It must have been a great deal for Min and his colleagues, with the exception of the American-educated Yun, to comprehend and digest fully. Nevertheless, as will be seen in later chapters, the experiences did not simply wash over Min but led him, on his return to Korea, to align himself more closely with agents for reform and modernization such as Sŏ Chae-p'il, the Western Christian missionaries, Yun Ch'i-ho, and even the young radical Syngman Rhee.

Min's Diplomatic Activity and Negotiations in Moscow

In Moscow the Korean mission was established at "the House of Mr. Holmsky, Troofnikovsky Lane, Pavarskaya Street, No. 42, Moscow."[66] Here the Koreans were attended by four liveried messengers and twenty-one servants, as well as being assigned two three-horse carriages. It was also from the top of this house that the Korean flag (t'aegŭkki) was flown for the first time in Russia's old capital.[67]

The day after their arrival the Korean party witnessed, from the house of the governor-general of Moscow, Grand Duke Sergei Alexandrovich,[68] the entry into Moscow of Tsar Nicholas II, together with his German-born wife, Alexandra Feodorovna, and his Danish mother, Maria Dagmar.[69] That evening Min was visited for the first time by Count Dmitrii Kapnist, the director of the Asiatic Department in the Ministry of Foreign Affairs. Once again nothing is recounted in *Haech'ŏn ch'ubŏm* of their conversation. According to Yun Ch'i-ho, however, it was at this meeting that Min's "five requests" were first presented. The requests were for the following items of support from the Russian government: a Russian military guard for the king; instructors to retrain the Korean army; governmental advisers, including a financial adviser; the establishment of telegraphic links between Korea and Russia; and a substantial loan of 3 million yen to repay a Japanese loan made to the Korean government during the Kabo reform period.[70]

On 22 May Min had his first audience with the tsar in the Kremlin. Although Kim To-il had been appointed by Kojong as the official Russian-language interpreter, Min decided to have Yun Ch'i-ho translate into English instead. In doing this Min appears to have been acting in contradiction to Kojong's orders, as he had earlier informed Yun that Kim To-il had been given "a secret telegraphic code" by the king, who had also instructed Min to "use him as interpreter in all important negotiations."[71] Yun, ever confident in his own superior qualities, was considerably offended to hear this and expressed his exasperation freely in the pages of his private diary:

> What a grateful King! He would rather trust a young man who had spent most of his whole life in Vladivostok, who cannot read a word of written Chinese or Corean, who was but a month ago an interpreter for the Russian sailors in the Legation, who was admitted to the Royal Presence only a few weeks ago—in short His gracious Majesty prefers trusting a youth of such an antecedence with the state secrets to counting on my fidelity. No wonder the King has no friends.[72]

Yun attributed Min's decision to go against his orders and to use him instead of Kim To-il to Kim's poor command of Korean. Yun, who like Min was from a *yangban* background, was particularly contemptuous of Kim's reference to the Russian empress dowager as the *huang jai aimi* [lit., "the emperor's mom"].[73] Ironically, at the outset of their journey, Yun had expressed approval of the "modern" attitudes and demeanor of Kim To-il, especially compared to the more conservative Kim Tŭng-nyŏn, but he was later to condemn Kim To-il for his lax morals and arrogance.[74]

Min's first audience with Tsar Nicholas II, at which the tsarina was also present, was a brief one. Min recited a congratulatory address and, according to Yun, "almost lost his voice and mumbled out his presentation speech in the most distressing manner."[75] Yun then translated the speech, and Min presented the tsar with King Kojong's personal letter and an inventory of the gifts that the mission had brought from Korea.[76]

The coronation gifts were a two-tier purple shell box, two embroidered screens, two white brass braziers, four bamboo blinds, four flower-patterned mats, and four hanging scroll paintings.[77] Concerning these gifts, Yun wrote bitterly, "These might pass for a present from a private Corean to a private Russian. But as the gift of a King to an emperor, they are shamefully poor. I had scarcely the cheeks [*sic*] to look at the officers who have the charge of the archives. Impoverished Corea!"[78]

During this audience the tsar spoke in English and asked Min about his journey and how he liked Moscow, questions to which Min gave polite replies. Yun, however, went beyond his role as interpreter and added on Min's behalf, "Whenever it shall please your majesty to inquire into the affairs of Corea, the envoy extraordinary is prepared and authorized by his government to present to Your Majesty in full the condition and needs of Corea."[79]

Yun's tendency to exceed his brief and his ever increasing frustration with what he perceived to be the dullness and inexperience of his superior, Min Yŏnghwan, was to lead to considerable friction between them. In fact, as negotiations reached a delicate stage toward the end of the stay of the mission, Kim To-il, much to Yun's chagrin, was suddenly reinstated as Min's interpreter.

In the afternoon of the same day Min also visited the minister of foreign affairs, Prince Lobanov-Rostovsky, for the first time. This visit appears to have been purely a courtesy call, during which nothing of moment was discussed. Yun made no record of any conversation but found Lobanov to be "a pleasant old man, with a strong face."[80]

On the following day, 23 May, Min set to work in earnest to fulfill his role as Chosŏn's first envoy to Russia. In keeping with Russian protocol, he first visited Grand Duke Sergei, the governor of Moscow. He then sent his calling card to the diplomatic representatives of all the countries with which Chosŏn had treaty relations at that time as well as those of Portugal, Turkey, Spain, and Persia. Min was pleased to find that all these countries' envoys reciprocated by sending him their calling cards. Although this was merely a diplomatic formality, it must have been encouraging for the Korean party to find themselves being treated on a par with other nations, including their more powerful neighbors, China and Japan.

On 24 May Min's diplomatic activity continued as he visited each Russian government ministry and had personal meetings with the minister of justice, M. V. Muraviev, and the minister of education, Pobedonosushev (Pobedonosüssep). As well as visiting the envoys of the United States, Britain, France, Germany, Italy, Austria-Hungary, Japan, and China, Min also had personal conversations with Li Hongzhang and Yamagata Aritomo. Although it is not known what Min and Yamagata spoke about, Yun Ch'i-ho recorded the conversation between Min and Li in his diary, evincing some disgust at Li's tactless questioning of Min in a crowded room, with many high-level Russian officials within earshot, on such matters as Kojong's flight to the Russian legation, the execution of Kim Hong-jip, and whether Min belonged to the Taewŏn'gun's party or the Japanese party at court. To Li's final question—whether Koreans liked the Japanese—Min replied tactfully, "Some of them like Japan and others don't, just as it is in China."[81]

What language was used during this exchange is not clear from Yun's account. We know that Min could not speak Chinese, as he specifically mentions this fact in *Sagu sokch'o,* the diary of his trip to Queen Victoria's Diamond Jubilee in the following year. It is highly unlikely that Li spoke any Korean. Yun, on the other hand, who had lived in Shanghai for several years while attending an English school there and had married a Chinese woman, may have known some Chinese. It is most likely, however, that Li used an English-speaking interpreter and that Yun interpreted for Min. The fact that the conversation probably took place in English might explain Yun's fear that Li's tactless questions were being overheard by Russian or Japanese officials in the same room. This conversation also shows that despite Min's advocacy of maintaining Chosŏn's traditional relationship with China in his essay *Ch'ŏnilch'aek,* he himself does not appear to have had any special rapport or affinity with Chinese officials themselves.

The first diplomatic crisis faced by Min and his colleagues was one of protocol. Should they remove their official headgear so that they could attend the coronation, which was to take place inside the cathedral of the Kremlin Palace? In fact, they were not the only envoys placed in such a quandary; the problem was also shared by the Chinese, Turkish, and Persian representatives. The Koreans were informed by their Russian assistants Planson and Paskov that the envoys of the three other nations would remove their hats and enter the cathedral. As the removal of headgear by Korean or Chinese officials was a sign that they had been disgraced and stripped of their rank, Min demonstrated considerable flexibility when he was initially persuaded by Yun and the Russian aides to set aside Korean court etiquette and do likewise.

Subsequently, however, the Turkish ambassador revealed that he would not remove his hat and that it was likely that the Persians and Chinese envoys would not either. Min, unwilling to lay himself open to the possible censure of the Korean court by discarding a time-honored tradition, opted for caution, reversed his previous decision, and blamed Yun for the confusion. Consequently, the relationship between the two soured further, as may be seen from Yun's diary entry for that day:

> Mr. Min is a spoiled Corean Yangban out and out. He is capricious, petulant, and self-willed. He behaves himself haughtily and ungraciously when he is humored as he has been of late. (He seems to think that it is really somewhat to be "His Excellency, the Special Ambassador of His Majesty, the King of Tai (?) [*sic*] Choson!")[82]

In the end the Korean party witnessed the imperial procession from a vantage point outside the cathedral in the company of the envoys of Turkey, China, and Persia but were unable to attend the coronation itself. After a journey of thousands of miles across two oceans and two continents to arrive in time for the coronation, Min must have felt some frustration at this unexpected turn of events. It was probably partly as a result of this experience that Min cut his hair and adopted Western military uniform in the following year before departing for Britain as minister plenipotentiary and envoy extraordinary for the Diamond Jubilee of Queen Victoria.[83]

On 28 May Min and the other foreign envoys offered the tsar congratulations on the conclusion of the coronation ceremony. In this second audience, Min exchanged pleasantries with the tsar and tsarina, and again Yun Ch'i-ho interpreted. While in Moscow Min's party attended balls, the theater, horse races, and the ill-fated "people's banquet" held on 29 May at Khodynskoe Field. From the diary entries it appears that the Koreans did not hear about the accident at Khodynskoe, in which more than a thousand Russian peasants had been trampled to death and many more injured as they rushed forward to receive free food, until 2 June. Although this event was an inauspicious beginning to the start of the reign of the new tsar, the text of *Haech'ŏn ch'ubŏm* omits the fact that so many had died, while emphasizing the tsar's magnanimous treatment of the victims:

> On the day of the people's banquet, when they were handing out food to the people, more than twelve hundred people were injured in the confusion. When the emperor heard this, he immediately provided every person with 1,000 wŏn from the privy purse to assist them. The people all praise him.[84]

On 1 June Min met Lieutenant General Sergei Dukhovskoi, governor-general of the Amur region. Min raised the issue of the repatriation of Korean immigrants in the Russian Far East but was told that most of the migrants were of mixed race and that they were all prospering.[85] From the brief mention of their conversation in *Haech'ŏn ch'ubŏm,* it appears that the Russian side, which was now intent on settling the region that it had acquired from China three decades earlier, had no wish to encourage those Koreans who were naturalized Russians to return to their own country. According to Ban Byung-yool, Dukhovskoi, unlike his predecessor, Baron Andrei N. Korf, "was an advocate of liberal policies toward Korean immigrants: (1) utilization of the Koreans for the colonization of the Ussurisk Krai; (2) welcoming them to Russian citizenship with allotments of land; (3) and Russification."[86]

On the journey back to Korea, Min passed through the Priamur region and was met by many of the Korean migrants settled there. Their diligence, prosperity, and continued sense of patriotism appear to have influenced Min's attitude, and in the end he refrained from urging them to return to their native land and instead recommended that a Korean consulate be set up at Vladivostok to provide additional support and protection for these Korean migrants, who had settled in Russia largely as a result of intolerable famine conditions in their own country.[87]

The second diplomatic crisis which Min faced after the affair of the headgear was that although he had presented Kojong's personal letter and gifts at his first audience with the tsar, Planson had advised him to present his credentials at a later date because this would provide him with a pretext for a further personal audience. As the days passed in Moscow, however, and the tsar retreated to one of his summer resorts, Min grew increasingly anxious about not having presented his credentials. He sent an official dispatch to Lobanov requesting an audience at the earliest opportunity.[88]

On 5 June, according to the entry in *Haech'ŏn ch'ubŏm*, Min met Lobanov to discuss the matter of the presentation of his credentials to the tsar. Yun's diary, however, provides a fuller account of what Min and Lobanov discussed. In addition to requesting an audience to present his credentials, Min also reiterated his five requests for assistance from the Russian government. Yun, who was also present at the meeting, recorded their conversation as follows:

> Min: The condition of affairs in Corea is such that I hope the Russian government may soon grant the five propositions which I have been authorized to lay before you, viz.
>
> 1. Guard for the protection of the King until the Corean army be drilled into a reliable force.
> 2. Military Instructors.
> 3. Advisers: One for the Royal Household to be near the King; one for the Ministry; one for mines, railroads, etc.
> 4. Telegraphic connections between Russia and Corea on terms beneficial to both: An expert in telegraphic matters.
> 5. A loan of 3 million yen to cancel the Japanese debt.[89]

As mentioned previously, these five proposals had already been translated into Russian by Stein and presented to the director of the Asiatic Department, Kapnist, to be shown to Lobanov two days after the arrival of Min's party in Moscow. Nevertheless, Lobanov, who was conducting concurrent negotiations with the Japanese envoy Yamagata Aritomo, appeared to have heard nothing of them before his meeting with Min on 5 June. Whether he had prior knowledge of the requests or not, his response to them was decidedly lukewarm. He told Min that he would need to discuss the requests with his colleagues and also place them before the tsar. Min responded by telling Lobanov that he needed to return to Korea as soon as possible to report to his government whether it could rely on Russian support or not. Before the meeting ended, he handed Lobanov the following memo:

> "Corea had concluded a secret treaty years ago,[90] with Russia, binding the countries into a close friendship. We did not consent to all that Japan demanded since 1894, because of our reliance on the support of Russia. Japanese, finding themselves unable to carry out their designs, were enraged. This drove them to commit, with certain Corean traitors the crimes of the 8th October.[91] Coreans feeling the wrong deeply, look to Russia for help: hence the five requests. Russia is the only country which Corea expects to take up the responsibility single-handed. Russia's help would place the government of Corea on a firmer basis." Her Majesty, the late Queen of Corea, because of her partiality to Russia, brought on her the hatred of the pro-Japanese party, resulting in her death. In some Eastern papers it is rumoured that Russia and Japan intend to exercise a joint influence on Corea. Such an arrangement would bring about a conflict. Corea would gain nothing by the arrangement not only but would find in it the embryo of another national calamity. "I beg that the five propositions might soon be granted."[92]

This memo clearly shows that the main motivation of the Chosŏn administration's attempt to gain Russian protection was its fear of increasing Japanese encroachment on Korean sovereignty in the wake of the Sino-Japanese War. In addition it shows that the Korean side were also engaging with the Russians in an effort to preempt any attempt by Russia and Japan to carve up Korea into separate spheres of influence. At the same time the weak position from which Min was negotiating is painfully clear. Min's unenviable task in this nineteenth-century version of "fighting barbarians with barbarians" was to offer the Russians just enough to prevent them from making a secret deal with Japan while ensuring that any increase in Russian influence would not jeopardize Chosŏn sovereignty. This task could not have been made any easier for Min by his view that, as we know from his policy essay *Ch'ŏnilch'aek,* Russia was an even greater potential threat to Chosŏn's continued independence than Japan.

On the following day, 6 June, Min was visited by the governor of Vladivostok, Unbyolgyol (Unbyŏlgyŏl), and of the Priamur region, Sergei Dukhovskoi, who were both about to return to their posts in the Russian Far East. At 3:00 P.M. on the same day Min was again given an audience by the tsar, ostensibly to present his credentials as is recounted in *Haech'ŏn ch'ubŏm.*[93] Once again, however, the candid account provided by Yun's private diary reveals what actually took place. At this meeting with the tsar, Min "practically recited the memo that he had given to Prince Lobanov."[94] According to Yun, the tsar listened attentively and remarked "Tai Won Kun" at the mention of "Certain Corean Traitors."[95] Once again Yun was unable to restrict himself to merely translating for his superior and added his own opinion on the condition of his country:

> "What Corea wants is a stable government. A Corean has not known a single day in the last three years in which he felt secure in life and property. It is now in the power of Russia to enable Corea to have a stable government. A joint influence of Russia and Japan would breed factional intrigues among Corean officials and produce irritating complications between Russia and Japan. Under such an arrangement, either in war or in probable peace, Corea would be the sufferer. May your Majesty never consent to such an arrangement." The Czar shook his head and said, "No. No!" every time the joint influence of Russia and Japan was mentioned.[96]

Min repeated the five requests, and the tsar told him to discuss the matter further with Lobanov and Minister of Finance Witte, while reassuring him that Korea could rely on Russian help. Min also delivered a personal message from King Kojong thanking the tsar for the services of Waeber and Speyer. In marked contrast to Yun's candid account, the record in *Haech'ŏn ch'ubŏm* provides only the barest outline of the audience as the following passage shows:

> A ceremonial official led us into the room just as when we had presented the personal letter. We went into the room. The emperor stood up. There was no one beside him. I stepped forward. The emperor shook my hand. I recited the congratulatory message and presented the credential letter. The emperor received it with his own hands while standing. Yun Ch'i-ho translated into English for me. I explained that because of the ceremony I had presented the personal letter first, and now I was presenting the credential letter. The emperor replied that he understood. The emperor told me as an envoy to return to His Majesty the King and convey his wishes for cooperation, trust, and eternal friendship. I replied that I would respectfully obey his instruction. I bowed three times and withdrew.[97]

A comparison of these two accounts shows how fortunate it is for our understanding of this pioneering phase in Korea's diplomatic dealings in the West that Chosŏn's official envoy to the Russian court was accompanied by such a compulsive diarist as Yun Ch'i-ho.

On 7 June the coronation celebrations finally came to an end, and the Korean party prepared to depart for St. Petersburg. Before leaving, Min awarded silver medals inscribed with the Korean national flag and the words *"Kŏnyang wŏnnyŏn"* (The founding year of Kŏnyang)[98] on the obverse and *"Tae Chosŏn Konggwan"* (The legation of Great Chosŏn) on the reverse to their twenty-seven Russian servants. He and the other members of the Korean mission also received different medals according to their rank from the Department of the Imperial Household by order of the tsar.

That day, however, more important business was discussed than is recounted in *Haech'ŏn ch'ubŏm*. At 10:30 A.M. Min and Yun visited the Russian minister of finance, Witte, repeating the requests that they had already placed before the tsar and Lobanov. Witte's response was also cautious. He reassured Min that Russia would not permit "Japan or any other country to take or trouble Corea."[99] Nevertheless, he emphasized Russia's need to proceed cautiously until the completion of the Siberian railroad, as Japan, although "a hundred times weaker than Russia," had more influence on the Korean peninsula because of its close proximity to it. Nevertheless, Witte reassured Min that "Russia would prevail in the end," and in response to the five requests, he informed Min as follows:

1. Military instructors will very likely be given.
2. As for advisers, we may increase the staff of officers in our legation at Seoul. They may help you.
3. The loan cannot be granted until the financial condition of Corea be examined. As the Corean finance is represented by the customs service, Russia must have more influence in customs so that a reliable guarantee might be secured for the loan.
4. As for the guard, if the King of Corea has not the character enough to protect himself, how can others protect him? . . . If I were in his place I would punish all my enemies beginning with Tai Won Kun.[100]

Witte apparently made no reference to the proposed telegraphic connection between Russia and Korea in Min's five requests at this particular meeting. It is clear that the Russian side had adopted a cautious policy for Korea at this stage and obviously wished to avoid antagonizing Japan. On the other hand, its desire for greater influence in the Korean customs service may well have put the Korean side on its guard. As will be seen later, Anglo-Russian rivalry over influence in Korea's customs service eventually became serious enough to bring nine British cruisers to the port of Inch'ŏn to prevent the replacement of the British commissioner of customs, John McLeavy Brown, by a Russian.

On 8 June Min's party left Moscow and headed for St. Petersburg by rail. At St. Petersburg they stayed at the home of Stein's family, No. 4 Kabinyesky

Street. The Steins' home was in fact an apartment, and after the luxurious conditions of the house put at their disposal by the Russian government in Moscow, Min and the others found it cramped and inconvenient. Nevertheless, it was here that the temporary Korean legation was established and here that the Korean flag was first flown in St. Petersburg.

The Chosŏn Mission's Diplomatic Activity and Negotiations in St. Petersburg

On 13 June Min met Lobanov again. Although this visit is merely mentioned in passing with no further comment in *Haech'ŏn ch'ubŏm,* Yun's diary provides a detailed account of the negotiations that took place at this meeting. In the first instance Lobanov gave Min the tsar's assurance that Russia would do its utmost to "protect the independence and peace of Corea from being endangered by Japan." He also told Min that Kojong could stay at the Russian legation as long as he wanted and that he would be guarded there.[101]

Min pointed out that the Korean king could not remain in the Russian legation forever and that it was imperative that he should return to the palace as soon as possible. He once again requested a Russian guard that could protect Kojong when he left the Russian legation. Lobanov replied that this was impossible as it would give offense to England and Germany, but he told Min that on his return to the palace Kojong would have Russia's "moral assurance of safety."[102] What Lobanov did not tell Min was that the provision of a Russian guard would have run counter to the spirit of article 2 of the Yamagata-Lobanov Protocol, which stated, "The Russian and Japanese governments will endeavor to leave to Korea, as far as the financial and economic situation of that country will permit them to do so, the creation and maintenance of an armed force and of a native police in sufficient proportions to maintain order without foreign aid."[103]

As Andrew Malozemoff points out, however, the phrase "as far as the financial and economic situation of that country will permit" was to provide the Russians with sufficient flexibility of interpretation to send a military mission to Korea.[104] Significantly, however, the final decision to send military instructors to Korea does not appear to have been taken until after Lobanov's sudden death on 1 September 1896, while Min and his party were returning to Korea via Siberia. Lobanov himself, therefore, appears never to have deviated from his original cautious approach of remaining strictly within the bounds of the protocol.

Min, unaware of the secret negotiations that had taken place at Moscow between Lobanov and Yamagata, persisted in his demands. As an alternative to a Russian palace guard, he requested two hundred military instructors, who would be able to perform the dual role of protecting King Kojong and training the Korean army. Lobanov once again rejected Min's request, arguing that such a move might give rise to conflict with the Japanese soldiers stationed in Seoul. He then went on to outline the Russian government's attitude to Min's previous requests. He told Min that an officer would be sent to "examine into the military affairs of Corea and the advisability of sending out Russian instructors."[105] Concerning the loan, he stated that the minister of finance would send out an expert to carefully examine "the condition of the Corean finance and of the state of commerce and agriculture of the country."[106] Depending on this expert's report, the Russian government would decide whether or not to advance the loan. In regard to the request for a telegraphic connection, Lobanov stated that his government was willing to connect a Seoul line with the Vladivostok line but that no submarine cables could be laid between China and Korea until more was known about the latter's circumstances. It is clear from this response that Lobanov was pursuing a course of prevarication as he had no wish to upset the Japanese by flagrantly going against the spirit of his recent agreement with Yamagata. On the other hand, he did not wish to forfeit the Russian advantage in Seoul by rejecting Min's requests out of hand.

Min did not object to Lobanov's response on the issue of telegraphic connections, but he questioned why Lobanov did not simply consult with Waeber in Seoul or the Russian naval authorities in the region concerning Korea's military affairs rather than sending out an officer and waiting for his report, a process that might take three or four months. "In the meantime," Min argued, "the King would have been in the Legation nearly a year and the country gone to pieces."[107]

Lobanov insisted on the necessity for specialists to be sent and pointed out that the process would not take so long because Russia had good telegraphic and postal services. He also complained that the Korean government had submitted its requests too late and demanded why they had not been made "when the king first went to the legation or even before it."[108] Nevertheless, he promised Min that his request for military instructors would receive due consideration. The discussion concluded with Lobanov asking Min if an armed force would be required to protect the telegraph lines in the north of Korea. Min, perhaps fearing that an affirmative answer might provide the Russians with a pretext for stationing troops in the Korean interior, did not give a direct answer but replied that the matter could be discussed at a later date when the details of the telegraphic connection had been worked out.[109]

After this discussion, Stein and Yun held a private conversation in which Yun lamented that he was not privy to the communications by telegram between Min and the Korean government even though the junior-ranking Kim To-il was. Stein informed Yun that the dispatch of a Russian financial adviser to Seoul would mean "putting the Corean Customs in the hands of a Russian."[110] This prediction was later borne out when Speyer attempted to have the British head of customs, John McLeavy Brown, replaced by the Russian Finance Ministry agent Kir Alekseev.

On 16 June at 2:00 P.M. Min and Yun visited Kapnist at the Foreign Office again. Min emphasized that the request for a royal bodyguard was the most important of the five propositions. As it had been rejected, he demanded to know why the Korean government should not have the right to hire as many military instructors as it wished. Kapnist reiterated Lobanov's opposition to the palace guard on the grounds that it would "evoke political questions whose consequence might be rather more injurious than helpful to the safety of the King."[111] He repeated that Kojong could continue to stay in the Russian legation and that he would have "the full moral assurance of Russia that nobody would harm him"[112] if he chose to return to the palace. Kapnist, therefore, also encouraged Min to accept the status quo in Seoul and refrain from making requests that might bring Russia into conflict with Japan or the Western powers.

When Min asked Kapnist whether the Russian legation guard would be permitted to enter the royal palace in the event of trouble, the latter again responded negatively. Min continued by asking what objection there could be to a large number of Russian military instructors temporarily taking charge of the safety of the king while the Korean army was being reorganized and retrained. Kapnist reminded Min that this would have political consequences and that as Russia had objected to the stationing of Japanese troops in the palace, it could not then do the same thing itself.[113]

When Min asked Kapnist how many instructors would be sent, he was again told that an expert would first have to be sent from the War Department to assess the condition of the Korean army. Finally, Min requested a written response from the Russian government to his five requests, and the meeting ended. According to Yun, after this meeting Min was "so depressed that he would not go anywhere or see anything. He fills the house with sighs. He begins to complain that his mission has so far been a failure because of his incapacity."[114] Significantly, there is no entry for this day in *Haech'ŏn ch'ubŏm*, and on the following day, Min chose to comment in his diary on Russia's expansionist tendencies:

> If we look at a map of Russia, we find that it has one-seventh of the world's land mass. Its population is 113,054,649 in all, but they still worry that their popula-

tion is insufficient. They have the intention of expanding their territory in the southeast because their land is near the Arctic Circle, and there is much wilderness and no people.[115]

Despite Min's frustration at the unresponsive attitude of his Russian counterparts, the negotiations progressed and resulted on 30 July in Lobanov's written response to Min's five requests. The substance of the document is again provided by Yun's diary:

1. The King may stay in the Russian Legation as long as he wants. In case he should return to his palace, the Russian government would answer for his safety. A guard will remain in the Legation at the disposal of the Russian Minister at Seoul.
2. For military instructors, the Russian government will send an experienced officer of high standing to Seoul to negotiate with the Corean government on the subject. His first object in view shall be the organization of a Corean guard for the King. Another experienced man will be sent to examine the economical conditions of Corea and to find out necessary financial measures.
3. These two confidential officers may act as advisers, under the guide of the Russian minister at Seoul.
4. The question of the loan will be taken into consideration when the financial condition of Corea and its needs be fully known.
5. Russia consents to connect the land lines of Corea with those of Russia and will give all possible assistance to the realization of the project.[116]

As can be seen by comparing the response with Min's original requests, Lobanov refused to change his original cautious stance and did not accede to any of Min's requests that might have brought Russia into conflict with Japan or the other foreign powers in Seoul. Unfortunately, after 5 July Yun was no longer privy to Min's negotiations with the Russian Foreign Office after being displaced by Kim To-il, the original interpreter for the mission. It seems, however, that although there were some further negotiations between Min and Lobanov, the outcome remained as outlined in the five responses above. Lobanov also decided that Min should be accompanied on his journey back to Korea by the military official Colonel Putiata, who was to make an assessment of Korea's military needs and help to retrain the Korean army. Colonel Putiata was a member of the Russian general staff and had served as a military attaché in Beijing. Ironically, he had been assigned to Marshal Yamagata Aritomo during the latter's visit to Moscow for the tsar's coronation and secret negotiations with Lobanov.[117]

As might be guessed, however, by the end of the mission's stay in St. Petersburg, Lobanov was beginning to find the Korean party increasingly importunate. According to the German chargé d'affaires Heinrich von Tschirschky und Bögendorff,

> Prince Lobanov in particular would be glad to see the departure of these people from the Far East. The less they are otherwise occupied, the more they honour the minister with their visits, which in accordance with Oriental custom they always drag out considerably. Prince Lobanov complains that they approach him with all kind of political requests which in most cases cannot be taken seriously at all, but which, in spite of all his efforts to dissuade them, the Koreans present anew again and again with tiresome stubbornness.[118]

The Koreans, on the other hand, were still ignorant of the Russo-Japanese negotiations in Seoul and Moscow that had resulted in the Waeber-Komura Memorandum and the Yamagata-Lobanov Protocol. These two agreements had tied the hands of the Russian Foreign Ministry to a great extent, and Lobanov's foot dragging in granting security guarantees for Kojong and Korea itself must also have become increasingly frustrating for Min and his colleagues. At the end of several months of negotiations with Lobanov, Witte, and Kapnist, Min's only concrete accomplishment was the appointment of Colonel Putiata to investigate the condition of the Korean army and the appointment of Dmitrii Pokotilov to examine Korea's financial situation. On the crucial question of a Russian guard for Kojong, enabling him to leave the Russian legation and return to the palace in safety, Min's mission appeared to have failed. This matter, however, was eventually solved by the relocation of the royal palace from Kyŏngbokkung, which was in the vicinity of the Japanese legation, to Tŏksugung, which was in the Chŏngdong area of Seoul and was surrounded by Western legations and missionary residences.

Min's Relationship with His Adjutant, Yun Ch'i-ho

As the mission's stay in St. Petersburg lengthened, the relationship between Min and Yun, which had never been close, deteriorated even further. In fact, during this period Yun seldom mentions Min in his diary without criticizing him. Nevertheless, the ambiguity of his feelings toward his superior are clearly demonstrated in the following passage:

> After all, I can think of nobody among the Corean officials of Min's caste who may behave himself as decently and as prudently as he has done. He is by na-

ture sensible, reasonable, liberal, and even confiding. But his unlimited success in the corrupting official life of Corea has spoiled him into a calculating, suspicious, peevish, and arrogant and selfish man.[119]

Yun's judgments, of course, should not be taken completely at face value. Yun was ambitious and intelligent, and he was obviously frustrated by the subservient role he had to fulfill as Min's interpreter. Furthermore, his command of English, his education and experience in the United States, and even his Christian religion must have made it difficult for him to be humble toward Min, who, although four years his senior, spoke only Korean, had never been abroad before in his life, was a "benighted" Confucian, and was powerful, Yun seemed to believe, only because of his birth.

Yun was himself nominally the scion of a prestigious clan, but he was handicapped by the fact that he was the descendant of a son of a secondary wife (sŏŏl) and that his father, Yun Ung-yŏl, was a military rather than civil official.[120] Earlier in the Chosŏn era being the descendant of a secondary wife would have been an insurmountable obstacle to entering the administration. Although it is clear that such prejudices were weakening by this period, Yun seems to have harbored a sense of grievance that probably contributed to the obvious resentment that he felt toward Min Yŏng-hwan during their visit to Russia. Furthermore, Yun was connected through his paternal grandmother to the Andong Kim clan, which had been displaced by the Yŏhŭng Min as the influential royal in-law clan in the Chosŏn court.[121] Members of these two clans, therefore, would have been natural political enemies.[122] Kim Ok-kyun, for example, whose coup of 1884 had resulted in the deaths of several leading members of the Min clan, was an Andong Kim.

According to Yun, Min often blamed him unfairly for the mishaps of the mission. On arrival in Moscow the Russian official assigned to the Korean mission, Planson, had advised Min to hold back his credentials so that he would have an excuse for an additional audience with the tsar. Min followed this advice but was then dismayed to find that arranging a further audience was not such an easy matter and eventually required the writing of a special dispatch to the Russian Foreign Office.[123] In Yun's account of the writing of this dispatch, Min had originally written that he had withheld the credentials on the advice of "'an official of your Department of Foreign Affairs (!)'"[124] As Planson's advice had been given confidentially, Yun urged Min to remove the phrase, which appeared to be placing some blame on Planson. Min finally agreed after Planson took offense on being shown the original draft, and the final draft read, "Because the coronation ceremony of His Majesty the Emperor of this esteemed country took place on the twenty-second day of the previous month,

I first presented the personal letter of His Majesty the King of my country and have not yet presented the credential letter."[125]

Yun came into conflict with Min again after Planson and Stein requested that Yun present a written version of his private view on the dangerous consequences of any attempt to partition Korea into separate areas of Russian and Japanese influence, a view that he had expressed to the tsar on the occasion of Min's audience on 6 June. Yun showed the memo to Min and received his approval, but on the day that they went to visit Lobanov, Min's attitude changed: "Min, with an ugly expression of pride and anger, said, 'If you give the Prince the memo, it would look like our mission had two envoys.' I [Yun] said nothing and kept back my memo. Then afterward he asked me why I did not give it to the Prince [Lobanov]!"[126]

The internal wrangling between Min and Yun continued throughout the mission's stay in St. Petersburg and undoubtedly contributed to Yun's decision not to accompany Min and the rest of the party on the homeward journey across Siberia. Instead Yun went on his own to Paris to continue his study of French.

There were other signs of a deepening rift between the two, including Yun's replacement by Kim To-il as Min's official interpreter in early July. As Yun admitted in his diary, however, Min might have made this change because of telegraphed instructions received from the court rather than his own personal preference. In fact, much later Yun expressed a sense of relief that Min had protected him from being involved in negotiations that may have involved compromising Korea's sovereignty. Furthermore, Kim To-il had, after all, originally been given the responsibility of interpreter for all official business in Russia.

In any event, King Kojong and his court appear not to have trusted Yun. He was not an orthodox member of his class. He was a Christian, educated in Shanghai and the United States, married to a Chinese woman, and had connections with the conspirators of the 1884 coup. Although it is unlikely that he had foreknowledge of the coup, he took the prudent step of leaving Korea after it failed. In addition, despite his undoubted patriotism and dislike of the racial prejudice that he had encountered in the United States, he also had a strong disdain for the Confucian attitudes of China and Korea and an admiration for the accomplishments of the West. It is hardly surprising, therefore, that he should have encountered frustration in his dealings with Min, who had passed his whole career in the midst of the machinations of the Korean court and had no experience of the modern Western world before his mission to Russia.

Eventually Min and Yun were able to find common ground in playing Korean chess together, and when Min praised Yun for his Chinese verse compositions and French ability, as well as providing him with 100 rubles for his trip to Paris, the latter was willing to judge his superior less severely.[127] Later, on his return to Korea, Min was to prove a valuable ally inside the court for the reform efforts of the Independence Club; he even won the praise of reformers such as Sŏ Jae-p'il and Chŏng Kyo, and Yun Ch'i-ho ultimately considered him a friend.[128]

The Chosŏn Mission's Encounter with Western Technology and Institutions in St. Petersburg

Not surprisingly, one of the first sights that the Korean party visited in St. Petersburg was the bronze statue of Peter the Great astride a horse on the banks of the River Neva. It was natural that he, an enlightened despot who had brought Russia at least partially into the modern world, should attract the interest of monarchists such as Min and Kim Tŭng-nyŏn, just as he had attracted the attention of the Meiji leadership in Japan. On the same day that the party visited the statue, Min recorded a short and eulogistic biography of the former tsar in his diary.[129]

Subsequently, Min's party visited the zoo and the botanical gardens, where they encountered a heated greenhouse for the first time. They had their photographs taken, had their portraits painted for Tsar Nicholas II's collection, and even rode on a nineteenth-century version of the roller-coaster. On a visit to Tsarskoe Selo, one of the tsar's summer retreats, they were beguiled by a trained elephant, which could play a harp with its trunk. Min noted laconically that "this is also one way of making a profit."[130] They visited a cinema and saw their first moving picture, which Min described as follows:

> We went into one building that was completely dark. Suddenly, on the front wall we could see a bright light and illuminated images. Sometimes there were people riding on galloping horses and sometimes men and women acting together, drinking wine or dancing. A thousand forms and ten thousand images moving just as in life. The people watching could not help but be amazed. They say that this method uses electricity and lenses to illuminate and move the pictures, but I could not understand the intricate details of how it worked.[131]

Min described the Russian script and the mixed nationalities and languages in Russia, which had arisen as a result of its military expansion. The party visited the house in which Peter the Great had lived during the construction of St. Petersburg and marveled at its humble dimensions. Perhaps with Kojong and his reputed extravagant lifestyle in mind, Min commented pointedly, "With this economical and frugal lifestyle, he [Peter the Great] left behind a good example for posterity."[132]

Tsar Nicholas II's habit of traveling around his numerous summer palaces rather than remaining at the capital seems to have surprised Min. Nevertheless, he noted that the business of government in Russia was delegated to numerous departments and that affairs of state were all punctually dealt with. He described this method of government with an elegant Chinese phrase: "the emperor lets fall his robes, and the empire is governed."[133] Just how aware Min and his colleagues were of the real state of Russia is not clear from *Haech'ŏn ch'ubŏm,* which contains scarcely a critical word about the country from which Kojong was desperately seeking protection from Japan. Even Yun's franker account of events in St. Petersburg provides a description of a Russia that was both enlightened and progressive. It is probable that the monarchic system of Russia and the other major European nations was a more acceptable model for Min and his colleagues than the presidential system of the United States.

Although there is no direct evidence in the text of *Haech'ŏn ch'ubŏm* that Min was familiar with the U.S. system of government, it is highly unlikely that he was not. In the first place, Korea and the United States had had treaty relations for fourteen years by 1896. Furthermore, Min's elder cousin Min Yŏng-ik had led the first Korean mission to the United States in 1883, where he had met President Arthur in New York on 18 September. Finally, Min was traveling with Yun Ch'i-ho, who had spent several years studying in the United States and was, therefore, familiar with the country.

Among the commercial enterprises that Min visited and described in detail in *Haech'ŏn ch'ubŏm* were a beer factory set up by a German with a monthly production of five million bottles, a cotton mill owned by an Englishman, Harry Howard, and a dye works owned by another German, Karle. In addition the Korean party visited numerous government-owned enterprises such as a candle-making factory, a porcelain factory, an agricultural implements exposition, a paper mill, the paper and coin mints, a stone-carving factory, a munitions factory that produced forty thousand bullets per day, a field artillery factory, a naval shipbuilder's yard, and the naval arsenal. In fact, the visits to so many factories dedicated to the manufacture of modern weaponry evoked a rare personal comment from Min, when he wrote after the visit to the naval arsenal,

> In the last few days we have seen military and naval weapons being produced incessantly. Every nation in the world is doing the same thing. Where will all these weapons be used? If Heaven wishes for the security and peace of living beings,

then one day all these weapons must be melted down and made into agricultural implements.[134]

As well as such visits to private and government manufacturers, *Haech'ŏn ch'ubŏm* provides detailed accounts of visits made by Min and his entourage to a forestry college, a prison, the water-pumping and filtration plant that supplied the whole of St. Petersburg, the gun batteries at Kronstadt, an army barracks, the observatory at Kolpino, the Winter Palace, and the vast St. Isaac's Cathedral in St. Petersburg. Min also made various purchases of books, seeds, a windmill, and even a whole set of instruments for a military band at a cost of three thousand rubles, to the great disgust of Yun, who wrote in his diary, "No wonder he doesn't like me. Because I never try to hide my disgust whenever 'His Excellency' (E.E. and M.P.)[135] wastes public money on things that are unnecessary, nay, even useless."[136]

In addition there are observations on topics as diverse as Greek Orthodoxy, the origins of Western alphabets, Russia's reference libraries, Russian marriage and funeral customs, military conscription, the Russian government's annual budget, the Arctic conditions of Russia's northern territories, the construction of pavements from wood in St. Petersburg, the five types of refined sugar found on sale in the markets, the custom of spraying water to prevent dust on the capital's streets, the stringent licensing of ships' captains and the shipping regulations of departments of trade in the West, the St. Petersburg constabulary, the compulsory education system, the institutions set up for the poor and disabled, and the diligence of even the poorest Russians, of whom Min wrote,

> Russian poor people all take goods and sell them on the streets. All of them are docile and do their best to earn a living from their jobs. A few have bowed heads and mournful faces and go about barefooted in rags and beg food by going from house to house. There are also some who play small musical instruments to get money. They play a tune and then wait for the people who have listened to them to give some money whether a lot or a little. So we can see the wealth of this country and the honesty of the common people.[137]

There was also time for entertaining, and Min frequently dined with staff from the Foreign Office and Admiralty. Despite Yun's account of tensions and misunderstandings between Min and Stein and the other Russian officials assigned to the Korean party, their emotional farewells at the end of their stay in St. Petersburg—about which Yun wrote, "Mr. Min and Kim D. N. were affected to tears"[138]—appear to have been genuine. Indeed, Min was presented with a flower by the Russian official only referred to by his Chinese-character name of Ko Ak-si and later composed a poem recorded in the collection appended to the diary: "I hate to see the willow leaf parting from its branch/Now I see this wonderful flower, I will not forget its branch/If I could wipe away the regret of parting in this transient life/I could plant this flower and not forget its branch."[139]

The Return Journey and Min's Encounters with Korean Immigrants in Siberia

Although Min had originally intended to return to Korea via the Suez Canal and the Indian Ocean, the Russian assistant Stein persuaded him to travel via Siberia because of the heat and cholera epidemics along the southern route. On 18 August Yun Ch'i-ho bade a cordial but relieved farewell to Min and his Korean and Russian associates and left St. Petersburg for Paris; on the following day Min and his party departed on the first leg of their return journey, as far as Moscow. From Moscow they traveled in the company of the Japanese envoy Nishi Tokujirō to the exhibition center at Nizhniy Novgorod. Later in 1898 this same Nishi, who by that time held the post of foreign minister, was to sign an agreement with the Russian minister at Tokyo, Baron Rosen, in which, among other things, both countries agreed to recognize Korean independence and refrain from interfering in Korea's internal affairs.[140]

As the guests of the Russian government the Korean mission was housed and guided around the exhibition at the former's expense. The main purpose of this exhibition was to display the agricultural and manufactured products of Russia. The Koreans encountered an extensive range of goods, including the inevitable military hardware, of which they had already seen so much in St. Petersburg.

It was at this exhibition that the Koreans first saw a man work under water in a diving suit, and it was here that they took their first balloon ride, an experience that seemed to have made a great impression on them:

> We went into one place where there was a balloon with a basket made of bamboo. It could seat four people and the balloon was inflated above it. It was tethered with a rope. The person in charge had prepared everything and invited us to get on with him and ride on the wind. We soared up and floated among the clouds in the sky. Flap, flap, we were flying as though we had been transformed into immortals! There was a machine and line that enabled us to come down ac-

cording to when we wished. We doubted what was happening and felt we had become flying immortals in a dream, sleeping on our pillows.[141]

On the day after the memorable balloon trip, they encountered what Min described as a "fish that understood human language."[142] On closer examination of the description, it appears to have been a trained seal. For five days they were fêted by the Russian authorities at Nizhniy Novgorod before departing on 26 August down the tree-lined Volga on the paddle wheeler *Pushkin,* heading for Samara. The journey was uneventful, and Min recorded little in the diary other than the names of the major towns, such as Nijat and Kazan, through which they passed.

At Samara they transferred to a train that had compartments reserved for the Korean party, enabling them to continue their journey in comfort and privacy. The journey was long and tedious, and the train traveled more slowly than the one that had taken them across Canada. Min and his companions alighted at Omsk, where they were entertained at the station by the vice-governor, Momonov.

After this short break they were back on board the train heading east through a landscape that was beginning to show the first signs of autumn. On 1 September they arrived at Novosibirsk, where they had to alight in order to cross the River Ob' by ferry in the shadow of the half-completed iron railway bridge. The following day was Kojong's birthday. "I and my colleagues are here on the Siberian railway heading east and longing for the palace," wrote Min; "we feel overwhelmed by sorrow and longing."[143]

At Achinsk they were again forced to disembark in order to cross the River Chulym by ferry. The train traveled slowly through the rugged countryside, its locomotive breaking down at frequent intervals. There were no stations or hotels in this region, and the Koreans survived on tea and such simple fare as was served on the train.

At Krasnoyarsk the railway came to an end, and the party halted before embarking by carriage on the next stage of its journey. It was here that Stein and Putiata received the telegram from the Foreign Office informing them of the death of Lobanov at Kiev on 1 September. After all his efforts to build a working relationship with the Russian foreign minister, Min must have received a blow on hearing this news. In a measured understatement Min wrote in the diary, "His death is truly regrettable."[144] As subsequent events will show, however, Russian policy toward Korea became bolder after Lobanov's death.

On 5 September the party set out from Krasnoyarsk in carriages that held two people. Min and his valet, Son, led, followed by the two Kims, then Colonel Putiata and Stein; another carriage for their luggage brought up the rear. They were escorted by the local police magistrate, Kobalyov (Kŏballyop'u), and two mounted constables.

The journey was not an easy one as they passed from post station to post station. There were no hotels or restaurants along the route, and they were forced to sleep on the carriages and survive on tea and whatever food they could buy at the staging posts. From Nizhneudinsk they traveled slowly along a broad dirt road cut through forest, the wheels of their carriages sinking into the soft soil and mud. Along the route they observed the construction of the Siberian railway, frontier houses built solely from wood, and a solitary cattle rancher herding a thousand head of cattle.

On 11 September Min's party arrived at Irkutsk, the home of the government general of the central Siberian region. Here they were able to rest at a hotel and recover from the rigors of the journey. They were impressed to find a city resembling St. Petersburg in the midst of the wilderness through which they had just passed. "This constant improvement and enlightenment," wrote Min, "is surely the result of model government at both higher and lower levels. One cannot help but be envious with admiration."[145]

Here they were visited by two young Koreans, Sin Ing-nok and Kang Sason (relatives of Kim To-il), who had lived in Vladivostok and were now studying at the university in Irkutsk. As they continued their journey home, Min and his companions were subsequently to meet many more Koreans who had left behind their own impoverished country for the promise of opportunities in the Russian Far East.[146]

On 13 September after dining with the governor of Irkutsk, the party set off for Lake Baikal, arriving early in the morning on the following day. Here they transferred to a steamer and crossed over to the eastern shore. They then resumed their journey by carriage over increasingly rocky and difficult terrain to Ulan-Ude, where they were forced to halt to repair a carriage wheel. As they traveled on to Chita, they passed pioneer villages and saw Mongolian herdsmen roaming on the pasture land.

Beginning to sicken from the long and arduous journey, Min and his party halted at Boburomaskatya and lodged overnight. The increasing muddiness of the road meant more frequent stops along the route to rest the exhausted horses. On 18 September after passing through a terrain of mountains and plains, the party arrived at Chita, a small town with a population of ten thousand, including many Chinese who had crossed over the border from Manchuria. Here they could rest in a hotel, a welcome relief after the cramped quarters of the staging posts.

Despite the hardships of the journey during which, wrote Min, "we have eaten wind and slept in the damp, suffering from coughs and influenza and a hundred aching bones,"[147] he was still able to appreciate the beauty of the land-scape through which they had just passed: "Along the route many of the birch trees have been dyed with frost, and their yellow leaves are mingled with the pine and cedar. It looks like a painting. The people traveling in this landscape make a marvelous scene."[148]

Finally, on 23 September they were able to leave behind their bone-shaking carriages and embark on the steamer *Besenak* along the Silka River. The next day they arrived at Ignashino, where the Silka joins the Amur River. From here the Koreans could see Chinese territory on the south bank and Russian terri-tory to the north. While they were traveling along the Amur they mourned the anniversary (according to the lunar calendar) of Queen Myŏngsŏng's death in a poignant scene recorded in the diary:

> Since entering western Siberia, I and my fellows have traveled day and night with all haste, but we are still in the middle of our journey and will be unable to par-ticipate. Today at dawn we mourned together and could hardly bear our intense sorrow. In the cabin inside the ship we hung our national flag and burnt incense and a bright candle on a desk. Wearing our official robes, we faced toward the east, bowed four times, and wept together.[149]

On 26 September the party arrived at Blagoveshchensk, where Kim To-il had lived as a student ten years earlier. They halted there to change ships and were visited by six Koreans. They had all immigrated more than ten years ear-lier, and although happy to meet their fellow countrymen, they may have been made anxious by Min's initial insistence that they would all have to return to their native land should the Korean government order it. It seems, however, that as Min met more and more of these immigrants and saw their patriotism and prosperity he resigned himself to the state of affairs and simply exhorted them to obey the laws and not cause any trouble for the Russian authorities.

The immigrants themselves, who were either residents of Blagoveshchensk or on business from Khabarovsk, all claimed to be intending to return to Ko-rea after they had made enough money in Russia to do so.[150] In fact, however, according to Patterson, the majority of Korean immigrants to Russia became permanent settlers.[151] Whatever their true intentions, Min remarked approv-ingly in his diary that some of them had retained their topknots and one of them still wore the traditional Korean headgear, the *manggŏn*.[152]

On 30 September Min's party set off again on the steamer *Magotpu*. After the rigors of their journey by carriage across Siberia, they were pleasantly sur-prised that the cabins were heated by steam pipes. At one of the stops along the route, they were met by a representative from the Korean immigrant village, Samari, which had more than two hundred homes. The Korean residents, this man told them, were all naturalized citizens. This village appears to be the same as that identified by Ban Byung-yool and Wayne Patterson as Samanri (Russian name, Blagoslovennoe), which was at the mouth of the Samara River about 547 kilometers from Blagoveshchensk. As early settlers, the inhabitants of this village were given the exceptional privileges of being exempt from poll tax forever and from land tax for twenty years. In addition they were granted Russian citizenship and were given approximately 270 acres of land per household. All these privileges were in accordance with the Migration Promotion Law of 1861.[153]

On 3 October the steamer arrived at Khabarovsk, a town with a population of six thousand people, half of whom were Chinese. The river was so shallow at this point that they were unable to anchor. The governor general, Dukhovskoi, whom they had met at the coronation ceremonies at Moscow, had had advanced warning of Min's arrival and had prepared a launch to take off the Korean party and had arranged for them to be lodged at a government residence. On the following day Min was once again visited by representatives of the local Korean population. This time he "carefully admonished them not to forget their country's righteousness."[154]

Later that day they received a visit from Dukhovskoi and General Gribskii, Ataman of the Amur Cossacks. Min and his party visited an exhibition that included some items of clothing and implements from Korea as well as from China and Japan. It was at this time that the Koreans heard of the exploits of Muraviev-Amurski, who had acquired the territory northeast of the Amur River from the Qing and brought it under Russian control. Seeing firsthand evidence of Russia's eastward expansion gained at the expense of the Qing empire might well have caused Min to wonder at the wisdom of his own monarch, for whose sake he had spent several months seeking Russian protection.

During their stay in Khabarovsk Min and his party received hospitable treatment from Dukhovskoi and Gribskii. They were taken to see the Cossacks training on horseback and inspected their barracks. In addition they visited the military academy; a girls' school, where the children were taught English, French, and German; and an institute for orphans and the destitute. There was also, of course, the inevitable visit to a factory making guns and ammunition. On his last day in Khabarovsk, Min went to an assembly hall in the Korean district and addressed more than a hundred people, instructing them that "they must behave themselves well now that the relations between [the] two countries were improving and that they must not cause any disturbances."[155]

That evening the Korean party boarded the steamer *Chikhachev* and departed for Vladivostok. Colonel Putiata and Stein, however, stayed behind "to attend to urgent business"[156]—probably to make the necessary arrangements for a detachment of military instructors to accompany Min and his party back to Korea. Between the time of Lobanov's death on 1 September and Min's departure from Vladivostok on 16 October, the Russian minister of war, Petr Vanovskii, revised Lobanov's original decision to withhold military instructors until after Putiata's investigation of the situation in Korea and authorized a contingent of two officers (First Lieutenant Afanas'ev I, Second Lieutenant Sikstel'), a military doctor, and ten noncommissioned officers to travel to Korea with Min's party.[157] No mention of this decision or of the presence of the additional Russian officers on the journey back to Korea from Vladivostok is made in *Haech'ŏn ch'ubŏm*. The arrival of Min's party accompanied by the Russian officers at Chemulp'o, however, was openly reported by the *Independent*.[158]

On 9 October Min and his party arrived at Nima and completed the final leg of their journey by train, arriving at Vladivostok on the following day. They were met at the station by several Russian government officials, including the vice-governor, Paulyenko. During their stay in Vladivostok they stayed at the Chikhotkasan Hotel.

Once again they received visits from Russian civilian and military officials and again they visited the local Korean community, of which Min wrote,

> There are several hundred homes belonging to immigrants from our country, as well as more than ten thousand homes scattered around the neighboring region. Probably because of the great famine of 1869, people from the north entered first, but now people are arriving incessantly from the eight provinces. The fact that they enter and do not return has resulted in this abundance of our people.[159]

Their leader, An Se-jŏng, told Min that the Korean flag was raised every year on the occasion of King Kojong's birthday. Min and his party met many other Koreans during their stay at Vladivostok, including one ethnic Korean, referred to simply as Grazdaniev, who had been adopted by a Russian family and had eventually risen to the post of auxiliary police magistrate. There were other Koreans of *yangban* background who had recently arrived with the intention of studying at the university in Vladivostok. Observing the scale of Korean immigration into the Russian Far East and particularly around the Vladivostok area, Min commented,

> There are several hundred homes belonging to immigrants from our country in this port, and I could not calculate the number of people traveling to and fro. Yŏnch'usa [Pos'et], Ch'uyesa, Such'ŏngsa [Suchan], and other places are called Chosŏn immigrant villages, and there are six or seven thousand homes. More

than half the people are naturalized Russians. They all wear Russian clothes and speak Russian, and the young people no longer know the customs of their home country. We cannot allow this to continue in this way. As quickly as possible we should establish a consulate and carefully decide on a treaty stipulation that if people wish to return to their home country, we should together help them to return. A settlement should be made where those who wish to engage in commerce may dwell. In this way we can avoid the problem of scattered immigrants stirring up problems. This is a very urgent business and is also what the immigrants desire.[160]

When Min had first met the governor-general of Vladivostok in Moscow, he had requested the repatriation of the Korean immigrants to Russia. Like Isabella Bird Bishop, the British travel writer, however, Min had also probably been impressed by the cleanliness, orderliness, and prosperity of the Koreans in Russia; their situation was in stark contrast to the conditions of their counterparts in villages in Korea, where the practice of squeezing the poor had reached such an extent that they had abandoned any attempt to better their living conditions for fear of becoming the target of tax gatherers and unscrupulous local magistrates. As Bishop, who was also returning to Korea in October 1896, wrote of the Korean underclass,

> The farmers work harder than any other class, and could easily double the production of the land, their methods, though somewhat primitive, being fairly well adapted to the soil and the climate. But having no security of their gains, they are content to produce only what will feed and clothe their families, and are afraid to build better houses or to dress respectably. There are innumerable peasant farmers who have gone on reducing their acreage of culture year by year, owing to the exactions and forced loans of magistrates and yang-bans, and who now only raise what will enable them to procure three meals a day. It is not wonderful that classes whose manifest destiny is to be squeezed, should have sunk down to a dead level of indifference, inertia, apathy, and listlessness.[161]

Stein and Putiata rejoined Min's party at Vladivostok on 13 October, and within three days all the necessary arrangements for the return to Korea had been made. On 16 October, Min and his entourage departed from Vladivostok, accompanied by the Russian military instructors under the overall command of Putiata, on the same Russian warship that had taken them from Chemulp'o to Shanghai in April, the *Gremiashchii*.

The weather grew warmer as the *Gremiashchii* passed Wŏnsan on the following day and sailed down the eastern coast of Korea. That day they passed a large island that Min was told was Matsu Shima. Min referred to it as a Japanese island, apparently unaware that Matsu Shima was the Japanese name for Korea's Ullŭng Island. Japan had come close to demanding the cession of this island in the wake of the Soldiers' Rebellion of 1882, and in 1905 during the Russo-Japanese War Japan seized its administrative dependency, Tok Island. The latter remains a contentious issue between the two countries to the present day.[162]

In fact, by 1898 Matsu Shima was also the name attributed to the island by the Edinburgh Geographical Institute in its General Map of Korea and Neighbouring Countries in Isabella Bird Bishop's *Korea and Her Neighbours*. As the European name for the island was originally Dagelet Island, it would appear that the Japanese government had, by the 1890s, had some success in getting the West and even a high-ranking Korean official to look at the region through its eyes.

The Russian warship halted at Pusan on the morning of 18 October and set off again that same evening, giving the Koreans no time to go ashore, although they were visited by the local officials. From their vantage point in the harbor, however, they were able to see the extent of the Japanese settlement at Pusan. It was perhaps this sight that caused Min to lament the abolition of the naval command that had once protected the Pusan region.[163]

The ship continued its journey up the west coast of Korea arriving at the port of Inch'ŏn on 20 October. Min's party was met by several Korean officials as well as by Waeber, the Russian chargé d'affaires. After disembarking, Min was welcomed by his younger brother Min Yŏng-ch'an and his elder sister's husband, Kim Yŏng-jŏk, who had been awaiting his arrival for several days. That night they were entertained by the customs intendant, Yi Chae-jŏng, and lodged with him overnight.

On the following day Min and his companions retraced their steps toward Seoul via Oryudong, where they were met by more of their relatives. At 5:00 P.M. they arrived at Map'o and were welcomed by an impressive group of high-ranking officials from the Korean court, including seven ministers, two state councillors, six vice-ministers, and the mayor of Seoul.

At 6:00 P.M. Min and his companions continued on their journey and entered Seoul through the Tonŭi Gate. Together with Kim Tŭng-nyŏn and Kim To-il, Min had an audience with King Kojong at the Russian legation to report on their mission and present Tsar Nicholas' personal letter.[164] At this audience Kojong asked Min and the members of his entourage about their mission. According to the *Kojong sillok*, King Kojong was particularly interested in Russia's military system. Min praised both Russia's military and educational systems, concluding, "Although we cannot adopt the laws of the West, which has different customs from us, we have to follow its example in military affairs, education, and politics."[165]

After this brief report the king finally gave Min and his party leave to visit their parents. Thus a journey of 68,365 leagues around the world lasting seven months had finally come to an end, and a new chapter of increasing Russian intervention in the administration of Chosŏn in the form of military and financial advisers was about to begin.

Conclusion

Haech'ŏn ch'ubŏm provides a unique record of Chosŏn's early steps in diplomacy toward a Western power. Together with Yun Ch'i-ho's account, it gives us a rare insight into the difficulties faced by Chosŏn's diplomatic representatives from a Korean point of view. Yet despite all the difficulties, Min and his associates managed to conclude an important agreement and gain valuable experience of the world beyond Chosŏn's shores. Had such steps been taken thirty years earlier and had Chosŏn been given sufficient leeway to modernize and reform as Japan had done, the history of the Far East might look very different.

Nevertheless, Min's mission to Russia was undoubtedly one of the most significant efforts in late-Chosŏn diplomacy before that nation was absorbed into the Japanese Empire. The Min-Lobonov Agreement was one concrete result, but Min's own personal change in outlook, which will be explored in the following chapters, was perhaps the more valuable and significant achievement of the mission. Through contact with the West, Min divested himself of some of the confined views that were an inevitable by-product of his neo-Confucian education and was able to invest himself wholeheartedly in efforts to reform Korea along Western lines.

Min's exposure to the Korean migrants in Russia on his return journey may also have opened his eyes to the real potential of the ordinary Korean people once they had been liberated from the deadweight of a strictly delineated class society where most of the people were the victims of exploitation and abuse. His meetings with the patriotic Koreans of the Russian Far East, therefore, may have helped him to accept the egalitarian views of the Independence Club that were so objectionable to some other members of Chosŏn's ruling élite.

The following chapter will explore in detail Min's relationship with the Independence Club before examining the background and outcome of his second and final diplomatic mission to the West to attend Queen Victoria's Diamond Jubilee in the summer of 1897.

4

EMBASSY TO QUEEN VICTORIA'S DIAMOND JUBILEE

Min's Activities in Korea between His Diplomatic Missions of 1896 and 1897

On 20 September 1896, even before his return from Russia, Min was appointed a minister in the State Council (Ŭijŏngbu ch'anjŏng),[1] and on 12 November, soon after his return to Seoul, he was appointed minister of war.[2] This second appointment was apparently at the prompting of the Russian military adviser Colonel Putiata, who had gained a favorable impression of Min during the journey across Siberia back to Korea.[3] For some reason, however, Min's appointment was opposed by the Russian chargé d'affaires, Karl Waeber.[4] According to Jordan there was "considerable friction between the Russian Minister, M. Waeber, and some members of the Mission. The latter have secured the appointment of Min Yung-huan, late Envoy to Russia, as Minister of War, against what M. Waeber declares to have been his express wishes."[5]

Waeber's reluctance might seem odd in light of what appears to have been a good relationship between the two, but Waeber might have thought that Min's character would be likely to bring him into conflict with the commander of the Russian military instructors, Colonel Putiata. Yun Ch'i-ho, also, on first meeting Putiata at a dinner in St. Petersburg, had felt that the latter would not be suitable for the task of training Koreans, describing him as "lacking in the most important article which a civilized man must possess in a barbarous land viz. Patience."[6] As will be seen, Min, in his position as minister of war, does not appear to have been as cooperative as the Russians had hoped. This is hardly surprising, however. Based on the views that he had already expressed about Russia in *Ch'ŏnilch'aek* more than two years earlier, Min must have believed that Russian intervention in Seoul was a threat to Korean independence.

During Min's absence the Seoul newspaper, the *Independent (Tongnip sinmun),* which was published both in the Korean vernacular and also in English, had become increasingly popular since its maiden issue of 7 April 1896. Its editor, Sŏ Chae-p'il, frustrated by his lack of influence in his role as a government adviser, was undoubtedly making every effort to influence the policy making and political appointments of the Chosŏn administration through his editorials. Consequently, the new publication was becoming a powerful if somewhat tactless engine for reform in Korea. As Vipan Chandra eloquently explains,

> The paper attacked the die-hard, pleaded with the recalcitrant, cajoled the complacent, and cheered the bold. There was no facet of national life that it did not scrutinize. The administration, the legal and judicial system, the educational tradition, the social and family mores, the perceived personality traits of Koreans, the economy, and the country's foreign relations and defense were all closely examined.[7]

Soon after his return from Russia, Min was interviewed by the *Independent* and gave a very favorable impression to the interviewer, who in all likelihood was Sŏ Chae-p'il himself. The interview, which appeared in the newspaper in English on 10 November 1896, provides us with an invaluable firsthand account of how Min's travels in the West had affected his mental outlook and why he was subsequently to become increasingly identified with the Independence Club and the movement for reform and modernization in Seoul. For this reason the interview is presented here in full:

> The representative of *The Independent* has had an interview with Mr. Min Yung Whan, who has just returned from his mission to Russia. Mr. Min has become a new man altogether, judging from his conversation with the interviewer. His trip through America and his four-month sojourn in Europe have given him an entirely new idea of the world. He says "Before I went abroad, I had heard a great deal of the wonderful things of Europe and America through those who have travelled in these places, but I will be frank with you, and tell you that I did not believe all that they told me. Now, after I have seen them for myself, I rather think that these travellers did not tell me half of the wonders that are existing in these countries. I firmly believe that energy and science can accomplish many things which unscientific men have never even dreamed."

"What impressed you more than anything else?"

"Many wonderful things impressed me deeply, but one or two customs made a forcible impression on me. First I never saw more than a half a dozen men during my trip through America and Europe who appeared to have no ambition to work for their bread and butter. Everybody seemed to be anxious to get employment and earn his living honestly. I am sorry to say it is not the case with the Koreans. We all like to live at the expense of others. I think this is what has made Korea so poor; and the people have a less independent spirit than the Americans and Europeans. Another thing which made me admire the foreigners is that even the men who occupy the lowest position in the community seem to have pride for their country and love their Sovereigns and their fellow countrymen. Most of them can read and write and understand arithmetic so that they are able to make an account of themselves in business."

"Then so you fully realize the necessity of introducing reforms in your Government."

"Not only the necessity of introducing them, but I am willing to do all I can for the accomplishment of them."

"Were you satisfied with the treatment that you received in Russia?"

"Perfectly. In fact at times, I felt that I was not worthy of being a recipient of such courtesies and kindnesses from the Russian officials and the people at large. In connection with this I would say that these foreigners know the art of entertaining strangers, and they are skilful in diplomacy as well as in all matters of education and culture." The writer came away much pleased with Mr. Min's views and his enthusiasm over Europe and America.[8]

Subsequently Min's activities as minister of war were closely watched by the *Independent,* which publicly supported his efforts to reform the Korean army. On 28 November the newspaper praised Min's instruction that vacancies among commissioned officers were in future to be filled by noncommissioned officers "who hold the highest record as to their education, behavior and faithfulness."[9] This was a practical application of the recommendations for the selection of military officials on merit that Min had made in his proposals for preparation and defense in his policy essay *Ch'ŏnilch'aek.*

On 1 December the *Independent* reported that Min had visited soldiers who had been wounded in a clash with rebels.[10] "This is the first time in the history of Korea," the reporter commented, "that the Minister of War called on a sick and wounded soldier."[11] In the same issue it was noted that Min had personally attended the drilling of the new Royal Bodyguard.[12] Four days later Min's generosity in providing a banquet for the officers and soldiers of the fourth and fifth regiments at his own expense was warmly applauded:

He [Min] made a speech to them by saying "that the effectiveness of an army lies in the united sentiment of love for the country. I hope that we will all make our untiring efforts for the strength and glory of our common country," etc. This generous treatment and encouraging words from the Minister produced a very favorable impression among the rank and file of the Korean army.[13]

Min Yŏng-hwan had undoubtedly been adopted as the main figurehead for reform within the Korean administration by the *Independent*'s editor, Sŏ Chae-p'il. Articles concerning his integrity and enlightened attitudes continued to appear in the pages of the newspaper into the following year. On 21 January, Min's attendance at "a grand sacrifice to the soldiers who lost their lives during the rebellions of the Tonghak and the 'Righteous Army,'" was reported appreciatively, and on 9 February, the War Office's refusal to accept the graduates of Confucian schools at the request of the minister of education, "as Confucion [*sic*] knowledge is of very little use,"[14] also met with the newspaper's approval. Min's last action as minister of war in early 1897 that was deemed worthy of the *Independent*'s attention was to ensure the strict punishment of two officers who had been "convicted of squeezing the people while they were stationed in P'yŏngyang."[15] Soon after this report, Min was granted temporary leave of absence for health reasons; his health apparently improved, and he was subsequently appointed to his post as minister plenipotentiary to Europe. In addition to all these plaudits in the *Independent*, its editor, Sŏ Chae-p'il, also privately confided to Yun Ch'i-ho his approval of Min's behavior "since his return from Europe."[16] In its consistent approval of Min's actions, the *Independent* went so far as to publish the following glowing account of Min's personal integrity:

> The Minister of War, Mr. Min Yongwhan, wanted to settle all of his private accounts at the end of the old year and paid out every cent he owed to different persons. He did not have enough money to meet the expenditure so he sold a number of his personal belongings to raise the necessary fund. One of his old friends, named Sin Taihin, who had received a great many kindnesses from the Minister in the years gone by, saw the difficulty of the Minister, sent him $600, asking him to accept it as a token of respect and friendliness. The Minister wrote him a courteous note, declining the offer by saying that the root of the trouble in the country today is solely due to the custom of giving and taking of valuable presents between the officials and private individuals. He for one would not and could not encourage the custom under any circumstances, therefore he returns the money with appreciation of his friendly spirit. This is the first time in the modern history of Korea that an influential Minister refused to accept such a substantial gift from his friend.[17]

On 14 February the *Independent* reported Min's attendance at a "progressive dinner party" at the house of an American missionary, Dr. Horace G. Underwood, who was well known for his support for modernization and reform in Seoul. According to Yun Ch'i-ho, it was "a delightful dinner"; those in attendance included Horace Underwood and his wife, Lillias; Sŏ Chae-p'il and his American wife, Muriel;[18] the British commissioner of customs, John McLeavy Brown; a missionary couple, referred to simply as the Reids; and Min and Yun himself. At this dinner, however, Min expressed a pessimistic but essentially accurate appraisal of Korea's future prospects. "Mr. Min," Yun recorded in his diary, "thinks the country is hopelessly gone *(naranŭn ta kyŏlttan nassŏ)*."[19]

Apparently Min's relationship with the Russian military adviser Putiata had deteriorated during the time that he held the office of minister of war. Waeber informed Yun in confidence that "Colonel Butchata [Putiata] is constantly complaining against Min Yong Huan, of his incapacity etc."[20] Even Mrs. Waeber, a confidante of the former Korean queen, criticized Min for talking "one thing to one person and another to another."[21] In her estimate the only people working for reform in Korea were her husband; the American legal adviser to the Korean government, General Clarence R. Greathouse; the British commissioner of customs, McLeavy Brown; and the editor of the *Independent*, Sŏ Chae-p'il.[22]

Given Min's original assessment of the Russian threat to Korean independence as revealed in *Ch'ŏnilch'aek*, it is probable that he never gave his enthusiastic support to the Russian party in Seoul, despite the fact that he was identified as a key figure in the so-called Chŏngdong group (Chŏngdongp'a).[23] Chŏngdong was the area in Seoul that contained the American, British, Russian, and other foreign legations, and Chŏngdongp'a was the name given to those Korean officials who had frequent dealings with the diplomatic representatives, missionaries, and other members of the European and American community in Seoul. Min's orientation within this group would appear to have been toward the United States and Britain rather than Russia. The fact that Min had amicable relations with various members of the Western community in Seoul seems to be irrefutable, and there is even documentary evidence that he was already entertaining Western guests at his home at least as early as 1891.[24]

By the time of Min's departure for England, his relationship with the Russian party had clearly weakened even further, and he was now seeking to win British and American support for Korean independence. According to Jordan, there was

considerable friction between Min Yung-hoan in his capacity as Minister of War and the Russian Military Mission, the members of which complain openly of his obstructive tactics. As is well known, His Excellency was Corean Representative at the Coronation of the Czar of Russia and was, I believe, honoured by the bestowal of a high decoration, but since his return to Corea he has been credited with somewhat anti-Russian proclivities although his relations with M. Waeber have remained very cordial.[25]

The Independence Club, also, which had initially expressed approval of Russian assistance, was by this time gradually exerting pressure on King Kojong and his court to sever their ties with the Russian legation. To this end, the editorials of the *Independent* began to proclaim ever more vociferously the newspaper's founding principle of "Korea for Koreans."[26] Kojong finally departed from the Russian legation on 20 February 1897, after just over a year of residence there. This was to prove the beginning of the end of Russian predominance at the Chosŏn court. Already, an uneasy condominium of the two competing powers of Russia and Japan was beginning to come into existence, based on the rather shaky foundations of the Waeber-Komura Memorandum (14 May 1896) and the Yamagata-Lobanov Protocol (9 June 1896). As will be seen, with the departure of Kojong from the Russian legation, the agreement of 1896 concluded between Min and Lobanov began to break down as the Korean side became increasingly distrustful of Russian intentions. In short, the Korean leadership, although desiring Russian protection from Japan, had no wish to become an actual Russian protectorate.

Min's Appointment as Ambassador Plenipotentiary to Queen Victoria's Diamond Jubilee and Minister Plenipotentiary to Six European Nations

The record of Min's second journey to Europe forms the fourth section of *Min Ch'ungjŏnggong yugo* and is titled *Sagu sokch'o*. It is a daily record of Min's journey to Europe from Inch'ŏn along the western route via Shanghai, Port Said, and Odessa on the Black Sea. From Odessa Min traveled by railway to St. Petersburg and then on to London via Germany and Holland. Although it is likely that Min kept this diary with the assistance of the legation secretary, Yi Ki, or another member of his entourage, the diary begins with Min's own personal preface. Consequently, we can imply that, unlike *Haech'ŏn ch'ubŏm,* Min was the principal, if not the sole, author of it. In his preface, Min explains his motivation for keeping the diary as follows:

For the last several years I have continuously traveled around many nations at the king's behest. This book is a record of those travels, albeit an ineloquent one. Alas! Since ancient times the duties of envoys have arisen from the difficulties of nations. Among envoys of the past only Qiao of Zheng, Xi of Jin, and a few others were able to sustain their nations by their eloquence and stratagems. Moreover, the present world situation is more difficult than at the time of Zheng and Jin, and I am not the equal of Qiao or Xi. My speeches and plans have been in the expectation of peace and in the hope that by carrying out my duties, I might benefit my country.

It has not been a simple matter, however, to describe the mountains, rivers, and geographical features of foreign climes, nor the abundance of people, things, and places, and to write it all down. Nevertheless, as those who come after me may wish to investigate what I attempted, I have made this record and kept it.[27]

Together with *Haech'ŏn ch'ubŏm,* Min's second travel diary, *Sagu sokch'o,* provides an invaluable record of the earliest diplomatic activities of a Korean envoy in Europe. The Chosŏn administration had attempted to send a diplomatic mission to Europe nearly a decade earlier, in August 1887, but had been thwarted by the intervention of the Chinese resident in Seoul, Yuan Shikai. Three officials, Sim Sang-hak, Cho Sin-hŭi, and Pak Che-sun, had been appointed in succession to the post of minister plenipotentiary to the five European nations of Great Britain, France, Germany, Russia, and Italy. Sim had resigned because of bad health. His replacement, Cho, had managed to get as far as Hong Kong before backing down in the face of Chinese pressure. On his return to Korea in February 1890, Cho was banished for his failure to depart for Europe and was replaced by Pak, who was prevented from ever leaving Seoul by Yuan Shikai.[28] Min Yong-hwan's appointment as envoy extraordinary and minister plenipotentiary on 11 January 1897 (Kŏnyang 2),[29] therefore, was the fulfillment of a long-held desire of the Chosŏn administration to be represented at the major capitals of Europe. Min's second mission to Europe was substantially different in character from his first mission of 1896. As has been shown in the previous chapter, the 1896 mission had been a primarily Russian initiative. It had been orchestrated in the main by Waeber to capitalize on Russia's advantageous position on the Korean peninsula resulting from the flight of the Korean monarch to the Russian legation. The 1897 mission to attend Queen Victoria's Diamond Jubilee, on the other hand, was a purely Korean initiative and was carried out in the face of considerable opposition from the British financial adviser, McLeavy Brown. In addition, the mission was also actively discouraged by the British consul-general, John N. Jordan.

To demonstrate the importance he placed on the mission and the respect that he felt for the British sovereign, King Kojong appointed Min to the post of ambassador plenipotentiary *(chŏn'gwŏn taesa[30])* rather than envoy plenipotentiary *(chŏn'gwŏn kongsa)*. The Korean monarch insisted on this point despite Jordan's muted opposition to the title, which he felt might cause problems of diplomatic precedence at the British capital.[31] It should be noted, however, that Min was to hold this higher rank only while carrying out his duties as Chosŏn's representative at Queen Victoria's Diamond Jubilee celebrations. His rank as Chosŏn's representative to the six European nations was to be that of envoy extraordinary and minister plenipotentiary *(t'ŭngmyŏng chŏn'gwŏn kongsa)*.[32]

Kojong's determination to send Min to participate in Queen Victoria's Diamond Jubilee also appears to have been further strengthened by the publication of the Waeber-Komura Memorandum and the Yamagata-Lobanov Protocol on 24 February 1897. Kojong's motivation for sending the mission and also Jordan's discouraging response are clearly revealed in the following dispatch:

> As you are aware from my previous despatches, I have always when an opportunity offered discouraged the project of sending a Mission to Europe on the score of the needless expense it would entail, but since the King's return to his Palace he seems more bent than ever in making an attempt to enter into direct relations with the Courts of Europe. This idea has gained strength since the publication of the Agreements made last year between Russia and Japan respecting Corea, which have doubtless attracted your attention. These instruments, the existence of which seems to have been unknown to the Corean Government, have given considerable umbrage to the King and his advisers and the Foreign Minister is said to be contemplating addressing a query to the Russian and Japanese Ministers on the subject. There seems to be a vague idea that the Mission to Europe may succeed in directing the attention of the other Powers to Corea and among the more sanguine spirits dreams of an international guarantee of independence are freely indulged.[33]

The publication of the Waeber-Komura Memorandum and the Yamagata-Lobanov Protocol was, of course, a Japanese initiative. Faced with the unilateral publication of these agreements by Japan, however, Russia was also forced to follow suit. The result of the publication of the two agreements was, as the Japanese foreign minister Okuma Shigenobu no doubt intended, to undermine the trust between the Korean court and the Russian government and its representative in Seoul, Karl Waeber, while at the same time demonstrating Japan's continuing political influence on the peninsula.[34]

Since its victory in the Sino-Japanese War, the Japanese administration had suffered a catalogue of serious setbacks. In the first place, it had lost face both at home and abroad as a result of the Triple Intervention in April 1895, when it had been forced to retrocede the Liaodong Peninsula under the combined diplomatic pressure of Russia, France, and Germany. Its public image had been further dented by the involvement of Miura Gorō and, by association, Inoue Kaoro and the Japanese cabinet itself, in the assassination of the Korean queen. It had lost its grip on the Korean administration as a result of King Kojong's flight to the Russian legation. Its pretensions of preeminence in Korea appeared to have been flouted by Russia's contravention of the spirit if not the letter of the Russo-Japanese agreements of 1896, which had resulted in the introduction of Russian military and financial advisers into Korea. But with the publication of the Waeber-Komura Memorandum and the Yamagata-Lobanov Protocol early in 1897, the Japanese political leadership finally outmaneuvered the Russians and created a stalemate on the Korean peninsula. This was to prove a turning point, as Japan quietly consolidated its position in preparation for a possible conflict of arms with Russia that eventually came about in 1904. The Japanese game plan bore an uncanny resemblance to its patient maneuverings in the 1880s vis-à-vis Chinese political domination of Korea, which had turned out to be a prelude to the Sino-Japanese War.

As well as attending Queen Victoria's Diamond Jubilee celebrations in London, Min was also on a mission to thank Tsar Nicholas II on behalf of King Kojong for granting him asylum at the Russian legation. In addition, he was unofficially charged with conveying the Korean monarch's request to the tsar that Karl Waeber be retained as the chargé d'affaires at the Russian legation in Seoul instead of being replaced by his more aggressive colleague, Alexis de Speyer. On the completion of his duties in London, Min was then to take up his post as Korea's minister plenipotentiary at St. Petersburg after making official visits to the six European courts of Great Britain, Germany, Russia, Austria, France, and Italy, to which he would also be accredited. The decision that Min should make St. Petersburg his base in Europe was made on Waeber's insistence and reveals that Russian influence still prevailed at the Korean court, but it was an influence that was already on the wane. According to Jordan, Min himself wished to travel directly to Britain. He was unable to do so, however, as he had to put King Kojong's request for the retention of Waeber as the Russian representative in Seoul to the tsar before Waeber left Korea. Min did, however, promise Jordan that he would maintain close relations with Sir Nicholas O'Connor, the British minister at St. Petersburg, and would consult with him on matters of importance.[35]

Min's appointment as minister plenipotentiary to these five European treaty powers in addition to Russia aroused some speculation among the foreign representatives in Seoul about the motives that lay behind the decision. The French minister, Collin de Plancy, surmised that Min may have requested the post to avoid further conflict with the Russian military adviser, Colonel Putiata, with whom he was at odds.[36]

Although Min's previous mission to Russia in 1896 might have given the appearance that Min was a member of the pro-Russian group of officials at the Chosŏn court, it is clear from his policy essay *Ch'ŏnilch'aek* that he viewed Russia as a serious threat to Chosŏn's independence. In addition, as may be seen from an examination of the negotiations that Min had conducted with Lobanov in the previous year, Min had emphasized a speedy end to the Korean sovereign's residence at the Russian legation and his return to his own palace.[37]

Jordan also considered Min's departure from Seoul for Europe to be a matter of political expediency and communicated this opinion to his superior, Sir Claude M. MacDonald, British minister to Beijing: "He [Min] is comparatively a young man, of pleasing manners, who professes to have been greatly impressed by his experiences abroad, but his desire to serve his country in a European post may possibly be based upon a prudent resolve to avoid the risks of official life in Seoul."[38]

Min was to be accompanied by Min Sang-ho, who was appointed legation secretary (first rank) on 5 February 1897.[39] Min Sang-ho, however, was also appointed a plenipotentiary committee member at the Conference of the International Postal Union in Washington, D. C., so it was arranged that he would first travel separately to the United States and join Min Yŏng-hwan's party in London after the conclusion of the conference. Min Sang-ho had been the vice-minister of agriculture, commerce, and industry, and his appointment met with the wholehearted approval of the editor of the *Independent,* who described him in glowing terms:

> Mr. Min is one of the best English scholars in the Korean government, and is considered as an enlightened statesman. He received his education in the Maryland State Agricultural College which is a few minutes from the city of Washington. He is thoroughly familiar with the customs and manners of the American people, and he has many friends in and near Washington. We are confident that Mr. Min will prove himself to be one of the most intelligent and popular foreign Delegate [*sic*] in the coming Conference. We congratulate the Korean Government for the selection of such a competent official to the international assembly.[40]

Min Sang-ho also later impressed William Sands as being "the most perfect type of Korean aristocrat one could choose."[41] Jordan, on the other hand, while admitting Min Sang-ho's "considerable intelligence" and fluent English in a report to MacDonald, added somewhat cynically that the young Korean official

> bears a rather indifferent reputation on account of a youthful escapade some years ago in Hong Kong by which he contrived, under doubtful authority, to procure sufficient funds from a foreign bank to enable him to make an extended tour in America. He has paid me several visits recently and speaks enthusiastically of the prospect his present appointment affords him of realizing his dream of foreign travel.[42]

Min's entourage was completed by Kim Cho-hyŏn, a French-language interpreter in the Ministry of Foreign Affairs, and Kim Pyŏng-ok, a Russian-speaking clerk from Hamgyŏng Province in the Department of the Royal Household, who were appointed legation chancellors (fifth rank), and Son Pyŏng-gyun, who was appointed legation chancellor (seventh rank).[43] Probably for reasons of economy, Min was not accompanied by a personal valet on this trip as he had been in the previous year.

On 1 March 1897 King Kojong issued an edict commanding Min Yŏng-hwan to depart for Europe as ambassador plenipotentiary to attend the congratulatory ceremonies for "the 60th anniversary of the ascension to the throne of the Sovereign of Britain and Empress of India"[44] and to reside in Europe as envoy extraordinary and minister plenipotentiary to the six nations mentioned above. On 11 March Yi Ki, a clerk in the foreign ministry, was appointed legation secretary (third rank). This belated additional appointment was probably made because of the temporary absence of Min Sang-ho from the mission while he was in Washington. Several days later, Min received his official instructions from the foreign ministry and an itemized estimate of the mission's expenses, which came to 17,100 yen.[45] This was less than half the amount of the 40,000 yen traveling expenses that had been allocated to Min's mission to Russia in the previous year.

The reduction was due to John McLeavy Brown's opposition to the mission, which he considered to be an extravagance that the cash-strapped Korean government could ill afford. In fact, Brown, the British chief commissioner of Korean customs, was only persuaded to allocate the funds for the mission when Kojong informed him that he was sending Min to St. Petersburg to persuade the tsar to retain Waeber in Seoul rather than replace him with Speyer, who was bent on pursuing an aggressive policy of asserting Russian preeminence on the Korean peninsula. Speyer was later to attempt to have Brown replaced by the Russian financial adviser, Kir Alekseev, and was only dissuaded from doing so by the timely arrival of nine British cruisers at Inch'ŏn. Brown, therefore, must have felt that despite the expense, it was in both Britain's and his own interest to release sufficient funds for the mission.[46]

According to Jordan, Brown had also been reluctant to release funds for the mission because the accounts of the previous mission to St. Petersburg had not been settled. Although Min had a reputation for integrity, it appears that even he was not entirely above reproach. In February Jordan wrote to MacDonald,

> It seems that there is still a balance of 5,000 dollars in Min's hands which he declines to refund. Mr. Brown made a personal appeal to the King on the subject, but His Majesty, who supplements his own Civil List by intercepting all the public revenue he can, seemed rather amused than otherwise at the action of a Minister who followed so successfully his own example.[47]

As the salaries for late Chosŏn officials were notoriously deficient and as Min appears to have been furnished only with travel expenses for his mission to Moscow, it is most probable that he retained this sum in lieu of any other form of stipend. Nevertheless, it appears that Min eventually relented as the *Kojong sidaesa* records that on 25 February 1897, "Out of 40,000 wŏn travel allowance granted Min Yŏng-hwan the minister to Russia sent by the Ministry of Foreign Affairs, Min returned a surplus of 4,987 wŏn, 72 chŏn, 8 pun to the Ministry of Finance (T'akchibu)."[48]

On 15 March Min received his official seals and orders, also from the foreign ministry. As well as being ordered to present his credentials at the courts of the six European nations, Min was instructed as follows:

> He [Min] should also carry out an envoy's duties and increase friendship and cooperation with each of those countries. If there is any important matter concerning this country, he should consult and take action to achieve a satisfactory compromise. In addition, he must maintain equitable relations with the envoys and other officials of friendly nations residing in those countries. If there are any matters requiring explanation, they should be reported in detail.[49]

Before leaving Seoul, Min visited all the foreign envoys to acquaint them with his impending departure for Europe. "It goes without saying," he wrote in the mission diary, "that all the envoys were delighted."[50] At daybreak on 24 March, Min went together with Yi Ki, Kim Cho-hyŏn, Kim Pyŏng-ok, and Son Pyŏng-gyun to Kyŏngun Palace[51] for an early-morning audience with the king. Min Sang-ho had already left the Korean capital for the United States one week earlier, on 17 March.[52]

At the audience, the members of the embassy took their leave of the king.

At this time Min received a personal letter and a congratulatory address for Queen Victoria, a personal letter of gratitude to Tsar Nicholas II, six credential letters in duplicate, a set of injunctions, and a letter of appointment. After they had left the audience chamber, Kojong summoned them for a second, more personal audience in his personal residence, where, wrote Min, he "spoke to us and even consoled us with kind words. My companions and I trembled with inexpressible awe."[53]

At 8:00 A.M. Min and his party departed from Seoul through the Tonŭi Gate, traveling toward Inch'ŏn. On arriving at Map'o, the embassy was greeted by a large group of government officials, and a farewell banquet took place on the banks of the Han River under a clear sky, just as had happened before Min's departure for Russia in 1896. Min received advice and encouragement from all quarters before the banquet broke up, and the officials dispersed. As they were preparing to leave, Min's younger brother, Min Yŏng-ch'an, caught up with the party. At the last minute King Kojong had appointed him as an unofficial member of the retinue so that he could gain experience abroad.[54] Like Yun Ch'i-ho, who had been Min's adjutant on the 1896 mission to Russia, Min Yŏng-ch'an had previously held the post of vice-minister of education. He was also an official who spoke English and, like his elder brother, Min Yŏng-hwan, and his cousin Min Sang-ho, was in receipt of the approval of the *Independent*:

> The newly appointed Vice Minister of Education, Mr. Min Yungchan [Yŏng-ch'an], is well known to the foreigners in Seoul. He is a member of the Seoul Union and speaks English very well. He is brother of Mr. Min Yungwhan [Yŏng-hwan], the Minister of War. We congratulate Mr. Min Yungchan upon the appointment and hope he will prove himself to be an energetic promoter of education in his country. We believe that Mr. Min fully realizes the paramount importance of educational reformation.[55]

The party crossed the Han River by ferry and traveled toward Inch'ŏn in sedan chairs. Along the way they happened to meet the British minister to China and Korea, Sir Claude MacDonald (Dou Nale), who resided at Beijing.[56] He had just arrived at Inch'ŏn from China and was being accompanied to Seoul by John Jordan. The two parties halted and exchanged pleasantries before continuing on their separate ways.

Min and his entourage arrived at Inch'ŏn by torchlight that evening and lodged at the Daibutsu Hotel. The following day Min met the customs intendant *(kamni)* Yi Chae-jŏng, the Russian chargé d'affaires Waeber, and Waeber's wife. As Waeber's wife was returning to Russia, it was agreed that she would travel to Odessa together with Min's party.[57] Min also happened to meet Yun

Ch'i-ho, who had accompanied him to Russia the previous year. They agreed to travel together as far as Shanghai, where Yun was going to visit his Chinese wife, Ma Xiuzhen, and her relatives.

At Inch'ŏn the former maritime customs intendant, Paul von Rauthenfelt (No Tŭng-bi), joined the Korean party. Rauthenfelt, a Russian national, spoke English, German, Italian, and French, and also had a knowledge of Chinese. He was, therefore, to fulfill the role played by Evgenii Stein the previous year as the foreign assistant and interpreter for the mission. Rauthenfelt's appointment also met the approval of the *Independent,* which described him as follows:

> Mr. Von Routenfeldt is a Russian subject and an accomplished linguist. . . . He came to the Korean Customs Service last year from the Chinese Customs, and has been working under Chief Commissioner J. McLeavy Brown. He is a refined gentleman of fine appearance and has proved himself during his short sojourn here to be a perfect gentleman in every sense of the word. We are glad to learn that the Government is sending him to Europe with the Minister, as he will be very helpful to the mission.[58]

According to Yun, on the night of Min Yŏng-hwan's arrival at Inch'ŏn, both he and his younger brother cut off their traditional Korean topknots in Yun's room, adopting a Western hairstyle. For such a high-ranking official as Min Yŏng-hwan to cut his hair was a significant gesture. Adult male Koreans traditionally wore their hair in a topknot. During the Japanese-led reforms pushed through by Kim Hong-jip's cabinet after the assassination of Queen Myŏngsŏng, an edict to cut the topknot had been put into force despite strong resistance from the Korean populace. This edict was subsequently revoked, but the cutting of the topknot remained a sensitive political issue in Korea and continued to be strongly opposed by conservatives. Yun, of course, had already taken the same step many years earlier and commented disparagingly, "They took a deal of unnecessary caution against any mention of the affair in the Chemulpo paper."[59] There is also no mention of this episode in Min's own diary, *Sagu sokch'o.* It would appear that Min, although unwilling to upset the conservatives in Korean society, was determined to avoid the embarrassment he had faced in Moscow the year before. As has been recounted in the previous chapter, Min and his entourage had been unable to enter the cathedral in which Tsar Nicholas II's coronation took place because Korean tradition had prevented them from removing their headgear, which formed an integral part of the Chosŏn court costume. Furthermore, the experience of having been the object of derision in the streets of New York while en route to Russia in the previous year probably had also contributed to his decision not to wear traditional Korean costume but to exchange it for a military uniform in the Western style for his mission to Europe.[60]

The Journey to St. Petersburg via Odessa

Min had some "unavoidable business" in Shanghai, and so it was decided that he would travel there on the Russian merchant ship, the *Vladimir,* together with his younger brother, Yŏng-ch'an, and the mission chancellor, Son. The rest of the party would go directly to Nagasaki on the *Sendai Maru* and await them there. On 28 March, after telegraphing the Department of the Royal Household, Min and his two companions, together with Yun Ch'i-ho, set off for Yantai, arriving on the following day. There they were met by a representative of the German trading company Anz and Company, who had been telegraphed in advance by a Western employee of Meyer and Company in Inch'ŏn.[61] The Koreans stayed the night at the company godown. Two days later they left Yantai for Shanghai on the Chinese merchant ship the *Haian,* arriving there on 2 April.

In Shanghai Min once again visited von Möllendorff and his elder cousin Min Yŏng-ik, just as he had done the previous year before setting off for the Russian emperor's coronation. The diary contains no information about what was discussed at these meetings, but according to Yun, in the previous year, Min had received $20,000, authorized by King Kojong, for his own expenses during the Russian trip from Min Yŏng-ik. It is quite possible that Min Yŏng-hwan's "unavoidable business" in Shanghai involving his cousin was also for a similar financial purpose, particularly as Brown had supplied the embassy with a less generous allowance than in the previous year.

Just as had happened in the spring of 1896, Min's party was again delayed in Shanghai after Min was unable to book a passage on the first steamer to Nagasaki. Finally, on 10 April, after several days of anxious waiting, he and his colleagues were able to leave on the British ship the *Empress of China,* which was the same ship that had taken them as far as Vancouver en route to Russia the previous year.

On board ship the Korean party met the Chinese envoy, Zhang Yinhuan, and his entourage, also on their way to Britain for the Diamond Jubilee. Despite the best efforts of the Chinese to strike up a conversation, Min recounts in his diary that he and his companions were unable to communicate with them.[62]

Early in the morning on 12 April, the *Empress of China* arrived at Nagasaki. Rauthenfelt came to take Min and his party by skiff to the Russian ship *Sara-*

tov, where the other members of the embassy were already waiting for them. Min had, in fact, arrived one day after the ship was scheduled to sail, but because of the intervention of Admiral Evgenii I. Alekseev, the commander in chief of the Russian Asiatic Fleet, the *Saratov*'s departure had been delayed. This news attracted the critical attention of the *Independent*, which, in line with its editorial policy of applauding the good deeds of government officials and chastising their mistakes, commented somewhat self-righteously,

> Minister Min ought to have remembered that the expense of a day's delay of the regularly scheduled steamer is considerably more than the price of two passages. This time he fortunately caught the steamer through the courtesy of the Russian Admiral, but as a rule the steamers and trains do not change the regular schedule for the convenience of one or two passengers. We hope he will not always expect the same accommodation from the steamship or railway companies.[63]

Nevertheless, despite his tardy arrival, Min was accorded a military salute as he boarded the Russian ship and was welcomed by the *Saratov*'s captain and officers. Rauthenfelt had already bought the tickets. Min was to have a first-class deck cabin for himself while Rauthenfelt, Min Yŏng-ch'an, and Yi Ki shared another first-class cabin opposite. The legation chancellors, Kim Pyŏng-ok, Kim Cho-hyŏn, and Son Pyŏng-gyun, shared a second-class cabin below decks. Min was surprised at the low cost of the tickets, 420 yen for the first-class cabins and 160 yen for the second-class cabin. Rauthenfelt informed him that fares were low because the *Saratov* was a government ship used for transportating railway materials, construction workers, and soldiers to and from the Russian Far East.[64]

The *Saratov* departed from Nagasaki that same morning, 12 April, bound for Odessa via the Indian Ocean and the Suez Canal. The first night of the voyage the ship began to roll heavily, and there was a torrential downpour of rain. "All through the night," wrote Min, "it was impossible to sleep because of the pattering of the rain, the roaring of the waves, the groaning of the iron girders, and the clamor of the sailors."[65]

Min suffered from seasickness and was unable to get up the following morning. The storm had died down, but the ship was now enveloped in fog. At midday he was able to go on deck and was told that the distant specks of land he could see on the northwest horizon were the eastern region of Xiamen on the Chinese mainland. Min, who had been appointed minister of war in the previous year after his return from Russia, remarked in his diary that Xiamen, Taiwan, and Penghu formed a protective barrier for all of Fujian Province and that it was here that the Ming general Zheng Chenggong (1624–1662) had harassed the Qing forces in Fujian and Zhejiang.[66] Korean sympathies in the conflict between the Ming and the Qing dynasties, of course, lay firmly with the former. The Ming were appreciated for their intervention during the Hideyoshi invasions at the end of the sixteenth century, while the Qing were seen as barbarian usurpers. This fact accounts for the ambivalence of Korean attitudes toward Qing China as Korea's suzerain in the nineteenth century.

That evening the fog thickened and visibility was reduced to zero. The ship could only move forward slowly while letting off repeated blasts from its foghorn. Around 7:00 P.M. the passengers could hear the sound of another foghorn, and for a while the two ships traded blasts in the pitch darkness. It was with some relief, no doubt, that a short while later Min heard the other ship's foghorn gradually fade into the distance.[67]

In the early afternoon of the next day, the fog dispersed and the *Saratov* began to travel more quickly. By this time it was sailing about five hundred leagues south of Hong Kong. After dinner, Min went to the rear deck to listen to the Russian soldiers' choir. In his diary he likened the sound of their singing to the chanting of Buddhist nuns and added a typically ambivalent assessment of the Russian soldiery:

I have heard that Russian soldiers are all stupid, ignorant, and fierce. They are not afraid of cold or heat. They are not particular about food or drink. Even if they spend the night on the damp ground, they do not become ill. At each meal they are provided with one lump of bread and a bowl of gruel. They have two meals like this a day. Nevertheless, they neither get tired nor hungry and are still able to fight courageously and well. Consequently, it is said that the soldiers of no other Western nation can match them.[68]

On the following day, 16 April, the ship sailed smoothly through a sea that was "pure green like oil." At the bow of the ship, Min saw flying fish skimming the tops of the waves, and in the evening he sat on deck enjoying the cool air and the scene of the moon rising, its light reflecting on the surface of a sea of jade. "It made me think," he wrote, "of the phrase in Wang Panshan's poem, 'The mountain moon enters the river, shattering into golden shards.'"[69] Min's choice of poet, the Song-dynasty official Wang Anshi (pen name: Panshan), who rose to the position of prime minister during the reign of Emperor Shenzong (r. 1068–1085), was an appropriate one. Wang's radical reform measures aimed at ameliorating the lot of the peasants and small traders and ensuring the solvency of the Song administration had been bitterly opposed by the wealthy landowners and merchants of his day.

The next day, 17 April, was also bright and hot. Min noticed that most of the passengers had changed into white clothes for the tropics. The sea was calm and the color of indigo. Min was told that the ship was now to the northwest of Annam (Vietnam). That evening he observed an Orthodox service, which involved placing fruit and cakes in front of an icon of Jesus (Yaso). The service was attended by passengers from both classes and lasted for two hours. Min was told that it was the custom on Russian ships to hold such a service on every second and seventh day.[70]

Min subsequently asked Rauthenfelt about Westerners' religious beliefs concerning the creation and teachings about heaven and hell, revealing that as a Confucian he nevertheless had some knowledge of Christianity. Rauthenfelt admitted that such teachings were not entirely logical, but like similar teachings in Buddhism, they encouraged people to do good and to avoid evil. Concerning the teaching that God was the creator of the universe, Rauthenfelt argued that if it were true that such a teaching was designed to deceive foolish people, "then why do nearly all Western people worship God and by developing all kinds of skills become daily richer and more powerful?"[71] Min admitted the reason in this argument in his diary, and it may well be that he was in sympathy with Christian beliefs: his aunt after all, the wife of the Taewŏn'gun and mother of King Kojong, is said to have been a Roman Catholic.[72] It is also known that Min had friendly relations with the American missionary community in Seoul.[73]

Min's Confucian sensibilities, however, were shocked when he heard on the same day that a sick child who had died on board ship during the night had been cast into the sea and that this had been done according to the ship's regulations. He was reminded of a story in Zhang Zaichu's *Si shu ji* (Record of the West), in which a missionary had died during a voyage. The missionary's wife had begged that his body be kept until the ship reached Aden one day later so that he could be buried on land. The captain refused her entreaties, however, arguing that when somebody died their soul went up to heaven, and that it was, therefore, immaterial whether the body went into the earth or the sea. "In general," added Min "most Westerners believe this."[74] Such an idea, of course, was anathema to a Confucian because there would be no grave at which the proper sacrifices could be offered to the deceased ancestor.

On 20 April Min got up early and described the sea as being "bright green like the color of a duck's head." In the afternoon he could see the mountainous island of Singapore on the northern horizon. That evening the ship anchored eighty leagues south of Singapore. Min could see the shoreline to the north and described it in his diary as "ten thousand dots of lamplight glowing red, penetrating to the bottom of the sea."[75]

The next morning the ship arrived at Singapore itself, and the passengers amused themselves by tossing silver coins into the sea for the local children to dive for. Min was captivated by the sight of the "rather black" children diving from canoes into the water and emerging with a coin in their grasp. "It was just as if they were catching the magic pill of Han," he wrote.[76]

The embassy went ashore to see the sights of Singapore. First they visited the Chinese quarter with its temples, guild halls, theaters, wine shops, and brothels. Then they traveled north along a road lined with bamboo groves to the zoo. The weather was exceedingly hot, and the party retired to a wine shop, where, according to Min, they consumed nothing stronger than several jugs of ice water. In his diary entry for this day, Min provides an account of how Singapore was seized from Malaya (Yubulguk) by the British in the reign of Jiaqing and how "Chinese people came here like tame ducks and built a huge port"[77] because the British did not levy any poll tax.

Min's description of the native people as "stupid, vulgar, and jet black" revealed that it was not only the white Westerners who were capable of looking down on other races. Nevertheless, Min went on to provide an accurate description of the local people's dress and ornamentation as well as a list of local products that would not have been out of place in a Western travel book of the period.[78]

On the same day Min went to visit the British consul identified only by his surname Mitchell, and after returning to the ship that evening, he was visited by the Russian consul, also identified simply as Kiremyorov. That Min chose to visit the former and waited to be visited by the latter may be interpreted as another indication of the cooling of relations between the Korean and Russian courts since the departure of Kojong from the Russian legation in February of the same year.

For the next two days the ship continued past Malucca, up the west coast of Malaya and the Dutch colony of Sumatra, erroneously described by Min as being a British colony. The straits were thronged with ships and countless islands. On the night of 23 April a thunderstorm struck and "the rain jumped like white pearls."[79] When Min went up on deck the next morning, he saw an expanse of jet black sea and foaming billows as the ship entered the Indian Ocean. By afternoon the weather had deteriorated, and the ship had to battle against a contrary wind. "The waves were as high as mountains," wrote Min, "and the ship rolled exceedingly."[80]

Surprisingly, according to the diary, it was announced that this day was Jesus' birthday. It appears that Min misunderstood Easter to be Christmas. At all events Min attended the service at 9:00 P.M. and was unable to leave until 1:00 A.M. when the ceremony finally finished. Exhausted and overheated, Min and his companions returned to their cabins, undressed, and lay down on their bunks. No doubt to Min's dismay, he had no sooner lain down when an invitation to attend a festive banquet arrived from the ship's captain. "I could not refuse," wrote Min laconically, and after changing into fresh clothes went to the dining hall, where he was regaled with handshakes and kisses and plied with drinks until the early hours of the morning.[81]

The next day the ship had begun to roll again, and by the following day, Min was again feeling slightly seasick. By 10:00 A.M. a storm was raging, and the contents of his cabin were flung from one side to the other, while the passengers "staggered about like drunken people."[82] On the morning of 27 April the cloudy peaks and dense, green foliage of the Ceylon shoreline came into view on the northern horizon. In his diary entry for this day, Min provides a synopsis of India's geography and history based on *Lei huan zhi lyue* (Historical summary of the world), with particular emphasis on how India had come under the control of the British at the time of the reigns of the Qing emperors Kangxi and Qianlong.

In writing about Ceylon, Min's references are again all Chinese: namely, *Bi yun ri ji* (Bi Yun's diary) and the *Tang zhi* (Tang annals). The ship was not scheduled to stop at Colombo, and so, to his regret, Min was unable to go ashore and see the "Buddha Country" for himself. Instead, he asked the sailors on the ship about the island. Once again his description of the local people betrays the prejudices of his time: "They are all dark black," he wrote, "and as ignorant as sheep and pigs."[83] From the descriptions he received about the dress of the Ceylonese, however, Min could recognize the origins of the dress style of the Buddhist monks and Lohan statues in his own country.

On the following day, it rained all morning, and a rumor went around the ship that there would be a cyclone. This rumor caused Min some anxiety, but he was reassured by one of the sailors that the weather would soon clear. He was then told about meteorological offices in the West, which could predict the weather seven days in advance and inform all the ports by telegraph so that ships could be prevented from leaving harbor.

Just as the sailor had predicted, the next few days were bright and hot. "It was just like traveling in a boat on the Yangtze River," wrote Min, characteristically drawing his simile from his vicarious knowledge of China rather than his own experience of Korea.[84] With the calmer weather, many parents must have brought their children up on deck, and Min was surprised to see babies less than a week old looking around and laughing. "Through this," he commented solemnly, "we can see that Western people's early development starts from when they are children in arms."[85]

Over the following days the weather became increasingly stifling, and it was difficult for Min to sleep at night. To the south, the mountainous contours of the Horn of Africa were clearly visible, and on 4 May at midday the *Saratov* arrived at Aden. Min and his party went ashore on a lighter to look around. The sight of the camels and donkeys that they passed along the road reminded Min of "a scene from Liao or Hopei."[86] Such references to China were, of course, purely literary as Min's actual experience of that country was limited to brief visits to the ports of Yantai and Shanghai.

The Koreans inspected a fortress built by the British, prompting Min to provide the following explanation of Aden's strategic importance to Britain:

> For sixty years the British have depended on this place as a coaling station as well as a vantage point to control the entrance to the Red Sea. In this way they have prevented Russia and all other countries from spying on the route to India. That is why even though it is a profitless and barren place which incurs a yearly increase of expenditure, it is being maintained in preparation for a time of trouble.[87]

Before returning to the ship, Min sent a telegram to the Department of the Royal Household. At 6:00 P.M. the ship got under way and after sailing north for two hours entered the Red Sea, where the Arabian and African shores were clearly visible to the north and to the south. For several days the *Saratov* steamed up the Red Sea, and Min had time to read Wang Jichun's *Shi e cao zai* (Record of an envoy to Russia). Min matched Wang's description of the Medina region and the "brother islands"[88] with the region through which they were traveling.

In the early hours of 9 May the ship arrived at the entrance to the Suez Canal. Min recorded that the tolls were two yen per ton of cargo and two yen per passenger. He noted that the toll office was run by the British and went on to describe how Britain was wresting control of the canal from the French:

> Ten years ago a Frenchman, de Lesseps, pioneered this canal. He sold share certificates and then began and finished the huge project. From this the French collected great profits. Because the land belonged to Egypt, they promised to give the king one-third of the profits. Later Egypt sold its share to the British for a great price. I heard, moreover, that because of France's expenditure in the Annam war, it will also sell its shares to the British so that all the rights and privileges will come under their control.[89]

On the evening of the same day, after passing through the Bitter Lake, with its shores of white salt and houseboats moored on the banks of the canal, the ship arrived at Port Said. The following day Min and his companions went ashore once again for sightseeing. They inspected an Islamic mosque and ascended a lighthouse built by the French. Min noted that some of the local people were fair skinned and that "the women generally cover their heads with blue cotton linen, barely exposing their eyes . . . like our country's women's long dress."[90]

The same afternoon the *Saratov* got under way once more, heading north across the Mediterranean Sea. Two days later it was passing through the Dardanelles. On either side Min could see the gun batteries that lined the Turkish shores. He recorded in his diary that Turkey was on the verge of war with Greece, but, in fact, war had already broken out in April that year and had ended in May. During the passage through these strategic straits, Min witnessed warning shots being fired at a Russian ship that had strayed too close to the shore.[91]

At 6:00 A.M. on 13 May the ship passed Constantinople on the western shore, evoking Min's admiring response:

We passed the old capital of Turkey, Constantinople. It is located along the western shore. Continuously for several hundred leagues there is luxuriant, bright countryside. The fields are like inlay or embroidery. Moreover, we passed two royal palaces. They were buildings of many stories that rose up halfway to the sky with white-washed brick battlements. They were exceedingly marvelous. There were gun batteries on both shores, scattered like stars or chess pieces. It is rightly called a great wonder.[92]

On hearing that they would arrive at Odessa on the Black Sea on the next day, Min recounts, all the passengers shook hands and congratulated each other. That evening the sailors prepared a banquet for the passengers, who would soon be disembarking. In his diary Min reflected on the journey:

I thought about how we had departed from the capital in March and of all the places we had passed on our journey, the poisonous vapors and the steep, fathomless billows of the sea. Because of His Majesty's support and liberal blessings our travel party has had a favorable passage, and we are exceedingly joyful.[93]

Early on the following day, 14 May, Min asked the sailors to fly the Korean flag from the ship's flagpole, and at 10:00 A.M. the *Saratov* docked at Odessa. The Koreans were welcomed by the local governor and two military officials and were then taken by carriage to their hotel. As they would be leaving for St. Petersburg the next day, the governor invited them to the theater that evening. Min was overwhelmed by the luxury of the auditorium. "On each of the floors there were hundreds and thousands of seats and benches," he wrote; "there were electric lights all around like a string of pearls. It was a wondrous sight!"[94] Although Min never found out the name of the play, he felt that it was not unlike a Korean dramatic performance. He was, however, particularly impressed by the lifelikeness of the stage scenery.

On the following day, 15 May, Min paid the hotel bill, which came to 150 rubles at an exchange rate of one silver yen to one ruble. On their arrival at the station Min found that the governor had allocated him and his party their own compartment on the train and that they would be accompanied by two servants. At 10:00 A.M. they departed for St. Petersburg and were able to sit back and enjoy the luxurious comfort of late-nineteenth-century rail travel in Tsarist Russia. That evening they were met en route by Min's relative Min Kyŏng-sik,[95] who had come from St. Petersburg with three telegraphed instructions from the king. Unfortunately, Min makes no mention in his diary of what those telegrams contained.

Min's Activities in St. Petersburg
and the Journey to London

On 17 May the train arrived at St. Petersburg and Min and his companions were met by Planson and Ko Ak-si, two of the officials who had been assigned to Min's mission the previous year. After settling into the Malniyamalshikai Hotel,[96] Min telegraphed the Department of the Royal Household and on the following morning sent a dispatch to the Russian Ministry of Foreign Affairs requesting an audience with the tsar to present Kojong's personal letter and his own credentials. He also sent a telegram to Min Sang-ho, who was now in Washington at the International Postal Convention. In Korea, the *Independent* reported that Min had also telegraphed the Korean government concerning his safe arrival at St. Petersburg.[97]

On the afternoon of 19 May, Min went to pay his respects to the minister of foreign affairs, Mikhail N. Muraviev. This was the first time the two had met as Min had, on his visit of 1896, conducted all his negotiations with Lobanov, who had died suddenly soon after Min's departure from the Russian capital. As the situation had changed between the two countries, Muraviev undoubtedly had less time for his Korean guest than had his predecessor. Nevertheless, it is likely that at this meeting Min acquainted Muraviev with Kojong's wish to retain Waeber at Seoul.

That evening Min and his entourage went sightseeing and once again found

themselves drawn to the bronze statue of Peter the Great on the banks of the
Neva. Perhaps wistfully reflecting on the powerlessness of his own country's
condition, Min recounted in his diary the enlightenment and military prowess
of the former tsar:

> Peter was born in 1672 according to the Western calendar. At the age of twenty-
> five he ascended the throne. He saw many rebellions in the country. He departed
> in disguise to tour Great Britain. He studied about ships, government, mathemat-
> ics, and all kinds of manufacturing and then returned to his own country. He
> transferred his capital to present-day St. Petersburg. Through trade he collected
> revenue, and by exercising the art of despotic leadership, he fought successive
> wars with many countries and won them all. So he attained wealth and strength.[98]

It seems that on this occasion, however, Min's praise for Russia was less complimentary than that expressed in the record of the mission of 1896, *Haech'ŏn
ch'ubŏm*. At the end of an explanation of the Russian government and military
system with its cruel punishments, for example, Min wrote ominously, "From
time to time the citizens demand reforms, and it is said that there are those
who are conspiring to oppose the government."[99]

There were further days of sightseeing before Min received a dispatch from
the Russian Department of Rites on 22 May, inviting him to an audience with
the tsar on 25 May. On the appointed day, Min, together with his younger
brother, Yŏng-ch'an, and the legation chancellor, Kim Pyŏng-ok, boarded a
train for Tsarskoe Selo, the tsar's summer retreat. The audience took place in
a residential section of the palace. Min and his younger brother were ushered
into the presence of the tsar, and Min presented first his credentials and then
the personal letter from King Kojong.[100] Min then read out the congratulatory address relating to the Diamond Jubilee of Queen Victoria, who was the
tsarina's grandmother. This address was then translated into English by Min
Yŏng-ch'an. When he had finished, the tsar welcomed Min, expressing his surprise and happiness at meeting him again. Min informed him that the purpose of his visit was to present his credentials at the various European capitals
and then return to St. Petersburg as a resident envoy. The tsar wished him a
safe journey and after shaking hands with them, the two Koreans withdrew.[101]
Although no mention is made in *Sagu sokch'o* of Min conveying Kojong's request for the retention of Waeber at this meeting, it is most likely that he did
so. From the variations between *Haech'ŏn ch'ubŏm* and *Yun Ch'i-ho ilgi*, as
shown in the previous chapter, it is clear that any transactions of a sensitive
nature between Min and the tsar and his officials were invariably omitted from
Min's official account. It is reasonable to assume, therefore, that Min did not

divulge the full contents of his meetings with the tsar and Muraviev in *Sagu sokch'o* either.

The next few days were spent visiting the envoys of those countries with which Korea had treaty relations including Japan, the United States, and Great Britain. Min also received visits from the ministers of Persia and Sweden. There were also outings to a factory for building model prototypes of warships and to one of the great churches of St. Petersburg. On 28 May Min received a visit from the chancellor of the British legation inquiring about the number of members of Min's party who would be attending the jubilee celebrations. The British Foreign Office, having mislaid the dispatches, had apparently been unprepared for the Korean mission's arrival. The confusion that existed is shown in Mac-Donald's somewhat garbled dispatch to Jordan on the subject:

> Sir, with reference to the Corean Mission to the Queen's Jubilee, I have to inform you that I telegraphed to you today to the effect that your tel of April 26 had been communicated to the F.O. In answer to my tel I had the honour to receive a reply from H.M. Sec. of State, stating that my tel of April 27 was the first intimation that had been received on the subject of a Corean Mission, that there were great difficulties about entertainment and accommodation, and asking whether it were possible to discourage the idea without giving offence. His Lordship added that if the Envoy came full particulars as to his rank and that of his suite and mode of living must be forwarded.[102]

The next day Min visited the American ambassador, referred to simply by his surname Breckenridge, and asked him if he would deputize for him while he was visiting the other European capitals. Breckenridge promised to pass on the request to his government. Min then went to the British legation for tea. On his return to his hotel Min wrote a dispatch to the American legation repeating the request that he had made to Breckenridge earlier:

> Be it known that this envoy intends on the first day of the following month to depart from this legation temporarily to go to Europe and present credential letters from his sovereign in each country with which our nation has a treaty. As soon as this business is accomplished I will return to this legation. During the period before I return, I would be grateful if you would temporarily take charge of our legation's affairs. I have already made this request personally. Please consider that usually any country that has treaty relations with another country may manage that nation's diplomatic affairs. Just as in our country there are the examples of the British envoy managing the affairs of Italy and the German envoy those of Austria.[103]

In this way Min appears to have made a point of exercising his rights as the diplomatic representative of an independent nation. After a further exchange of dispatches, which showed no sign of enthusiasm on behalf of the American ambassador or his government, it was, nevertheless, finally settled that the embassy of the United States would handle the diplomatic affairs of Chosŏn until Min's return. From this dispatch we can also clearly see that at this stage in his mission, Min still intended to visit the other European capitals to present his credentials and then return to St. Petersburg, where he would reside as the Korean minister plenipotentiary to Russia and all Korea's European treaty partners. As shall be seen, however, Min was only to present his credentials in London, abandoning his mission soon after the end of the jubilee celebrations and departing from Europe for the United States.

On 31 May, the final day before Min and his entourage were to depart from St. Petersburg, they visited the zoo and the coin mint, where they observed the production of gold, silver, bronze, and nickel coins. On their way back to the hotel they passed by the imposing Fortress of St. Peter and St. Paul, which overlooks the Neva River.

That afternoon Min sent his younger brother to thank the American minister for agreeing to deputize for him, while he himself went to take his leave from the minister of foreign affairs, Muraviev. Also on this day, Min received a telegram promoting his younger brother to the rank of deputy lieutenant-colonel in the Ministry of War.

On the morning of 1 June Min sent a dispatch to the Russian Ministry of Foreign Affairs informing them officially of his intention to leave St. Petersburg for three or four months to attend the Diamond Jubilee in London and then to continue traveling around Europe to present his credentials at the capitals of Germany, France, Italy, and Austria. He informed the ministry of his arrangement with the U.S. minister and, also, that one of the legation chancellors, Kim Pyŏng-ok, would be remaining at the Malniyamalshikai Hotel during his absence. Then at 8:00 P.M., leaving behind Min Kyŏng-sik and Kim Pyŏng-ok, Min Yŏng-hwan boarded a train together with his brother, Min Yŏng-ch'an; secretary Yi Ki; legation chancellors Kim Cho-hyŏn and Son Pyŏng-gyun; and the party's Russian assistant, Rauthenfelt.[104]

The journey to Germany was an uneventful one. Just before the Russo-German border, a military official boarded the train to check passports. When they reached the border itself, everyone transferred trains after a one-hour wait in the station. On the evening of the next day they arrived in Berlin. As they had some time before they had to catch their next train, Min and his companions, rather predictably, went to visit the zoo. Min was impressed by the way in which the enclosures of the animals were landscaped in such a way as to recreate the animals' natural habitat. He took particular note of a giraffe, about which he wrote whimsically,

> In one place there was a horned animal shaped like an ass and about several *chang* high. Its hide was yellow with black markings. It is sometimes called a giraffe. The people of old said that giraffes were originally holy people. Are these truly giraffes? How is it then that the West has so many holy people?[105]

At 11:00 P.M. Min and his companions boarded a train heading westward. Min occupied the long hours of traveling listening to Rauthenfelt's account of German history. Rauthenfelt recounted how Frederick Wilhelm III of Prussia had been defeated by Napoleon and then humiliated by him in front of the Russian tsar. He told how the Prussian monarch had sworn revenge at the tomb of his ancestors and how after imposing a system of conscription on his people, he had finally regained all the territory taken by Russia by helping the latter defeat Napoleon in the Franco-Russian war.

The conscription system, which had begun in Germany under Frederick Wilhelm III and been perfected under the political and military leadership of Bismarck and Moltke respectively, was particularly impressive to Min, as was Germany's education system. Concerning the former, Min wrote,

> After the appointment of Bismarck, a martial spirit has been encouraged in everyone. Even the children of nobility between the ages of fifteen and twenty-five enter the army for a period of three years, after which they are permitted to return to their homes. If there is some crisis, all the soldiers throughout the country can be recalled within three days, producing an army ranging from three million soldiers up to a maximum of five million. On the other hand, their customs are extravagant, and many of the people are impoverished and thin.[106]

At midnight the train reached Holland. Before embarking for Britain, Min and his colleagues took a short sight-seeing trip. En route they came across a statue commemorating Admiral Michiel A. de Ruyter, celebrating his defeat of the British in 1652.[107] Min also noted Holland's geography and its prowess as a trading nation. At 10:00 P.M. they set off for England aboard the Dutch ship *Koningin Regentes* and arrived at Queenborough at 9:00 A.M. on 5 June. As a diplomatic party they were exempt from customs inspection and immediately boarded a train for London. Once in London they stayed at the Cecil Hotel, situated between the Strand and Victoria Embankment, just a short distance from Charing Cross Station and Trafalgar Square.[108]

Min's Participation in the Diamond Jubilee
and Other Activities in London

The next few days were characteristically foggy and rainy, and Min and his party do not appear to have gone out sightseeing. Concerning his impression of the British capital, which he had briefly visited the previous year, Min wrote, "London is located on either side of the River Thames. The country is originally very cold, but is warmed by a warm sea current. Also the smoke and heat from several million houses lingers continuously, so that the air is seldom clear and often foggy. Lamps are lit even in broad daylight."[109]

Because of the poor British weather, the diary entries comprise impressions of the hotel, an outline of British history, and a conversation with a guest on modern methods of coastal defense. The hotel was a luxurious building of eight stories and, according to Min, was where princes and envoys stayed on their visits to London. He was very impressed by the hotel elevator, but even more surprising was the presence of telephone kiosks in the hotel and the discovery that "in the whole of the London region there are telephone lines that connect several million houses inside the city."[110] Min marveled at the convenience of the hotel's bank, telegraph office, and printed stationery, while the luxurious dining hall, smoking room, and reading room and their electric lighting caused him to write, "It is just like entering the Flower Pearl Palace."[111]

On 8 June Min wrote and sent two dispatches to the British Foreign Office, enclosing copies of his credentials with the first and King Kojong's personal letter in Chinese and English with the second.[112] The first dispatch announced Min's arrival at the capital and requested an audience with Queen Victoria so that he could present his credentials; the second requested an audience so that he could present Kojong's personal letter. Min perhaps hoped in this way to gain the opportunity for two audiences with the British Queen, as he had done the same in Russia the previous year on the advice of one of his Russian assistants, Planson.

At midday, an official from the Foreign Office, identified in Min's diary simply as Sheen (Si-in), visited and informed Min that the foreign secretary, Lord Robert G. Salisbury, was absent from London but that he would be back in a few days.[113] The rest of the diary entry for 8 June is dedicated to a brief history of the United Kingdom, which Min described somewhat inaccurately as being "basically three islands in the Atlantic Ocean completely cut off from all other places"[114]—the "three islands" being England, Scotland, and Ireland, with no mention of Wales. Tactfully, considering Kojong's own shaky hold on power, Min omitted to mention the Civil War and the execution of Charles I from his account of British history, jumping from Elizabeth I to William of Orange. In addition, he chose to conclude his account by emphasizing Queen Victoria's role in the success of the British Empire:

> She [Victoria] has now ruled for sixty years. The territory has expanded, covering each colony in Africa, Australia, India, and in the Southern Seas. Even though the territory is not connected together, it is almost equal in extent and size to that of Russia. Although all the official orders proceed from Parliament, it cannot be denied that it is the empress' fortunate destiny that sustains the nation.[115]

On the following day, it rained again, and Min "in a melancholy mood" was confined to the hotel once more. During the day he got into conversation with a Westerner and asked him why Western cities had no defensive battlements. He was informed that because of the nature of modern artillery "even if a city were to be protected by walls of metal and a scalding moat, it would not be strong enough." Min learned that modern British defenses relied on gun batteries placed strategically along shorelines and at the mouths of river estuaries.[116] Min may have included this account because it corroborated his own recommendations for the defense of Chosŏn that he had made several years earlier in his policy essay *Ch'ŏnilch'aek.*

Several days later Min and his party were invited by the Foreign Office to move from the Cecil Hotel to a house in Kensington, where they would be lodged at the government's expense. According to the *Independent* and the *Times,* Min and his party stayed at Kensington Mansions, De Vere Gardens, which is just south of Kensington Gardens in central London.[117] Inasmuch as Min and his entourage had been immediately lodged at the Russian government's expense in the previous year, Min may well have wondered why such an invitation had not come earlier, particularly as their hotel bill came to the princely sum of 70 pounds, or 700 silver yen, which they could ill afford.

Sheen conducted the Koreans from the Foreign Office to their new lodgings. The house in De Vere Gardens had five stories and was neatly furnished. Min and his entourage were also provided with one gold-wheeled carriage with grooms in red uniforms. Coincidentally, among the neighbors of the Korean mission was the American novelist Henry James, who also lived in De Vere Gardens at this time. On the day following the move, Min received a dispatch granting him an audience with Queen Victoria at 3:30 P.M. on 21 June.

On the following day, Min Sang-ho, having completed his duties in Washington, arrived in London. "We shook hands in a strange land," wrote Min Yŏng-hwan; "his delight was clear to see."[118] On 19 June the Foreign Office allocated the Koreans a military official, Major Alfred Edward John Cavendish (Kabinnisi), as an assistant during their stay. Major Cavendish had been a military attaché to the Chinese army in 1894 and to the British legation at Beijing in 1895. In 1891, when he had been stationed in Hong Kong, he had visited Korea while on leave from the army and had even written a book, *Korea and the Sacred White Mountain*, based on his travels there.[119] During his time in China he had been highly critical of the state of the Chinese military and had tried in vain to warn his superior, Lord Kimberley, the foreign secretary, of the menace posed to British interests in the Far East by Japan.[120] Later that day Min paid his first visit to Foreign Secretary Lord Salisbury. It was also on this day that the Korean flag was first flown from the temporary Korean legation at De Vere Gardens.

On the next day, 20 June, Min was occupied visiting the other foreign legations in London, and as he was expected to ride on horseback in the jubilee procession around London, he took the opportunity to practice at a nearby horse-riding ground, which was most probably in Hyde Park. That day Min was also visited by Lord Salisbury, but made no mention in his diary of what they may have discussed.[121]

At 2:00 P.M. on 21 June, Major Cavendish accompanied Min and his companions to Buckingham Palace for their first audience. At the palace they joined a banquet for about fifty envoys, who were all receiving audiences that day. After the banquet finished, Min was led to the audience chamber. As no accompanying officials were permitted to go in with the envoys, Min was without his younger brother, who had acted as interpreter in his audience with Tsar Nicholas II. Nevertheless, Min appears to have managed on his own, as his account suggests:

> After the banquet finished, a ceremonial official led us forward. Only ambassadors were permitted to be presented. We were not permitted to take in subordinate officials with us. I entered the private chamber in my turn, carrying the credential letter and personal letter. The empress was already standing waiting. I saw that the empress had a round face and a rounded chin. Her spirit was vigorous with few signs of aging. I advanced in my turn and presented the credential letter. The empress also received it in turn. I then presented the personal letter. The empress then asked if his majesty the sovereign of our country was safe and well. I replied that he was and then in my turn retired.[122]

That evening Min and his companions returned to the palace for a dinner with all the other ambassadors and the British royal family. After the meal was concluded, Min joined "a great gathering of all nations' costumes and hats."[123]

The envoys waited outside the audience hall before once again being presented before the aging empress, who "simply nodded, and that was all."[124]

The next day, 22 June, was the day of the Diamond Jubilee celebration itself. Min and his companions put on ceremonial dress and went to the palace with Major Cavendish. After a twenty-gun salute, the procession left the palace. Queen Victoria's carriage, surrounded on all sides by the Household Cavalry, led the way, while Min rode alongside the other envoys in the procession that followed.[125] The jubilee ceremonies at Westminster Abbey were followed by another procession around the flower-strewn streets of London. Min, who was well aware of the tragic crowd accident that had occurred during the tsar's coronation the previous year, was particularly impressed by the orderliness of the crowds in London and wrote, "There were no fewer than one million spectators today. All of them had a seat, and there was not even the slightest disorder."[126]

The following day Min witnessed the enthusiastic reception that the queen received from a crowd of schoolchildren who were waiting for her as she departed from Buckingham Palace for Windsor, and that evening he caught a glimpse of the queen again as he and his entourage walked around Kensington Gardens together with Major Cavendish. "The empress came in and out of view from time to time under the flowery shade of the willows," wrote Min and added, perhaps for King Kojong's edification, "The intention of this gathering was for the sovereign and her people to enjoy themselves together."[127]

That same day Min visited a large greenhouse in the park and went into some detail about how such buildings made it possible to cultivate all sorts of tropical plants and trees despite the British weather. Min and his party then visited what appears to have been the Natural History Museum, although Min called it the International Museum *(man'guk pangmulwŏn)* and described it as being to the northeast of the park. Here he was surprised to find grass sandals, oiled hats, and bamboo pipes from Korea on display as well as more gruesome exhibits, such as "the sinews, bones, and entrails of people, all immersed in medicinal water."[128]

The next few days saw Min attending banquets given by the Prince of Wales, the Lord Mayor of London, and a London millionaire, who, Min noted with some astonishment, "received twenty thousand pounds in interest payments each month."[129] On 26 June Min attended the naval review at Spithead, where he boarded a steamship along with the other foreign envoys and cruised among the massive flotilla of warships, witnessing their devastating firepower. He recorded his impressions of the review in his diary entry for that day:

> After lunch I took a train together with both secretaries and traveled twenty minutes to the estuary mouth. On the surface of the sea on the left and right, we

saw warships packed together and stretching out over one hundred leagues. All were large iron ships. I counted more than 180 of them altogether. On board the ships sailors moved about urgently. Some wore red and some wore black. They carried weapons and stood in ranks as though they were on the point of the outbreak of war.

The heir apparent and all the ministerial officials met together with the ambassadors of each nation. We boarded a steamship and sailed leisurely across the surface of the sea. All the soldiers fired ceremonial cannons. Their crashing sound and the shuddering of the sea billows was truly an awesome sight.[130]

The following day, 27 June, Min presented the Department of the Imperial Household with "one pair of finely engraved white copper braziers, five scrolls embroidered with pearls, and ten ornamental purses as congratulatory gifts."[131]

As in St. Petersburg in the previous year, Min appears to have had considerable time for sightseeing, but this time without the pressure of conducting negotiations. Together with Major Cavendish, Min saw the sights of London, including Tower Bridge, the British Museum, and the British Library. On 29 June, he witnessed the queen returning from Windsor and noted, again perhaps for King Kojong's benefit, that "it is a Western custom that when the monarch goes out, there is no difference between her entourage and that of ordinary citizens."[132] That afternoon, Min also attended a royal garden party at Buckingham Palace.

The next few days were rainy and foggy, and Min appears not to have gone out. Instead the diary entries are concerned with various statistics about Britain and London and a very complimentary description of the British people: "Their physique is tall and big, and they have a white complexion. Their hair, beard and pupils are either black or brown. Their mind is precise, and they work with firm endurance. They have a brave, martial spirit and are the best out of all the European nations."[133] Min went on to list some salient aspects of British society—for example, the equal division of inheritance between men and women; the prohibition of secondary wives; the custom of removing one's hat and shaking hands as a greeting; the absence of the kowtow when meeting the monarch; the fact that nobility and commoners shared the same tables at banquets; and the custom of toasting the queen before beginning a banquet.[134]

In the next few days Min attended a military parade and a military tattoo before the celebrations came to a close on 5 July. On this day Min awarded silver medals to all the servants and staff allocated to their party. These medals were engraved with the words *Tae Chosŏn Kŏnyang Yi Nyŏn* (Great Chosŏn: Second Year of Lustrous Inauguration). The next day Major Cavendish also departed. Although Min mentions in *Sagu sokch'o* that his relations with Cavendish had been cordial, Yun Ch'i-ho, in his diary, recorded conversations that he had had in Seoul with Waeber and Brown that indicated that the same could not have been said for the relationship between Cavendish and Min's younger brother. According to Yun, Brown had told him,

> "There is no doubt that Min Yong Huan's failure was due to the evil influence of his brother. Major Cavendish, who was authorized by the British government to look after the Corean embassy, wrote me saying that he found Min Yong Chan the most disagreeable personage he had ever seen. Rautenfelt wrote out here saying that unless Min Yong Chan were suppressed, he would not serve the embassy."[135]

The following days were again given over to sightseeing as Min visited such diverse places and events as the Crystal Palace, a ball given by the Lord Mayor of London, Windsor Castle, the National Gallery, a factory that manufactured torpedoes and machine guns, and a final ball for foreign envoys given by Queen Victoria about which Min wrote,

> Above and below, the building was illuminated by ten thousand lamps as though it were daylight. All the palace ladies wore long, beautiful dresses with pearls and jewels that dazzled the eyes. All had bare arms and chests. Their fine brocade filled the hall and fluttered in the candlelight. I wondered if I was in the Pearl Palace or the Shell Tower.[136]

In the days following the ball, Min began to make preparations for the homeward journey via the United States. Before leaving he was awarded a commemorative gold medal and his entourage silver medals, which they received from the Foreign Office. At 7:00 A.M. on 17 July Min and his companions departed from London, at which point *Sagu sokch'o* comes to an abrupt end; there is no record of the return journey.

The Outcome of Min's Mission

According to Yun Ch'i-ho, Min's departure from London was in contravention of his official instructions. On 19 July, two days after Min's departure from London, Yun had an audience with Kojong in Seoul, during which the following conversation about Min's mission took place:

> Then His Majesty said, "Is Min Yong Huan sleeping? Why doesn't he telegraph me anything? Have you heard anything about his military uniform being ob-

jected to by the English F.O.?" To the last question I answered; "Yes Sir, I have heard that the English Government objected to Min's military uniform, but I can't believe it. For if so, why should he not let your Majesty know? Min Yong Huan is a careful man and he would have let Your Majesty know all about it if there were any difficulties concerning the uniform."[137]

Yun presumed that the pro-Russian group at the court, led by Kim Hong-nyuk and Chu Sŏng-myŏn, was behind the story concerning Min's military uniform, as they were opposed to Min and his foreign dress. These two pow-erful officials had, Yun surmised, "invented the story to prejudice His Majesty against Min and foreign costume."[138] On 26 July Yun met McLeavy Brown and asked him if there was any truth in the story and duly recorded in his di-ary that "Brown denied it emphatically and assured me that Min had been well received in London."[139]

Yun later discovered further details about the mission to Europe from a con-versation he had with Min Yŏng-ch'an on the latter's return to Korea, in which Min confided that his elder brother's main task in St. Petersburg had been to urge the tsar not to transfer Waeber and that he had curtailed his mission in Europe for reasons that he explained as follows:

> From Russia we went to London where we had a fine time. While there we re-ceived telegrams from the Seoul Court instructing my brother to work for the emperor business. We had no cheek to go around different courts begging to be allowed to call our King Emperor. So we didn't say a word about it. Later on a telegram came through the French Legation at London telling us that we should proceed to Paris and Berlin to conclude a certain military convention with France and Germany. This scared my brother so much that, in spite of the united ad-vice of Min Sang Ho and myself to visit the other court [sic] without mention-ing the convention, we left London in July for America.[140]

The exact nature of the proposed military conventions is not clear but, based on a report from Kir Alekseev, the Russian financial adviser in Seoul, B. A. Ro-manov reveals that Kojong had been so disillusioned by the failure of the Rus-sians to fulfill their promises to provide Korea with adequate security guaran-tees against Japanese interference that in May 1897 "he applied simultaneously to France and to Germany for aid and it was proposed to ask France in par-ticular to send a shore detail and a permanent guard ship to Chemulpo."[141] It is likely, therefore, that Min had been ordered to enter into negotiations on such matters with these two countries while he was in Europe.

Min's sudden departure from Europe was expressly contrary to the wishes of King Kojong as can be seen from the royal edict dismissing him from office that read as follows:

> We are told that the Envoy Extraordinary and Minister Plenipotentiary to Great Britain, Germany, Russia, Italy, Greece and Austria, Min Yungwhan, is returning home before completing his mission without order from the Government. We consider his action as insolent in the extreme. We hereby dismiss him from the office which he now holds.[142]

Min's unexplained abandonment of his official responsibilities in Europe was also commented on in the *Independent:*

> We are with many others puzzled over the movement of Mr. Min Yungwhan, the Envoy to the European Courts. There must be some reason underneath which made him take the erratic movement, as no sane person would so wilfully place himself in such a ridiculous position. It is evident that his course has displeased His Majesty and the Cabinet so that he is now placed in a very embarrassing predicament.[143]

Yun Ch'i-ho, who had succeeded Sŏ Chae-p'il as the editor of the *Independent,* feared that Min's dismissal was the result of a conspiracy by the pro-Russian party in the court.[144] Further light is cast on Min's decision to cut short his mission, however, by a confidential dispatch from the British consul-general Jordan to the minister at Beijing, Sir Claude MacDonald, in which he wrote,

> Both the King and his Ministers profess themselves unable to account for the strange behaviour of the Corean Representative, but some telegrams received from Mr. Min, copies of which have been furnished to me confidentially and are inclosed herewith, seem to throw some light on the matter.
> As far as can be gathered from these mutilated messages, the Envoy would appear to have received instructions to procure some sort of an international guarantee of Corean integrity, and he may very probably have shrunk from undertaking such a difficult task.[145]

The source of Jordan's information may well have been the Japanese legation. During Min's mission to Russia in 1896, the Japanese naval attaché, Lieutenant Yashiro, had revealed to Yun Ch'i-ho that he was aware of the contents of Min's telegram to the Korean government concerning the fact that military instructors were to be sent to Korea and had even boasted, "Ah, the Corean Cabinet can't keep any secrets. We know all about what they do."[146]

It would seem from the texts of the telegrams in Jordan's possession that Min was concerned that any secret convention that he was being asked to make with France and Germany would have been in direct contravention of the secret agreement that he had negotiated with Lobanov in St. Petersburg the previous year.[147] Min may have considered breaking this secret treaty a matter affecting his personal honor, or he may simply have considered it to be politically rash. Min's sudden abandonment of his diplomatic duties might be considered irresponsible in the extreme, particularly if his subsequent sojourn in the United States was paid for by funds allotted for his official mission in Europe. Nevertheless, it must be remembered that Min made his decision at a time when there was intense confusion at the Chosŏn court. A traditional Confucian court official had a sacred duty to remonstrate with his sovereign even at the risk of his life or career if he felt that the ruler was acting wrongly. In the light of Min's subsequent opposition to the 1905 protectorate treaty, it does not seem out of character that he placed his own sense of caution and integrity above the wishes of his sovereign and his government. The apparent failure of his mission to make any impression on the British sovereign or her government may also have led Min to believe that Europe was a lost cause and that Chosŏn's last hope lay with the United States. In fact, despite the fact that he had been disgraced at court, he even went so far as to request that he exchange places with the Korean minister at Washington.[148]

Min was subsequently replaced by his elder cousin Min Yŏng-ik, who had been living outside Korea for many years in Hong Kong and Shanghai. The latter's appointment, however, was opposed by the French minister, who informed the Korean Foreign Office that Min Yŏng-ik would be a "persona non grata" if appointed minister to France because he had "resided for ten years outside Korea" and "had been involved in an irregular transfer of $40,000 from the French Bank in Hong Kong 'some years ago.'"[149] In January of the following year the secretaries of the embassy returned to Seoul, and Min Yŏng-ik abandoned any attempt to travel to Europe.[150]

Thus, Min Yŏng-hwan's second visit to Europe ended in disappointment and even disgrace. In St. Petersburg in 1896, he had been courted by the Russians to some extent as they had a vested interest in increasing their influence in Korea. In addition the young tsar himself was personally interested in affairs related to the Russian Far East. In comparison, Min's visit to London must have been disappointing. He appears to have had no clear purpose other than putting in a presence at the great courts of Europe to uphold Korea's claim to be a sovereign, independent nation. The aging Queen Victoria, however, took no personal interest in Min, and in her eyes he must have appeared to be just another envoy among many others from a faraway land about which she knew little.

According to Hwang Hyŏn, it was even rumored in Korea that Queen Victoria was disappointed that Min had cut his hair and had not worn his national costume. In *Maech'ŏn yarok,* Hwang provides this somewhat inaccurate account of Min's return to Korea, which may be considered as reflecting prevailing hearsay rather than strict historical fact:

> The minister to Britain returned to this country. As he could not complete his ministerial responsibilities, Kojong made him return early and dismissed him from office. When Min went to London and saw all the members of the other congratulatory missions with short hair and wearing Western suits, he hated to be different, so he also cut his hair and put on a Western suit.
>
> One day the British queen, who had heard that in Chosŏn people did not cut their hair, invited Min to an audience in order to see the dignified mien of the Chosŏn minister. When he attended the audience, the British queen was disappointed and told him to go away.
>
> Afterward people heard this rumor and blamed Min for discarding the dignity of his fatherland. He also was so filled with regret that even after returning to this country, he continued to cut his hair and wear Western suits.[151]

Hwang's account here is inaccurate in several respects: first, as we know from Yun's firsthand account, Min had already cut his hair and adopted a Western-style uniform before he left Korea. Second, Min was not recalled because of any failure in Britain, but because he refused to travel to France and Germany to conduct secret negotiations. He also did not return home early but remained in self-imposed exile in the United States for more than a year. The rumors were probably connected to the alleged British disapproval of Min's military uniform mentioned previously. Some credibility may be attached to such rumors, however, on the basis of the following dispatch from Jordan concerning the 1902 mission to London for the coronation of Edward VII:

> I did all I could to persuade the Emperor to let them go in their native costume which is really pretty and would have made an effective display of colour. But he would not yield, and they are now in Japan getting rigged out in foreign uniforms. They then proceed to London to complete their foreign outfit before the ceremony commences.[152]

Despite such patronizing attitudes, however, it is known from a conversation between Queen Myŏngsŏng and Isabella Bird Bishop before the former's murder that both the Korean queen and King Kojong longed for Britain to lend its influence in the protection of Korea's independence:

The Queen spoke of Queen Victoria, and said, "She has everything that she can wish—greatness, wealth, and power. Her sons and grandsons are kings and emperors, and her daughters empresses. Does she ever in her glory think of poor Korea? She does so much good in the world, her life is a good. We wish her long life and prosperity"; to which the King added, "England is our best friend." It was really touching to hear the occupants of that ancient but shaky throne speaking in this fashion.[153]

This account by Bishop is also corroborated by Jordan. In fact, according to Jordan, Min Yŏng-whan shared similar feelings for the British sovereign. When a Korean mission was sent to the coronation of King Edward VII in 1902, Jordan wrote the following dispatch to the British assistant undersecretary for foreign affairs Sir Francis L. Bertie:

> The Emperor [Kojong] takes much interest in the coronation. He had certainly a genuine respect for the late Queen and this feeling was shared by many Coreans. Let me give a trivial instance.
>
> A little time ago I was calling upon Min Yung-hwan who was Corean Representative at the Jubilee of 1897. The reception room being cold, he took me into a small private apartment, and there hanging up beside his desk was a neatly framed and very simple and natural picture of the late Queen surrounded by a few of her grandchildren.[154]

Although Kojong had undoubtedly sought the support of the British government by sending Min to Britain, by 1897 the stage was already being set for the future Anglo-Japanese alliance of 1902. The only consolation for Min's efforts appears to have been a speech given to Parliament by George N. Curzon, the British undersecretary for foreign affairs, on 19 July 1897, just two days after the departure of Min and his entourage from London. In this speech, which was reported in the *Times,* Curzon insisted that the British government would maintain Korean independence, neither allowing it to be absorbed by any of its neighbors nor permitting it to be used by any other power for gaining control of the eastern seas.[155] The *Times* correspondent in China, George Morrison, strongly criticized this speech, which was surprisingly at odds with subsequent British policy, as being unwise in the light of the strategic and political situation in the region. That is to say, Morrison seems to have believed that by 1897 Britain was no longer in a position to enforce its will in the region and was inviting humiliation at the hands of either Russia or Japan.[156] And, unfortunately for Korea, Curzon, who had extensive knowledge of the Far East and had visited Korea itself, left the Foreign Office to become viceroy of India in the following year.

The subsequent indifference to the plight of Korea shown by the British Foreign Office, however, did not escape Isabella Bird Bishop's criticism, when she wrote, with a foresight far greater than that of her contemporaries in government, a prescient critique of British policy in Korea:

> The effacement of British political influence has been effected chiefly by a policy of *laissez-faire,* which has produced on the Korean mind the double impression of indifference and feebleness, to which the dubious and hazy diplomatic relationship naturally contributes. If England has no contingent interest in the political future of a country rich in undeveloped resources and valuable harbours, and whose possession by a hostile Power might be a serious peril to her interests in the Far East, her policy during the last few years has been a sure method of evidencing her unconcern.[157]

Conclusion

Min's embassy to Britain was only his second diplomatic mission abroad, but it was also his last. The motivation behind his mission and its exact purpose cannot be clearly determined from the documentary evidence. Nevertheless, it can be assumed that the Korean administration wished to sound out the British and possibly the other European nations' governments concerning the possibility of an international agreement for the neutralization of Korea. It is highly unlikely, however, that Min was able to broach such a topic in either of his two brief meetings with the British foreign secretary Lord Salisbury. Although there is no record of what may have been discussed at these meetings, in all likelihood nothing more significant occurred than an exchange of courtesies.

If Min did discuss the issue with Major Cavendish, the British officer assigned to the Korean mission, the latter would probably have informed him of the difficulty of achieving a goal that relied on a degree of international goodwill and cooperation that did not exist. It should always be borne in mind that Min's two missions to the West in 1896 and 1897 took place during the years that led not only to the relatively limited conflict of the Russo-Japanese War but also to the far more devastating international conflict of World War I a mere ten years later. A contributing factor to Min's decision to abandon his mission in Europe entirely may well have been a clear realization that the idea of Korean neutrality guaranteed by the European powers was simply an impossible dream.

When Min finally returned to Korea in 1898, after spending more than a year in the United States, he continued to hold important posts in the government and sought to mediate between those working for Korea's reform and modernization and the court officialdom. As will be seen in the following chapter, in the final phase of his career from 1897 until his death in 1905, Min played an important role in Korean domestic politics as one of the main proponents of reform during the short-lived Taehan Empire (1897–1910) and as the highest-ranking Korean official to stand in opposition to the protectorate treaty forced on Korea by Japan on 17 November 1905.

5

THE FINAL PHASE

Min's Sojourn in Washington and Return to Korea in September 1898

After leaving Britain in July 1897, Min Yŏng-hwan traveled directly to the United States and spent almost a year in Washington, D.C., where, according to the *Independent,* he stayed together with Min Sang-ho and Min Yŏng-ch'an at "the Hamilton House."[1] To avoid the displeasure of King Kojong and possible punishment if he returned to Seoul, Min Yŏng-hwan and his colleagues remained in Washington in self-imposed exile for more than a year. As has been mentioned in the previous chapter, Min even requested that he be appointed Korea's minister at Washington, a post that he had originally been chosen for in 1895 but had been prevented from taking up because of the assassination of Queen Myŏngsŏng. His request, however, was rejected, and he and his fellow exiles appear to have spent their time acquainting themselves further with aspects of Western modernization. Min Yŏng-hwan himself even became quite fluent in English.

Significantly, Min was also present at the deathbed of Sŏ Kwang-bŏm, a former conspirator in the coup of 1884 and a progressive official, who had come to prominence during the Kabo-Ŭlmi reforms of 1894–1895. Min also attended Sŏ's funeral, which was boycotted by Yi Pŏm-jin, a pro-Russian official who had replaced Sŏ as the Korean minister at Washington in 1896.

Another of the leaders of the coup of 1884, Sŏ Chae-p'il, was also in Washing-

ton at this time, having resigned from his post as an adviser to the Korean government in 1897 under pressure from conservative forces within the Korean
court. After his return to the United States, Sŏ had continued to write letters
to the new editor of the *Independent,* Yun Ch'i-ho. These letters were published
in that newspaper under the rather pretentious pseudonym "Columbus." In
one of his "Letters from Washington," Sŏ, after criticizing the conservatism and
incompetence of Yi Pŏm-jin, who had to rely on his twelve-year-old son to in-
terpret for him at official functions, wrote an approving, if somewhat patronizing, account of how both Min Yŏng-hwan and Min Sang-ho were spending
their time in the American capital:

> Gen. Min Yungwhan also speaks English quite fluently and he seems to have ac-
> quired a great deal of useful Western ideas. It is simply marvellous to notice how
> the American atmosphere works such wonderful changes in one's ideas! Col. Min
> Sangho is reading law and I would not be surprised if he turns up in Seoul one
> of these days and tells his friends that the law of the country must be made for
> the interests of the inhabitants thereof and it must be obeyed by the ruler as well
> as the ruled. It will sound strange to many of his friends will it not.[2]

Apart from this tantalizing piece of information from Sŏ Chae-p'il, there is
sadly no other record available to trace the activities of the three Mins in the
United States. Nevertheless, it is clear that the experience of life in both Britain
and America was an important one for Min Yŏng-hwan and, as will be seen in
this chapter, led him to adopt a basically Anglo-American orientation in his
efforts to maintain his nation's sovereignty and independence during the final
phase of his career.

On 22 May 1898, Min Yŏng-hwan was granted a special pardon by Kojong
and was appointed to the rank of lieutenant general (*pujang*).[3] As a consequence
he, Min Sang-ho, and Min Yŏng-ch'an returned to Seoul via Hawai'i on 14 September of the same year.[4] The country to which Min Yŏng-hwan and his entourage returned, however, was no longer the Kingdom of Chosŏn (Chosŏn wangguk), but was now the Taehan Empire (Taehan cheguk). Almost one year earlier,
on 12 October 1897, while Min was still in Washington, Kojong had been crowned
emperor. The Korean sovereign had taken this step apparently only after the presentation of nine memorials by the prime minister, representing the entire government. It is clear, however, from the fact that while Min Yŏng-hwan was in
Europe, he had been instructed at least as early as July 1897 to gain the acceptance of the treaty powers for this transition from kingdom to empire, that Kojong thoroughly approved of the action and may well have initiated it himself.[5]
Kojong's elevation from king to emperor had also been supported by the

leadership of the Independence Club and its newspaper, the *Independent*. The purpose behind this transition from kingdom to empire was to assert Korea's parity with the neighboring empires of China, Japan, and Russia. The action was, therefore, seen by the leading progressive, Sŏ Chae-p'il, as "upholding the dignity of the nation as an independent state."[6] In terms of Korean foreign policy the decision to elevate the nation's status to that of an empire may also be seen as reflecting an abandonment of the Korean court's search for a benevolent protector as a result of its disillusioning experiences with Russia. Instead, Kojong and his court now sought to secure some form of international guarantee for Korean independence and neutrality, and to this end looked to Great Britain and the United States to lead the way. Min Yŏng-hwan, who had good relationships with many members of the foreign, diplomatic, and missionary communities in Seoul, appears to have been one of the leading proponents of this policy, and on his return to Korea, he actively worked to gain the interest and sympathy of the American and European representatives at Seoul for the cause of Korean independence. Meanwhile, on the domestic front, he gave his full support, albeit mainly from behind the scenes, to the Independence Club's efforts to reform the administration.

Min's Alignment with the Independence Club

The late 1890s were turbulent times for the Chosŏn dynasty as it sought to preserve itself and Korean independence in the face of irresistible external forces and its own internal contradictions. On his return from the United States, Min Yŏng-hwan became increasingly involved with the Independence Club and provided it with tacit support from within the court, despite the antipathy this caused among more conservative members of the Min clan, such as Min Chong-muk and Min Yŏng-gi. On 29 September 1898, Min Yŏng-hwan was appointed special entry officer *(tŭkchin'gwan)* in the Department of the Royal Household (Kungnaebu).[7] Soon after, in October, he was once again appointed minister of war and, according to the *Independent,* put forward the following ten-point reform program to Emperor Kojong:

> We learn from a reliable source that Mr. Min Youngwhan, the new Minister of War, advised His Majesty the other night (1) to clear the Palace of special courtiers (whisperers) of all grades, sorcerers, sorceresses and fortune-tellers, reissuing and limiting the number of gate-passes; (2) to throw the responsibility of the government upon the Ministers; (3) to select qualified officers with longer terms of service; (4) to appoint capable governors and magistrates; (5) to economize ex-

penses, stopping work on the Empress, [*sic*] grave, etc.; (6) to enforce laws without fear or favor; (7) to make trials fair and prompt; (8) to prohibit secret bribes and requests; (9) to investigate into the number, etc., of the Koreans who have become naturalized under foreign governments; (10) to employ men according to ability irrespective to caste.[8]

If we examine these ten points individually and compare them with the recommendations that Min made four years earlier in *Ch'ŏnilch'aek,* we can see the basic consistency of Min's political thinking. The first point appears to address the problem of the demoralized state of Kojong after the death of his wife and is, therefore, a recommendation that did not appear in his earlier essay. Points 3, 4, and 8, however, correspond to the first and second of his ten proposals for preparation and defense in *Ch'ŏnilchaek,* "employing talented people" and "awakening the fundamental principles of government." Point 2 reflects his positive appreciation of constitutional monarchy in Russia and Great Britain, which may be found in *Haech'ŏn ch'ubŏm* and *Sagu sokch'o.* Point 9 shows Min's concern for the growing number of Koreans living overseas and reflects his direct experience of the problems faced by Korean emigrants in Russia during his travels through Siberia in 1896 and in Hawai'i during his return from the United States in 1898. Point 5 was, of course, addressing another result of the assassination of Queen Myŏngsŏng but is in line with Min's general concern for the economic state of Korea. Points 5 and 10, however, clearly reflect the concerns of the leadership of the Independence Club for justice for all and the abolition of the sharply delineated class system, which still prevailed in Korea. It is clear from these proposals, therefore, why the Independence Club leaders should have viewed Min, with his extensive experience in the West compared to other leading members of the court, as their most valuable ally in the Taehan government.

According to the *Independent,* however, Min's "too progressive views . . . displeased His Majesty,"[9] and he was relieved of his post as minister of war and appointed state councillor on 21 October 1898.[10] By this time the Independence Club was increasingly coming into open conflict with the Imperial Association (Hwangguk hyŏphoe). This association had been formed from the Peddlers' Guild, an organization with strong traditional links to the Chosŏn monarchy, as a means of counteracting the increasing popularity and vociferousness of the Independence Club. The organization was controlled by reactionary forces in the court and was used to suppress the leadership and supporters of the Independence Club by violence and intimidation. As a consequence of his efforts to push through reforms at court, Min himself became a target of the Imperial Association's persecution and was temporarily forced into hiding in October 1898, soon after his return to Seoul.[11]

On 24 November 1898, however, Min successfully established the Hŭnghwa Private School (Hŭnghwa sarip hakkyo). The school, which was in front of the Hŭnghwa Gate in Seoul, emphasized practical study. The foundation endowment was contributed by former magistrate Kim Sin-yŏng; its governors were Min Yŏng-hwan, Im Pyŏng-gwi, and one of the leading figures in the Independence Club, Chŏng Kyo. The subjects studied were English, Japanese, arithmetic, geography (topography), history, composition, debating, and gymnastics. Its first headmaster was another Independence Club activist, Namgung Ŏk.[12]

According to the *Hwangsŏng sinmun,* by 13 July 1900 the student body numbered approximately 130 students. No land survey based on modern scientific techniques had been carried out on the Korean peninsula at that time, and the school was unique in providing its students with training in land surveying. Min and the other progressive governors and teachers of the school were probably motivated to introduce this subject in order to provide trained personnel for the Kwangmu Land Survey, which was carried out from 1898 to 1904 to enable the Taehan administration to reassert its rights to taxable land that had been omitted illegally from the land registers.[13] Land surveying, however, was commonly taught in private schools throughout the period before Korea's annexation in 1910 and was possibly promoted not only with a view to reestablishing the government's tax rights but also to prevent Japanese settlers from taking advantage, either by force or by stealth, of the confused state of land ownership records at that time.[14]

After the signing of the 1905 protectorate treaty, the school focused on inculcating a patriotic spirit in its students and educating them for the task of restoring Korea's national sovereignty. The school survived only until 1911, however, when lack of funds prompted the Japanese colonial administration to shut it down.[15]

To placate the increasing mistrust of the administration among the general populace in Seoul in late 1898, Kojong subsequently appointed Min vice president of the Privy Council (Chungch'uwŏn); but by late November the situation had deteriorated and on 26 November the *Independent* reported,

> Kim Hongkiu the Acting Premier followed by several of his colleagues went to the palace in the night. They again begged the Emperor to grant the popular demands by dispersing the pedlars, appointing new and popular Minister of War. His Majesty after many hours of hesitation appointed Mr. Min Yongwhan, the Minister of Home Affairs, the Acting Minister of War. . . . While the people have confidence in Mr. Min, it is rumoured that he refuses to take the acting Ministership of War as it does not give him full power.[16]

The cabinet was constantly reshuffled over the following weeks, and Min was finally appointed vice president *(ch'amjŏng)* of the State Council on 4 December.[17] Again he was unable to introduce any reforms in the government because of the concerted opposition of the court, and on 11 December 1898, he and his long-time political ally, Han Kyu-sŏl, the minister of war, sent in their resignations.[18]

On 15 December Yun Ch'i-ho, who had been the editor of the *Independent* since the departure of Sŏ Chae-p'il, was elected vice president of the Privy Council, and his name was sent to the State Council so that he could receive his appointment from the emperor. At the same time the "Privy Councillors took the bold step of recommending candidates to the Council of State for the various Ministries of the Government."[19]

According to the same report in the *Independent,* each of the thirty privy councillors was asked to write down the names of eleven people who they thought were "most worthy of the Cabinet positions." More than two hundred people were nominated, with Min Yŏng-hwan receiving the second most nominations among all the candidates. The results of the ballot, which were published by the *Independent,* were as follows: "Min Yŏng-jun, 18 votes; Min Yŏng-hwan, 15 votes; Yi Chung-ha, 15 votes; Pak Chŏng-yang, 14 votes; Han Kyu-sŏl, 13 votes; Yun Ch'i-ho, 12 votes; Kim Chong-han, 11 votes; Pak Yŏng-hyo, 10 votes; Sŏ Chae-p'il, 10 votes; Ch'oe Ik-hyŏn, 10 votes, and Yun Yong-ku, 8 votes."[20]

The result of this ballot clearly reflects a wide variety of opinion among the privy councillors. Min Yŏng-jun was undoubtedly a conservative, yet he garnered the most votes, perhaps because he was considered the most effective politician. At the other end of the spectrum were two nominees who had led the coup of 1884, Sŏ Chae-p'il and Pak Yŏng-hyo. Even Ch'oe Ik-hyŏn, the diehard Confucian conservative, who had so adamantly opposed the opening of Korea two decades earlier, received as many votes as the progressives Sŏ and Pak. Representing the two poles of the middle ground were Yun Ch'i-ho, who had had peripheral connections with the conspirators of the coup of 1884 and, of course, Min Yŏng-hwan himself, with his background in the Korean court. That Min garnered fifteen votes, despite lacking the political power base of his elder relative Min Yŏng-jun or the progressive credentials of Yun Ch'i-ho, Sŏ Chae-p'il, and Pak Yŏng-hyo, shows that Min was the candidate most likely to unite both ends of the political spectrum in Seoul.

Unfortunately, this early experiment in limited democracy ended in failure. Because of the nomination of Pak Yŏng-hyo, the president of the Privy Council, Yi Chŏng-gun, declined to submit the recommendations to the State Council. The nomination of Pak, who had been implicated in a plot to assassinate Queen Myŏngsŏng and had been forced to flee to Japan in 1895, proved to be a serious tactical error as it appeared to give credence to the assertions of the enemies of the Independence Club that it was in some way subversive. The Privy Council's efforts to establish an elected body with legislative powers finally failed, and the Independence Club was disbanded in December 1898 as a result of government suppression backed by an imperial edict and the evaporation of public support. Yun Ch'i-ho compromised with the court and took a magistrate's post in Wŏnsan, while Min Yŏng-hwan was reduced to working behind the scenes to curb the excesses of the court and to encourage Emperor Kojong, who had been demoralized by the violent death of his consort in 1895, to adopt enlightened policies.

Min's efforts to guide his sovereign, however, do not appear to have met with much success, and the demoralized state of the Korean emperor became increasingly apparent even to the foreign community. In January 1904 Jordan wrote to Sir Ernest Satow, "Our Emperor is quite hopeless. Nero fiddling when Rome was in a blaze was a dignified performance compared with what goes on in the Palace enclosure adjoining us."[21]

Nevertheless, evidence of the extent to which Min Yŏng-hwan used his influence at court to intervene on the behalf of Korea's movement for political reform is given by Yun Ch'i-ho, who recorded in his diary entry of 1 January 1899,

In the P.M. (about 2) Jung Hang Mo [Chŏng Hang-mo] called on me. He said that Messrs. Han Kiu Sul [Han Kyu-sŏl], Kwon Jai Hyong [Kwŏn Chae-hyŏng], Min Yong Whan [Min Yŏng-hwan] and Min Byeung Suk [Min Pyŏng-sŏk] succeeded yesterday evening in obtaining the promise of Min Yong Kui [Min Yŏng-gi] to make peace with the People's Party (Manminhoe). Min Yong Kui was to present a memorial to the throne withdrawing the charges of treason that he had made against the popular leaders.[22]

This kind of support earned Min Yŏng-hwan the enmity of conservative elements in the court, and three days later in a memorial presented by Im Tŏk-ki, he was criticized together with Pak Chŏng-yang and Han Kyu-sŏl for "covering up the crimes of the Independence Club members."[23] Soon afterward Min, who was minister of finance at this time, handed in his resignation along with another ally of the reformers at the court, Minister of Education Pak Chŏng-yang.[24]

Nevertheless, despite such opposition within the court, between 1898 and 1905 Min continued to hold important posts, including those of state councillor (ŭijŏngbu ch'amjŏng), minister (taesin) of Home Affairs (Naebu), of War

(Kunbu),[25] of the State Council (Ŭijŏngbu), of Finance (T'akchibu), and of Education (Hakpu); president *(ch'ongjang)* of the Bureau of Accounts (Hoegyeguk) in the Department of Military Affairs and president *(ch'ongjae)* of Military Reform (Kunbŏp kyojŏng); master *(kyŏng)* of Ceremonies and Rites (Chang'yewŏn), president *(ch'ongjae)* of the Department of Medals and Awards (P'yohunwŏn); and police commissioner *(hŏnbyŏngsa yŏnggwan)*.[26]

In 1900 the flow of memorials resumed. As president of the Accounts Bureau in the Department of Military Affairs, Min was awarded the title "Defender of the Nation" *(poguk)*.[27] Characteristically, Min declined to accept the title on the grounds that he was unworthy to receive such an honor. Needless to say, the emperor saw otherwise, and the title remained. In the eighth month of the same year, Min again offered his resignation from the position of president of the Accounts Bureau in the Department of Military Affairs, and all his other duties. His resignation was duly rejected, and Min subsequently offered his resignation from his concurrent appointment as composer of the motto for the imperial apartment *(ch'imjŏn sangnyangmun chesulgwan)*. Min insisted that he had no literary skill and likened himself to "a blind person being asked to write elegant calligraphy or a deaf person being asked to play harmoniously on the pan pipes."[28] In this particular case permission to resign was granted.

The Final Phase of Min's Official Career and His Declining Health

In 1901 Min offered seven memorials in succession resigning from all his official duties. In the first instance he argued that he lacked the basic capacity to undertake his responsibilities. In the later memorials, however, he placed increasing emphasis on his chronic bad health, which prevented him from carrying out his duties. Despite his pleas, the emperor insisted that he remain in office and refused to excuse him on the grounds of his illness.[29]

In the following year, Min resigned from the post of president of the Department of Medals (P'yohunwŏn), insisting on his lack of ability in the fields of military affairs, accounting, and the management of personnel. He mentioned his deteriorating health again and pleaded with the emperor to be relieved of all his duties. As before, he was ordered to continue in his post.[30]

Later in the same year Min presented a memorial demanding the punishment of Kim Yun-sik, Yi Sŏng-o, and others for their part in the plot that had resulted in the death of the queen seven years earlier. This was followed by a second memorial on the following day, in which he once again urged the emperor to apply the full penalty of the law to Kim and Yi. He was informed in the official response to his memorial, however, that the matter had already been settled by the government.[31]

Min's Activities in the Bureau of Emigration

The Bureau of Emigration (Yuminwŏn) was established by imperial edict on 16 November 1902. The bureau was set up within the Imperial Household Department rather than the Foreign Office and consequently came under the overall control of the most powerful official in the Korean government, Yi Yong-ik. Yi was originally from a very humble background and was described by William Sands, the American adviser to the court, as "the Peng Yang [P'yŏngyang] ruffian miner."[32] Nevertheless, Yi had gained the trust and gratitude of the royal family after he had acted as a go-between for Queen Myŏngsŏng and Min Yŏng-ik while the former was in hiding during the Soldiers' Rebellion of 1882. He had gradually risen through the ranks of the court until he came to control the royal finances. An ambivalent figure, considered one of the most corrupt officials in Kojong's court by Western observers, he is generally regarded as a patriotic figure in Korean historiography and respected as the founder of Korea University.[33] Yi Yong-ik and Min Yŏng-hwan were both among the founders of the so-called Reform party (Kaehyŏktang) in 1902. This organization, however, does not appear to have had any significant impact on the period, possibly because of Yi's clash with Min over Korean emigration to Hawai'i.[34]

The Bureau of Emigration came into being as a result of the lobbying of the American minister in Korea, Horace N. Allen, on behalf of the Hawaiian Sugar Planters' Association's representative, Ebon Faxon Bishop. Bishop had arrived in Korea in October 1902 with $25,000 "to take the necessary steps toward inaugurating the Korean immigration."[35] Korean emigration was approved by Min Yŏng-hwan, who became the president of the Emigration Bureau on 10 December 1902, and was also supported by Yun Ch'i-ho, Yi Ha-yŏng, and, in its initial and final stages, Emperor Kojong. Its greatest opponent was Yi Yong-ik, the de facto controller of Korean finances. Yi had been out of power at the time of the bureau's establishment, but after regaining his post as head of the Department of the Imperial Household, he finally persuaded Kojong to abolish the emigration bureau in 1903. He argued that the emigration of Koreans to Hawai'i and Mexico was akin to their being sold into slavery. Although it was true that Koreans who had emigrated to Mexico, under the auspices of a Japanese company, had been mistreated, those who went to Hawai'i undoubtedly had better prospects than if they had remained in Korea.

Patterson reveals, however, that it was much more likely that Yi opposed emigration both because he gained no personal profit from it and because a mass exodus of Korean laborers abroad would mean a diminution of Korea's taxable population.[36] Yi's opposition to emigration also received support from the Japanese. It is possible that Japan deliberately involved itself in promoting Korean emigration to Mexico, where it was known that laborers were mistreated, in order to give emigration a bad name in Korea. Some Japanese may also have wished to divert the competition posed to Japanese laborers in Hawai'i by Korean emigrants to another destination.

Behind the scenes in Seoul, Korean emigration was actively opposed by the Japanese minister Hayashi Gonsuke and was eventually stifled by the Japanese financial adviser, Megata Tanetarō, who prevented the necessary finances from being forwarded to Yun Ch'i-ho during his fact-finding mission of September 1905 to determine the conditions of Korean contract laborers in Hawai'i and Mexico.[37] As a result of the termination of Yun's mission and the withholding of funds for any additional Korean diplomatic missions abroad, Japan effectively prevented the establishment of a Korean consulate in Hawai'i. In addition, the true fate of the Korean laborers in Mexico was never ascertained.

After Korea's foreign relations came under Japanese control with the signing of the protectorate treaty in November 1905, the Japanese government prohibited Korean emigration so that Koreans would not compete with Japanese laborers in Hawai'i and, what was more important, so that the community of overseas Koreans in the United States could not expand and become an effective source of opposition to Japanese plans to colonize Korea. As it happened, the small Korean community in Hawai'i was later to play a key role both in attempting to enlist the support of the United States in opposing the establishment of a Japanese protectorate in Korea and also in keeping alive Korean aspirations for independence during the colonial years from 1910 until 1945.

Min Yŏng-hwan's active support for Korean emigration to Hawai'i, which was considered an abandonment of filial duty by Confucian conservatives, seems to have been motivated by his desire to enable Koreans to escape from impoverishment and also to establish stronger links with the United States by the establishment of a significant Korean community there. During his trip across Siberia in 1896 and his stopover in Hawai'i on his return to Korea from the United States in 1898, Min had seen how Koreans freed from the oppression of misrule in their own country could flourish and adapt. He must have hoped that Korean emigration to Hawai'i would also strengthen Korea's links with the United States and prevent Japan from deciding the fate of Korea unilaterally.

Min's plan was hindered, however, by the fact that the U.S. government, which had annexed the island nation in 1898, was opposed to further East Asian emigration to Hawai'i, preferring to see it populated by people of European origin. According to Wayne Patterson, the Hawaiian Sugar Planters' Association's recruitment policy in Korea, which involved the payment of passage for the Koreans and a loan of $50 to satisfy American immigration requirements, was in fact illegal according to U.S. immigration law and placed the whole project on a shaky foundation from the outset.[38]

In 1903 Min resigned all his official duties largely because of his poor health but was only permitted to stand down from his post as vice president *(puch'ongjae)* of the Department of Emigration. Min repeated his request to be relieved of all his duties on the following day but was told that he could not be spared.[39]

At the end of the same year Min resigned from the post of president of the Office of Rites (Yesig'wŏnjang). The Yesig'wŏn was an office established within the Department of the Imperial Household in 1900 and was responsible for the translation of diplomatic documents, including the emperor's personal letters to foreign sovereigns *(ch'insŏ)* and credential letters *(kuksŏ)*. This office was eventually abolished after Japan's annexation of Korea in 1910. In an anguished memorial of resignation from this office, Min informed the emperor that he was so ill that he could scarcely eat or get up from his bed and begged to be excused from his official duties. His poor health must have been obvious to Kojong at this stage as this was one of the rare occasions in Min's career that he was granted permission to resign.[40]

Min's Loss of Influence at Court and His Protest against the 1905 Protectorate Treaty

In 1904 Min held the posts of minister of home affairs, minister of education *(hakpu taesin)*, acting president *(ch'ongjae)* of the Department of Awards (Imsi sŏri p'yohunwŏn), and head of the welcoming committee for the Japanese ambassador extraordinary *(Ilbon t'ŭkp'a taesa yŏngjŏp wiwŏnjang)* (Itō Hirobumi). In relation to this latter appointment, it is worth noting Min's continued involvement in diplomatic affairs after his return from the United States in 1898, as he also played a major role in the welcoming committees for Prince Heinrich of Prussia in 1899 and Prince George of Bavaria in 1904.[41]

In addition to the above appointments Min also held the posts of president of the Bureau of Accounts in the Department of Military Affairs, head *(p'ansa)* of the Office of Royal Connections (Tollyŏngwŏn), minister of finance, and head *(kwanjang)* of the Royal Bodyguard (Sijongmu).[42]

In his role as head of the welcoming committee for Itō Hirobumi, who led

a special mission to Seoul in March 1904, Min was privy to the intention behind the mission, which appears to have been the distribution of bribes to the
Korean emperor and other palace officials. On 31 March Min confided his observations to the British Minister, John Jordan, who duly reported to his superior, the Marquess of Lansdowne, "The whole object of the mission was, according to General Min, who belongs to the party of Corean reformers, to
propitiate the Palace and the Emperor, regardless of the interests of the Corean
people."[43]

Throughout this time, Min continued to act as a bridge between moderate
progressives such as Yun Ch'i-ho and the Korean emperor. On 12 April 1904,
Yun Ch'i-ho recorded how Min had introduced him to Emperor Kojong:

> This a.m. at about 4 had the honour of being introduced to the presence of the
> Emperor by General Min Y. Whan [Min Yŏng-hwan]. His Majesty said to Min
> "Wae injŏsŏ wannŭi?" [What brings you here now?] He asked where I lived. He
> was in good spirit laughing and talking as if nothing of consequence has hap-
> pened. I was involuntarily moved to tears at his kindly words. Such the power
> of an autocrat over a common mind?[44]

In the same year Min, together with his progressive ally, Han Kyu-sŏl, was
responsible for obtaining a pardon for the young Christian political activist Syngman Rhee, who had been condemned to life imprisonment in Chongno Prison
for his part in antigovernment demonstrations around the time of the popular movement for a National Assembly in late 1898.[45] According to Rhee's American biographer, Robert Oliver, after his release from prison,

> Rhee urged Prince Min and General Hahn to go to the United States to plead
> for invocation of the mutual defense article in the Amity Treaty. The emperor,
> however, was so tightly in the toils of his Japanese captors that he could not give
> them an official appointment. Prince Min and the few others who were work-
> ing together in a last desperate effort to save Korean independence decided that
> Rhee should be the one to go. He was provided with a student passport and with
> messages to the Korean legation in Washington, which he concealed in the false
> bottom of his trunk. Then accompanied by Lee Chung Hyuk (who took the an-
> glicized name of Howard Leigh), he left Korea ostensibly to study in the United
> States.[46]

Rhee's plea for the "invocation of the mutual defense article in the Amity
Treaty" is a reference to the controversial "good offices" clause in the Korean-
American treaty. This clause, contained in article 1 of the treaty, read as fol-

lows: "If other Powers deal unjustly or oppressively with either Government, the other shall render assistance and protection, or shall act as mediator in order to ensure the preservation of perfect peace."[47]

Although it has been subsequently argued by some modern historians that this was simply diplomatic "boilerplate" and that the Koreans were naïve to place any faith in the clause, the former American minister in Seoul, Horace N. Allen, was of a different opinion. In his book of memoirs of his twenty-one years spent in Korea, the last eight of which were spent as minister of the U.S. legation, Allen wrote,

> Korea has taken that treaty to mean just what the words say, while we seem to have utterly disregarded the solemn promise we therein voluntarily made, that we should lend her our good offices should she be oppressed by a third power; thus breaking our faith with a people who trusted us implicitly, and who consented to the opening of her doors on this our guarantee of friendly aid.[48]

Rhee arrived in Washington on 31 December 1904 and met the first secretary at the Korean legation, Hong Chöl-su. Hong had already received a letter from Min asking him to "give Rhee every possible assistance."[49] While he was in Washington, Rhee presented letters from Min and Han to Senator Hugh A. Dinsmore, a former American minister in Seoul. According to Oliver, "Dinsmore was delighted to hear from his two old friends and promised to arrange an interview for Rhee with Secretary of State John Hay."[50] Hay was the author of the Open Door policy for China and was considered by Dinsmore to be in favor of continued Korean independence. Rhee subsequently met Hay at the State Department together with Dinsmore and was given Hay's full assurance that the United States was in favor of an independent Korea. Oliver continues the story:

> As they left the State Department, Senator Dinsmore said that he was fully satisfied with the conference, and so was Rhee. Rhee wrote out full reports on the meeting addressed to Prince Min and General Hahn, and Senator Dinsmore had them sent to Seoul in the American legation diplomatic pouch. Rhee always felt that this assurance from Hay would have resulted in saving Korea's independence except for the tragic fact that Hay died that summer and was succeeded as secretary of state by Elihu Root. So close did events come to averting the tragic destiny that led from Japan's seizure of Korea to Manchuria and on to Pearl Harbor![51]

Although Rhee subsequently managed in August 1905 to gain an interview with the U.S. president, Theodore Roosevelt, at his summer retreat at Oyster

Bay on Long Island, the president simply acknowledged his request and asked him to present his case formally through the proper diplomatic channels. As it happened, the Korean minister in Washington, Kim Yun-jŏng, had come under the influence of the Japanese and refused to act without explicit instructions from the Korean court, which, of course, was no longer free to issue any instructions contrary to the will of its Japanese advisers. Consequently, Rhee's mission ended in failure. On 10 September "Rhee received a note from Prince Min Young Whan commending him and Yoon for their efforts and enclosing $300 for their expenses."[52]

Unbeknown to Rhee or the United States Congress, Secretary of War William Howard Taft, who had supplied Rhee and Yun Pyŏng-gu with a letter of introduction to Roosevelt while they were in Hawai'i in June 1905, had, in fact, been on his way to a meeting with the Japanese prime minister, Katsura Tarō, at which he concluded a secret agreement. Although this was not a legal agreement but a private "understanding" between the Katsura government and the Roosevelt administration, it effectively acknowledged Japanese interests on the Korean peninsula in return for a similar acknowledgment by Japan of U.S. interests in the Philippines.[53]

In the final year of his life, Min Yŏng-hwan was appointed to various high-ranking posts, including member *(mugwan)* of the Royal Bodyguard, prime minister *(ŭijŏngbu ch'amjŏng taesin)*, minister of foreign affairs *(oemu taesin)*, and head of the Royal Bodyguard.[54]

While Yun Pyŏng-gu and Syngman Rhee were striving to gain support for Korean independence in the United States, Min Yŏng-hwan himself came into direct conflict with the Japanese chargé d'affaires in Seoul, Hagiwara Moriichi, who in May 1905 was attempting to acquire the concession for free coastal and inland navigation in Korea. According to Yun Ch'i-ho, "The Korean Cabinet, headed by Min Yong Whan, flatly refused to grant it," and as a result Min was forced to resign from his post as prime minister under pressure from Hagiwara.[55]

Around this time, Min also expressed his determined opposition to Japanese attempts to terminate Korean diplomatic representation abroad, including the post of his own brother, Min Yŏng-ch'an, who was the Korean representative in Paris. In his entry of 4 August 1905, Yun Ch'i-ho records: "When Mr. Min Yong Whan was the acting prime minister, some months ago, Hayashi actually told him that he (Hayashi) had persuaded Brown not to pay the salaries of the Korean ministers abroad. Mr. Min said, 'I hope my brother would starve to death than withdraw from Paris.'"[56]

Although Min continued to hold high office, it is clear that he was powerless to resist the increasing Japanese influence in the Korean administration as the Russo-Japanese War progressed toward a victorious conclusion for Japan.

The fact that toward the end of his life Min merely held the post of head of the Royal Bodyguard is evidence of the way in which he was sidelined in the administration as a result of the pressure exerted by Japanese advisers within the Taehan government.

The Japanese defeat of Russia in the Russo-Japanese War rang the final death knell for Korean independence. This time there was to be no Western intervention to rob Japan of the fruits of its victory, as had happened ten years earlier after the Sino-Japanese War. By the time of the conclusion of the war with Russia, Japan had already obtained the tacit acceptance of the two great powers that might have prevented it from realizing its ambitions on the Korean peninsula: namely, Great Britain and the United States.

The first Anglo-Japanese alliance, concluded in January 1902, saw Britain abandon its previous policy of "splendid isolation"; and in article 3 of the second alliance treaty, concluded in August 1905, the British government explicitly recognized Japan's paramountcy on the Korean peninsula: "Japan possessing paramount political, military, and economic interests in Corea, Great Britain recognizes the right of Japan to take such measures of guidance, control, and protection in Corea as she may deem proper and necessary to safeguard and advance those interests."[57]

This acceptance of Japanese ambitions in Korea was given in return for Japan's recognition of British interests in India as well as its tacit support for Britain in the latter's rivalry with Russia. In effect, this meant that Britain would place no impediment in the way of Japan's making Korea its protectorate. This was a view with which the British minister in Seoul, Sir John Jordan, concurred in a private letter dated 7 July 1905 to Sir Claude MacDonald, the British minister to Japan:

> It may be heresy to say so but I feel certain that nothing short of a protectorate will ever save the situation here. In the interests of the Coreans themselves this is the only possible solution and the people as distinguished from the officials would I believe infinitely prefer it to the Government which they have had during last 10 years of nominal independence.[58]

It is worth noting, however, that Jordan still felt that his superiors might consider the idea of Korea's becoming a Japanese protectorate "heresy" as late as July 1905.

The disastrous consequences for Korea of the British government's decision to rely on the Japanese to make up for its own inability to project naval power into Northeast Asia was not lost on the Korean chargé d'affaires, Yi Han-ŭng, in London. After numerous efforts "to enlist the support of the British government for the independence of Korea," Yi committed suicide in a state of despair on 12 May 1905.[59] The connection between the unprincipled pragmatism of British foreign policy and Yi's death, however, was conveniently ignored by the report in the *Times,* which stated blandly: "The Chargé D'Affaires had recently been unwell and greatly depressed, and it is known that whatever may have happened lately, he for some time had no sort of communication with his Government, and was left without resource from them."[60]

Britain was not alone in making common cause with the Japanese to counter what was seen as the threat of Russian expansionism. As has been mentioned, Theodore Roosevelt, while presenting a façade of impartiality to Rhee on his visit to Oyster Bay, in fact also favored the Japanese and fully concurred with the secret "memorandum of agreement" drawn up by Secretary of War William Howard Taft and Prime Minister Katsura Tarō, in which Japan's interests in Korea were to be respected in return for Japanese recognition of America's newly acquired interests in the Philippines, which were the result of its victory in the Spanish-American War in the summer of 1898.

The conclusion of the Treaty of Portsmouth on 5 September 1905 was a devastating blow to Korean hopes for continued independence. Russia relinquished its claims on the Korean peninsula, removing the last obstacle to the establishment of a Japanese protectorate. With the signing of the Ŭlsa Treaty of Protection on 17 November 1905 the protectorate became a reality. The foundations for the Ŭlsa treaty had already been laid during the Russo-Japanese War by the Japanese-Korean Protocol and the Agreement on Advisers signed in February and August 1904 respectively. Ironically, the United States, which had been the first Western power to make a treaty with Korea, was also the first to withdraw its legation after Japan transferred control of Korea's foreign relations from Seoul to Tokyo.

The Korean people, including most, if not all, Korean historians, have never accepted the legitimacy of the 1905 protectorate treaty.[61] Kojong never applied his seal to the document despite the continuous browbeating of Itō Hirobumi and Hayashi Gonsuke. Also, the cabinet ministers themselves, the so-called five traitors of Ŭlsa (*Ŭlsa ojŏk*), only applied their seals under duress, as may be seen from the following account of the signing of the treaty sent by the German minister-resident in Seoul, Conrad von Saldern, to the German imperial chancellor, Bernhard Prince von Bülow, on 20 November 1905:

> The treaty is signed by the Japanese envoy Hayashi and by the Korean foreign minister Pak Che-sun.
>
> This minister was empowered to negotiate with the Japanese but was not authorised to sign a treaty. The emperor is sticking to his "No". Incidentally an-

other Korean gentleman close to the emperor has just told me that the foreign minister never signed it, but that only the seal of his office was placed on the document by Japanese officials with threats of violence and the collusion of the Japanese gendarmes.[62]

The meticulousness of Japanese planning, the skill of the Japanese in preparing the field ahead of time, as well as the extent of the cooperation that they managed to elicit from the Western powers in making Korea their protectorate is partially revealed by Gottfried Ney, who replaced von Saldern as the German minister resident in Seoul. In Ney's account of the British chargé d'affaires Cockburn's justification to the Korean government of Britain's inclusion of Korea in article 2 of the Anglo-Japanese treaty of 1905, he wrote, "In his note the chargé d'affaires pointed to the agreement concluded between Japan and Korea in 1904 and stated that article 2 was simply an acknowledgement of the actual relationships created by that agreement."[63]

The wording of this justification bears an uncanny resemblance to the excuse for the nonintervention of the United States given by Secretary of State Elihu Root to Min's younger brother, Min Yŏng-ch'an, who had been sent by Emperor Kojong after Syngman Rhee in December 1905 to invoke the "good offices" clause of the Korean-American treaty of 22 May 1882. In his reply to Min Yŏng-ch'an's request for American assistance, Root wrote that the existing

> treaties between Japan and Korea appear to be of such a character as practically to give Japan control over the foreign relations of Korea, and to make the latest treaty of November 17, 1905, which is now called in question, but a slight advance upon the relations of control previously existing. Those previous relations of control amount to a complete bar to any interference by the United States under the treaty of 1883.[64]

Although no documentary evidence has yet been revealed, it is difficult to avoid concluding that the Western powers were deliberately briefed to respond to Korea's appeals in this way by the Japanese government, especially when it is noted that a copy of the above communication was sent to the Japanese chargé d'affaires ad interim in Washington, doubtless as a gesture of the full cooperation of the State Department in the matter.[65]

It was against this background of coercion, collusion, and international indifference to Japanese ambitions in Korea that Min Yŏng-hwan, who held the post of head of the Royal Bodyguard, and a group of officials took up the protest against Japan's diplomacy of force majeure. Min had been away from Seoul at the time of the signing of the treaty, attending the reburial ceremony of his first wife in Yongin.[66] He returned to Seoul on the evening of 18 November and heard for the first time that the protectorate treaty had been signed on the evening of the previous day by the Taehan cabinet ministers: namely, Minister of Foreign Affairs Pak Che-sun, Minister of Home Affairs Yi Chi-yong, Minister of Military Affairs Yi Kŭn-t'aek, Minister of Education Yi Wan-yong, and Minister of Agriculture Kwŏn Chung-hyŏn. Only the prime minister and long-time political ally of Min Yŏng-hwan, Han Kyu-sŏl, refused to sign. According to the *Min Ch'ungjŏnggong sillok,* Min "fainted several times, vomiting blood,"[67] on hearing this news and was forced to retire to his room.

Eight days later, on 26 November, Min met with Privy Councillor Cho Pyŏng-se to discuss ways to oust the officials who had signed the treaty and have the treaty itself annulled. Min and Cho subsequently led a large group of officials into the palace, where they waited for a response to their protestations from Emperor Kojong at the Department of the Imperial Household. Cho Pyŏng-se twice sent in memorials to the emperor, but he and the other protesting officials were finally ordered to disperse by an imperial edict.[68]

On 28 November Min Yŏng-hwan replaced Cho as the chief signatory of a further memorial demanding the abrogation of the treaty and the execution of those who had signed it. After receiving a reply from the emperor, Min addressed the large gathering of officials with him, insisting that they had to continue their protests until they received the emperor's mandate to put an end to the crisis. He then presented a second memorial and simultaneously handed in his resignation.[69]

Min remained in the courtyard of the palace throughout that night. Despite being ordered to leave repeatedly, "he straightened his robes and, adamantly setting his countenance, finally stated that even if he died, he could not comply."[70]

Police Magistrate O Chin-sŏp read out an imperial command demanding the immediate withdrawal of all the officials. The command stated that the protesting officials had an overriding duty to protect the emperor, regardless of their desire to preserve Korea's sovereignty.

Min then delivered an impassioned reply to this edict:

"As your humble servants have informed you, if your imperial sanction were to be granted to us, our national territory would be restored and your imperial person preserved. If your servant's words are without virtue, I beg you to cut off your servant's head and let it rot as a reward for his crime." Then turning around to the many people gathered there, he said, "What is your opinion of what I have just spoken?" Everyone was deeply moved, and there was no one who did not weep. They replied, "We all admire your absolute loyalty. Is there anyone who would dare to transgress to protect his own life?"[71]

At dawn on 29 November, however, a second imperial edict was issued in response to Min's protest:

> What you have stated is a fair opinion but to stay several nights in the palace and refuse to leave is outrageous conduct such as has never been seen in our court before. You have been reasoned with repeatedly but still have not withdrawn. How can such behavior be seen as the loyal duty of ministers? You are all placed under arrest by order of the Ministry of Justice (Pyŏngnyŏng pŏppu).[72]

In compliance with this edict, Min and the other officials waited outside the High Court of Justice (P'yŏngniwŏn) until dusk, when Yi Kyu-hwan, the High Court prosecutor *(kŏmsa),* emerged and pronounced judgment on the officials. Because of the mitigating circumstances, however, they received an immediate pardon and were at liberty to leave the palace. The protesting officials then went to the Cotton Merchants' Club (Paengmok chŏndoga) to prepare another memorial. As it was already too late to present it that night, the officials decided to wait until dawn the next day.

Min, however, whose health was already weak, had caught a chill from spending several nights out of doors in the palace grounds. As he had a violent headache, he decided to rest at the house of Privy Councillor Yi Wan-sik in Hoemokdong. He told his wife to return home but ordered his major domo Hwang Nam-su to go with him. Realizing the ineffectiveness of the memorials and recognizing the desperate straits into which his country had fallen, Min was unable to sleep. Just before dawn, at about six o'clock in the morning on 30 November, he ordered Hwang Nam-su to fetch his servant Ch'oe Sŏg-in. While Hwang was away from the house, Min committed suicide by cutting his own throat with a short dagger, "sacrificing his body to preserve his integrity."[73]

According to the author of *Min Ch'ung jŏnggong sillok* and also the contemporary diarist Hwang Hyŏn, at the time of Min's death, "a large star fell from the western sky, and more than a hundred magpies gathered at the house and cried loudly for a while and then scattered."[74] Min's body was taken to his own house, where many government officials and other men and women came and wept "until they lost their voices." A place for people to come and mourn away from Min's home was set up at the house of County Magistrate Yun P'yŏng-san. People went there continuously to mourn Min's passing. It is said that all the diplomatic representatives and many other Westerners also went there to express their condolences.[75]

Min Yŏng-hwan's suicide was quickly condemned by the pro-Japanese correspondent of the *Times* in Tokyo, Frank Brinkley, who wrote, in line with the attitude of the Japanese government, "Nothing makes the future look gloomier than the fact that men like Cho and Min lose their self-command instead of labouring to correct the situation produced by their own fault."[76]

Min's death, however, was reported from a Korean point of view in the *Korean Daily News* and the *Taehan maeil sinbo,* published by the Englishman Ernest Bethell.[77] Western governments also received detailed reports from their representatives in Seoul, who were well aware of the reasons for Min's action and also his standing in Korean society, as the following report from the British chargé d'affaires in Seoul Henry Cockburn shows:

> One of the leaders of the agitation was General Min Yung-huan, a cousin of the late Queen of Corea, and a man well known to foreigners, partly owing to his having at various times occupied a prominent position in the Corean Government, and partly to his having attended the 1897 Jubilee in England as Corean Envoy. On the evening of the 29th ultimo he parted from his friends with a promise to meet them next day, but then betook himself to the house of a friend and there committed suicide by cutting his throat early yesterday morning.[78]

In another report from von Saldern to Prince von Bülow, the former described Min as being "undoubtedly the first Korean after the emperor."[79] Even the flag of the Japanese embassy in Seoul was flown at half mast out of respect for Min when the news of his death became known.[80]

Min's death was followed by the suicide of former prime minister Cho Pyŏng-se; former vice-minister Hong Man-sik; a clerk in the Ministry of Education, Yi Sang-ch'ŏl; and a private in the P'yŏngyang garrison, Kim Pong-hak. Min's example also became an inspiration for the leadership of the "righteous armies" *(ŭibyŏng),* which rose up throughout Korea to resist the Japanese in the wake of the Ŭlsa treaty.[81]

That first night after Min's death, when his body was being clothed in a shroud, six calling cards, on which messages had been written, were found among his clothes. Five of the messages were addressed to the representatives of China, Great Britain, the United States, France, and Germany. They read as follows:

> Yŏng-hwan has failed his country. The state of this nation and his plan for the people have come to this end. Only by dying can he repay the emperor's grace and apologize to his twenty million fellow countrymen. He is already dead. Our twenty million citizens may be annihilated in the midst of their struggle for survival. Noble envoys, how can you fail to recognize Japan's purpose and also ignore Japan's actions? Noble envoys, Your Excellencies, if only you will take our

people's opinion seriously, report to your esteemed governments and people and assist our people's freedom and independence, even I, who am dead, will rejoice in the other world and be grateful. Oh Excellencies! Do not look upon Taehan lightly nor mistake the utter sincerity of our people.[82]

Another message, addressed to Min's "twenty million fellow citizens of Taehan," stated:

Alas! The nation's shame and people's disgrace have come to this point, where our people are in the midst of a life and death struggle. Usually those who demand to live die, and those who pledge to die live, so, gentlemen, how can you not respond [to this crisis]? Yŏng-hwan alone by dying repays the emperor's grace and offers an apology to his twenty million fellow countrymen, his brothers, so that even if Yŏng-hwan dies, he is not dead but without fail will help you gentlemen from the nether world. If you, my fellow brothers, make one million times more effort, strengthening this will and spirit, exercising your learning, making an all-out effort with a resolute mind and restore our freedom and independence, then the dead will rejoice from afar and laugh. Oh, do not lose one iota of your desire; these are my parting words to my twenty million fellow countrymen of the Taehan Empire.[83]

That night Emperor Kojong issued an imperial edict in praise of Min's loyal service and patriotism:

This chief minister was of a gentle disposition with an upright will and spirit. We received many benefits from his loyal service when he was in Our court. His long-standing, dedicated service for the nation was exceptional, and he was a person We turned to on Our left and Our right for support. When this distressing anxiety came upon Us, he gave counsel and exhortation. Without thinking of himself, he acted decisively, and finally out of patriotic grief he sacrificed himself. His loyal and righteous soul will surely become a sun and star, but Our heart is utterly cast down.[84]

Kojong gave orders for Min to be honored with a first-rank funeral and bestowed on him the posthumous rank of head of the State Council. He also commanded the Translation Office (Yesig'wŏn) to establish a memorial gate (chŏngmun) and to select a suitable posthumous name (siho) for Min as quickly as possible. Kojong made it known that he would compose the funeral ode and that it was to be read out at Min's funeral by one of his chief ministers, Imperial Secretary Yi U-myŏn.

Kojong issued further orders for a palace eunuch *(chungsa)* to be sent to Min's elderly mother to offer his condolences and for an imperial secretary *(pisŏsŭng)*, Cho Han-wŏn, to be sent to comfort his children. Yi Chae-gŭk, minister in the Department of the Imperial Household and a state councillor then reported that the posthumous name selected to be bestowed on Min was *Ch'ungmun*, "*ch'ung* meaning loyalty and referring to a thoughtful and gentle man who had preserved his integrity unto death, and *mun* referring to his diligent study of the great classics."[85]

The funeral officiator *(kyŏm changye)* was Cho Pŏm-gu, who stayed at Min's house to take charge of the funeral affairs. Min's mother also sent a telegram to his younger brother, Min Yŏng-ch'an, who was stationed in the Korean diplomatic and consular office in Paris at that time.

On 30 November, according to the custom of *taeryŏm,* Min's shroud was removed, his body dressed again and covered with a blanket, which was then tied with hemp. On the following day, somewhat ironically, Megata Tanetarō (Mok Ha-jŏn), the first Japanese financial adviser *(chaejŏng komun'gwan)* to Korea, was the first person to offer a funeral ode *(chemun)* at Min's coffin. He was followed by a long list of Korean dignitaries including former *chusa*[86] Sin Hyŏn-ju, who composed a funeral lament *(manjang)*, and former *chwarang*[87] Sin Yong-jin, who composed a *chŏlgu*[88] as a funeral lament. The Confucian scholar Sŏ Sŭng-ik offered a funeral ode as did Yi Hun-jin, Yi Kyŏng-ho, Yi Sŏn-jik, and others.

Major Sim Hong-t'aek, Captain Kim T'ae-jin, First Lieutenant Cho Chung-sŏk, and others were offering funeral odes as the ceremonial coffin *(tongwŏn pugi)* arrived. As Yun P'yŏng-san's house was too small to serve as a reception hall *(sa'min chohoeso)*, the reception was moved to the house of Min's army colleague Paek Hak-chin.

On 2 December, Kojong commanded that ten bolts of each color of silk, fifty bolts each of linen and cotton, one thousand wŏn of cash, thirty sacks of rice, ten bolts of white cotton cloth, and ten bolts of hemp cloth be provided at Kyŏngsŏn Palace for Min's funeral.

Instructor *(kyogwan)* Kim Sang-t'ae, Chusa Yi To-hŭng, former *chusa* of Ch'ungju Ch'oe Chŏng-gŭn, the teachers and students of Hŭnghwa School, which Min had established in 1898, and others all offered funeral odes and offerings.

On 3 December the imperial secretary was sent with offerings and a funeral ode from Kojong. Kojong also gave orders for Min's posthumous name to be revised as he felt that it did not suitably reflect Min's "exemplary loyalty and fidelity" in discarding his own life for the sake of his country. Min's posthumous name was subsequently altered to *Ch'ungjŏng,* "because to completely forget your own home in thinking of your country is *ch'ung* [loyalty] and to make people struck with wonder at your righteousness is *chŏng* (*jŏng*) [righteousness]."[89]

During the following days numerous dignitaries visited the place where Min's coffin lay to pay their respects, including Yun Ch'i-ho, many members of the foreign community and, as the anonymous author of the *Min Ch'ungjŏnggong sillok* records, "the *kisaeng* Ok-hŭi," who fittingly offered a funeral ode in Korea's native script *han'gŭl*.

On 17 December the funeral procession departed. It was a bright clear day, and the weather was warm and calm. As the bier was departing, the entire imperial court and government officials in attendance wept. The ministers and consuls of the various foreign legations and other distinguished persons took hold of the ropes attached to the bier and led it forward as a military band played in the middle of the courtyard. The master of ceremonies held the rite of departure outside the front gate with solemn devotion, his voice filled with sorrow and grief. Cho Pŏm-gu and Kim Han-jŏng presided over the funeral procession at the command of Emperor Kojong. Both sides of the bier had been beautifully decked with colored flowers by the students of the Hŭnghwa School. On one side of the bier was written, "A name that will be transmitted throughout history: loyalty that pierces the broad daylight" *(myŏngjŏn ch'ŏngsa, ch'ung'-gwan paeg'il),* and on the other side were the words "Your humble and superficial pupils all adore their teacher" *(pich'ŏn huhak ham'ang sŏnsaeng).*

After the bier was lifted up, the students all raised their funeral banners aloft as the soldiers blew their bugles. Crowds of people carrying lanterns spread out along the sides of the street to pay their respects as the bier went past. As the mourners left the reception hall, singing the pallbearers' dirge, the flags of the six military camps unfurled like butterflies in the north wind. It was as though the numerous funeral banners were proclaiming the people's grief and sorrow as they flapped in silhouette against the western sun. The multitude of mourners together with their wives wept out loud until they lost their voices. It was as though they were children who had lost a parent. When the bier arrived at Chongno, the merchants took it in turns to help to carry it through Namdaemun to Tolmoru.

The procession halted there for a while so that the foreign diplomatic representatives and other distinguished funeral guests could pay their last respects. The procession then headed toward Min's final resting place in Yongin County. At every village along the way, people from all walks of life presented odes and offerings and helped to carry the bier through the night. Whenever the road became rough and treacherous, the people accompanying the funeral procession would rush forward without a thought for their own safety, and seizing hold of the bier would lead it from the front and support it from behind.

On the following day, 18 December, the procession finally arrived at an inn in P'ungdŏkch'ŏn just as it was growing dark. After the local dignitaries had presented funeral odes and offerings, people from every household brought out lamps and torches. Lining the route on the left and the right, they escorted the bier to the top of the mountain. The funeral procession finally came to a halt at the grave site. Chŏng Chu-yŏng, the provincial governor of Kyŏnggi-do, and the Yongin County magistrate Hyŏn Ch'an-bong each presented a funeral ode and made an offering.

On 19 December at about two o'clock in the morning, the coffin was lowered into the grave and Min's ancestral tablet was completed. The company commanders and their soldiers fired three rifle salutes. Finally, Cho Pŏm-ku offered a libation on behalf of the emperor, and the procession returned to Seoul bearing Min's ancestral tablet.

When they reached Sŏbinggo, the commanding officer, Yi Ki-p'yo, received an imperial edict of consolation for the grieving soldiers. When they arrived at Tolmoru, crowds of people from the Seoul area attended the returning funeral procession in tears. Forty cavalry troopers, each carrying the Korean national flag, accompanied the procession to Min's home.[90]

The British chargé d'affaires Cockburn was also present at Min's funeral and made the following report to the foreign office:

> On the 17th. General Min's funeral took place, and was a really impressive ceremony. The Emperor was not personally represented in the cortège, but in all other respects the funeral was a national one, detachments of Corean troops marching in the procession with arms reversed. All the arrangements were carried out with a dignity I had not expected to witness, while in picturesqueness both of colouring and grouping the procession itself and the great crowds of people that watched it would be difficult to surpass.[91]

Min Yŏng-hwan was honored by his countrymen and many in the foreign community in Seoul for his patriotism and integrity. After his death he was to become a symbol of Korean independence, and it was his photograph that Syngman Rhee chose to place at the front of his book *Tongnip chŏngsin* (The spirit of independence). Nearly one year after his death, on 4 July 1906, Min's reputation was further enhanced by the discovery of bamboo (an East Asian symbol of integrity) growing from the place on the floor of his room where his bloodstained clothes had been placed.[92] Hwang Hyŏn provides us with the following contemporary account:

> After Min Yŏng-hwan committed suicide, the knife that he had used and his blood-soaked clothes were kept on the wooden floor behind the bed on which

his body had been laid before his burial *(yŏngsang)*. In the middle of the second month,[93] when Min's wife Pak-ssi went to fetch the clothes in order to dry them in the sun, fresh bamboo shoots were sprouting from beneath the clothes. There were four bamboo plants with a total of nine stems. Each one was the thickness of a knuckle. There was a mass of roots like threads that were lodged between the oiled paper and the floor boards. They were too weak to support the plants, which seemed to make the shape of *chuk* [the Chinese character for bamboo].

For about ten days to one month a human tide of Seoul's citizens came to see. Western merchants also came, and the people once again poured out libations and wept in mourning. The people of Seoul also painted pictures or made wood carvings of the scene and sold them, while the Chinese people in our country composed poems and even collected them together in a volume of verse.[94]

The skeptic might say that this miraculous bamboo had simply grown there naturally, or had even been planted there by a member of Min's family to enhance Min's reputation, or that at best it was simply a chance accident, but at the time it was to become a potent and enduring symbol of Korean resistance to Japanese oppression.

Conclusion

Today Min Yŏng-hwan's statue stands near Piwŏn in Waryongdong looking out across one of the busy thoroughfares of Seoul. The story of his death, though not his career as Chosŏn's first official diplomatic representative to Russia and the United Kingdom and possibly the highest-ranking supporter of reform at the court of King Kojong, may be found in most of the standard textbooks of the history of Korea. In 1962 he was posthumously awarded the Kŏn'guk medal by President Pak Chŏng-hŭi, and if one searches very carefully, his burial site may still be found hidden away in the outskirts of Yongin, a small town in Kyŏnggi Province.

This study has traced the story of Min's life and death in an attempt to put across a small part of the Korean side of the story in that nation's painful transition from the nineteenth to the twentieth century. Min Yŏng-hwan was born in the reign of King Ch'ŏlchong and spent his formative years under the rule of the Taewŏn'gun. As he grew up, he must have been aware of the Catholic persecutions, heard rumors of the destruction of the *General Sherman,* and been shocked by reports of the invasions of Kanghwa by the French and then the Americans in 1866 and 1871. Korea concluded its first modern treaty with Japan in 1876, when Min was just fifteen years old, and its first treaty with a Western power in 1882, when he was just twenty-one years old.

As one of the closest relatives of both Kojong and his consort, Min must have enjoyed a privileged status at the Chosŏn court and, as has been shown by this study, early promotion through the ranks of officialdom. On the other hand, he was also exposed to the intrigues of the court and the violent enmity of the Taewŏn'gun toward the Min clan, an enmity that resulted in the death of his own father, Min Kyŏm-ho. In fact, Min had scarcely reached adulthood when his father was brutally assassinated during the Soldiers' Rebellion of 1882. It is hardly surprising, then, that his memorials reveal a certain reluctance to participate in the pursuit of power at Kojong's court.

Nevertheless, Min strove against the corrupting influences that characterized the *sedo* politics of his day.[95] He memorialized for the strict regulation of the civil examination system and strongly condemned the avarice and cruelty of the provincial magistrates in his essay *Ch'ŏnilch'aek*. Among all late-Chosŏn politicians, he appears to have retained the trust and respect not only of the Korean people but also the foreign diplomats and missionaries in Seoul. In 1896 and 1897 he faced the difficult challenge of upholding Korean dignity abroad, while at home his country was in almost constant crisis. Even his ardent critic Yun Ch'i-ho had to admit that he could not think of a single other person in the Chosŏn court who could have handled the task of envoy to Russia as well as Min. Perhaps Min's greatest contribution, however, was in his efforts to traverse the gulf between Kojong's court and the Independence Club in the late 1890s.

Of course, Min was a human being with numerous faults and limitations. As has been seen, the American-educated Yun Ch'i-ho found it very difficult to work with him during the mission to Russia in 1896, although it is clear from Yun's diaries that he himself was probably not the easiest of people to work with either. In Min's failure to immediately return the unused funds from his mission to Russia in 1896, there are, perhaps, some grounds to claim that Min was not entirely free from the financial irregularities that seem to have been almost inseparable from office holding in the late-Chosŏn administration. The sudden abandonment of his mission to Europe also seems to betray a certain weakness of temperament, and his sojourn in the United States may have entailed the misuse of funds allocated for the expenses of his original mission. Furthermore, although Min was responsible for the Korean armed forces, he himself had received no modern military training and demonstrated a fair degree of naïvety in military matters in the early phase of his career. His political effectiveness also appears to have been hampered by his poor health.

Nevertheless, as one of the most privileged members of the ruling élite of Korea at the turn of the last century, Min Yŏng-hwan could easily have ignored the plight of his country, sought personal gain when in office, and come to an arrangement with the Japanese leadership in order to retain his status after the Ŭlsa treaty. Sadly, many leading figures in the Min clan and Korean society at large, including such distinguished patriots as Yun Ch'i-ho, Paek Nak-chun, and Yi Kwang-su, were eventually forced into compromising their integrity in some way. Min, however, assumed responsibility for the failure of his own efforts to prevent Korea's subjugation by Japan, and chose instead to sacrifice his life to appeal to the Western powers to protect Korean independence and awaken the national consciousness of his own people.[96] In doing so he bridged the two worlds of the Confucian conservative and progressive nationalist and won the respect of both camps.

On the other hand, Min's death was also a symbol of the death of the aspirations of a whole nation to transform itself. Faced with the fait accompli of the 1905 protectorate treaty, Min was forced to respond according to an older code of honor, and like his own country was prevented from making an autonomous transition into the modern world. In the Christian worldview, which was rapidly making inroads into Korea at the time of Min's death, suicide is seen as an act of despair and even a mortal sin. Yet for Min it was an assertion of his integrity and the integrity of his twenty million fellow Koreans in the face of overwhelming circumstances and his final act of protest against the seizure of his nation by Japan.

Perhaps he could have fought at the head of a righteous army or perhaps he could have tried to work from within to ameliorate the effects of the Japanese takeover. But Min was not a soldier, even though he had often held the post of Minister of War, and he was perhaps only too well aware how the Japanese would manipulate and compromise Korea's traditional status groups once they were in power. As the prevailing perception of Korean politics in this period is of a nation polarized between conservatives and reformers, Min's life and death presents us with the apparent anomaly of a well-connected monarchist who nevertheless sought to bring Korea into the twentieth century as an independent and modernized nation. If judged objectively, his failure and that of other like-minded officials and reformers was due more to the intensely self-interested rivalry of foreign powers for control or exploitation of the Korean peninsula than to any innate inability of the Koreans to modernize and govern their own country, as was claimed by Japanese and other foreign commentators of the day.

It cannot be denied, of course, that Korea was incapable of solving all its problems alone. It undoubtedly required the goodwill and support of the Western powers. Such support was not forthcoming, however, and in 1910 Korea was finally annexed by the Japanese Empire. With annexation Korea lost its last vestiges of sovereignty and self-determination, but it was not the only loser. Although it is no longer fashionable to draw lessons from historical precedents, it is, nevertheless, worth noting that the pragmatic decisions made by the United States and Great Britain to cooperate with Japan and withhold even the barest minimum of support for Korean independence and neutrality in 1905 were later to be paid for in full in the Pacific and Korean wars less than half a century later.

APPENDIX 1.
Min's Family Tree

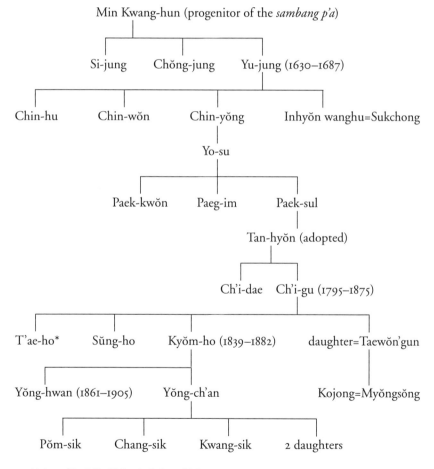

Min Kwang-hun (progenitor of the *sambang p'a*)

Si-jung   Chŏng-jung   Yu-jung (1630–1687)

Chin-hu   Chin-wŏn   Chin-yŏng   Inhyŏn wanghu=Sukchong

Yo-su

Paek-kwŏn   Paeg-im   Paek-sul

Tan-hyŏn (adopted)

Ch'i-dae   Ch'i-gu (1795–1875)

T'ae-ho*   Sŭng-ho   Kyŏm-ho (1839–1882)   daughter=Taewŏn'gun

Yŏng-hwan (1861–1905)   Yŏng-ch'an   Kojong=Myŏngsŏng

Pŏm-sik   Chang-sik   Kwang-sik   2 daughters

*Adopted by Min Ch'i-rok, father of Myŏngsŏng

SOURCE: Based on a tabulated analysis of the descendants of Min Kwang-hun according to the *Yŏhŭng Min ssi chokpo* in Yi Sang-ch'an, "1896 nyŏn ŭibyŏng undong," pp. 82–85.

APPENDIX 2.
English-Language Works on the Late Chosŏn Era

The period 1860 until 1910, the final fifty years of the Chosŏn era, has undoubtedly attracted the most attention from Western historians of Korea.[1] Perhaps the single most obvious reason for this is simply that, at least from 1882 onward, there are many Western diplomatic sources available for this period. Two early works that examine the opening of Korea to the West, *God, Mammon, and the Japanese: Dr. Horace N. Allen and Korean-American Relations, 1884–1905,* by Fred Harvey Harrington, and *Korea and the Old Orders in Eastern Asia,* by Frederick M. Nelson, rely almost exclusively on Western diplomatic archives.[2] These two works, first published in 1944 and 1945 respectively, are undoubtedly the most important pioneering works of Western historical scholarship on the period of the opening of Korea to Japan and the West. Nevertheless, because of their reliance on Western source materials, there is an inevitable sense of one-sidedness and even cultural bias despite the sympathy with which both authors view their subject. Harrington in particular is prone to adopting a mocking tone, which is only mitigated by the fact that he uses it as much against the Westerners in Korea as against the Koreans themselves.

Hilary Conroy's controversial work, *The Japanese Seizure of Korea, 1868–1910: A Study of Realism and Idealism in International Relations,* published in 1960, used Japanese sources for the first time in a Western study of this period of Korean history. This study, however, provoked a fierce response from Korean historians, who felt that it was overly sympathetic to Japanese justifications of their actions in Korea: namely, their security fears vis-à-vis Russia. In addition, Conroy's claim that there was no economic motivation behind the annexation of the Korean peninsula in 1910 has been vigorously rebutted by one of Korea's leading contemporary historians, Ki-baek Lee (Yi Ki-baek).[3]

With the appearance of Lee Kyung-sik's translation of *The History of Korea* by Han Woo-Keun (Han U-kŭn) in 1970 and in 1984 the more extensive work *A New History of Korea* by Ki-baik Lee (translated by Edward Wagner with Edward Shultz), the voice of indigenous Korean historians began to be heard more clearly in the

United States and Europe. Such general histories as these had, of course, been preceded by earlier pioneering works of Korean scholarship in English, such as George Paik's (Paek Nak-chun) *History of Protestant Missions in Korea, 1832–1910.* Although this work was first published in 1929, it has never been superseded.

Significant progress in the development of the study of this period in Korean history in the West came in the second half of the 1970s with the publication of James Palais' *Politics and Policy in Traditional Korea* and Martina Deuchler's *Confucian Gentlemen and Barbarian Envoys: The Opening of Korea, 1875–1885.* Both works are significant for their extensive use of Korean, Chinese, and Japanese sources, bringing the scope of Western scholarship onto a new level. These two works themselves undoubtedly came on the foundation of one of the most outstanding works on this period, *Korea and the Politics of Imperialism, 1876–1910,* by C. I. Eugene Kim and Han Kyo Kim, published in 1967, and *The Rule of the Taewŏn'gun, 1864–1873: Restoration in Yi Korea,* by another Korean scholar, Ching Young Choe, who, like Palais and Deuchler, studied under professors John K. Fairbank and Edward Wagner at the East Asian Research Center at Harvard University. This work was published in 1972, the same year that saw the publication of another pioneering work by a Harvard alumnus, *Korea's 1884 Incident: Its Background and Kim Ok-kyun's Elusive Dream* by Harold F. Cook.

In 1980 two more important works were published: *The Last Phase of the East Asian World Order: Korea, Japan and the Chinese Empire, 1860–1882,* by Key-Hiuk Kim, and *Mandarins, Gunboats, and Power Politics: Owen Nickerson Denny and the International Rivalries in Korea,* by Robert R. Swartout, Jr. These two books are complementary, the former providing a broad picture of the opening of Korea based on East Asian and Western sources, and the latter being an in-depth study of an American adviser in Korea based mainly on Western diplomatic archives, but with some reference to Korean and Chinese primary and secondary source material.

In 1988 another monograph on a Western adviser at the Korean court appeared: *West Goes East: Paul Georg von Möllendorff and Great Power Imperialism in Late Yi Korea,* by Yur-Bok Lee. This work is based on an impressive array of East Asian and Western sources. The same year saw the publication of a lively study by Vipan Chandra on the reform movement in Seoul—*Imperialism, Resistance, and Reform in Late Nineteenth-Century Korea: Enlightenment and the Independence Club*—and an impressive two-volume study based entirely on Russian, European, and American diplomatic sources of Russia's role on and around the Korean peninsula during the last two decades of the nineteenth century, George A. Lensen's *Balance of Intrigue: International Rivalry in Korea and Manchuria, 1884–1899.* These were followed two years later by Jongsuk Chay's well-researched and highly readable *Diplomacy of Asymmetry: Korean American Relations to 1910.* The most recent work, however, to make a substantial contribution to our understanding of this period, albeit from a Japanese perspective, is Peter Duus' work published in 1995, *The Abacus and the Sword: The Japanese Penetration of Korea, 1895–1910*. Finally, no overview of this period would be complete without mentioning the large body of journal articles in English by Young Ick Lew focusing on the nature and pivotal significance of the Kabo-Ŭlmi reform movement of 1894–1895.

The historiography of works in English of this period, therefore, can be looked at as developing in two directions as Western historians, initially relying on Western archives, have increasingly mastered Korean and other East Asian sources, while Korean domestic scholarship has not only been published in translation but has also been enhanced by Korean scholars, who have usually taught in the United States, publishing well-researched monographs on modern Korean history in English.

APPENDIX 3.
Diplomatic Correspondence and Dispatches

My dear and virtuous brother, Your Majesty the Tsar of Russia, on this occasion of Your Majesty the Tsar and Her Majesty the Tsarina's ascension to the throne and coronation ceremony, I respectfully offer my sincere congratulations.[1] I respectfully admire both Your Majesties and feel affection for your beloved Imperial Family.

Over a period of years I have heard of the great projects arising from your noble country's newly increased prosperity. I am overjoyed that these projects are for the purpose of promoting good friendship. Therefore, I command my intimate minister, Special Entry Officer First Rank Min Yŏng-hwan, to be appointed Envoy Extraordinary and Minister Plenipotentiary and to visit Your Majesty in my name, reverently participate in this congratulatory occasion, and humbly present this personal letter in order to extend my sincere congratulations.

I hope that both Your Majesties will receive this envoy Min Yŏng-hwan with favor and occasionally bestow an audience upon him. Please listen to him and trust his words.

May both Your Majesties be blessed with eternal happiness.

Signed by the Royal name of Your Majesties' good brother at the capital Hanyang (Seoul) on the 1st day of the 4th month of the 33rd year of my ascension to the throne and the 505th year since this nation's foundation.[2]

TSAR NICHOLAS II'S REPLY TO KING KOJONG'S PERSONAL LETTER

From Tsar Nicholas II of Great Russia to His Excellent Majesty the King of Great Chosŏn, Min Yŏng-hwan Envoy Extraordinary and Minister Plenipotentiary of your noble country safely arrived at Moscow and was able to attend on the day of the coronation. We were delighted that the envoy Min Yŏng-hwan immediately presented himself at court and read out the personal letter from Your Majesty, expressing affectionate friendship and sincere intimacy. In addition he brought many kinds of precious presents, which I and the Empress received with gratitude.

We are grateful to Your Majesty and from henceforth our deep friendship will increase as we enjoy tranquillity together and eternal, boundless protection. I often saw the envoy Min Yŏng-hwan. He conducted affairs by means of harmonious discussion, faith, and mutual confidence. Now that he is about to return, I have employed him to convey this letter of reply. I respectfully wish Your Majesty the King peace, prosperity and that Your reign may flourish forever.

Personally signed and sealed, Nikolai II on the 21st day of the 6th month of the 2nd year of my ascension to the throne at Illyinsk.

Minister of Foreign Affairs by Imperial Appointment, Lobanov.[3]

MIN'S OFFICIAL DISPATCH OF INQUIRY TO LOBANOV

Official dispatch [of inquiry; *chohoemun*] from the Great Chosŏn Envoy Extraordinary and Minister Plenipotentiary Min (Yŏng-hwan). Be it known that this envoy, in respectful obedience to the orders of His Majesty the King of his country, has been sent to negotiate the affairs of his country, having been conferred with the authority of Envoy Extraordinary and Minister Plenipotentiary. On the twentieth day of the previous month I arrived at this capital city. According to the usual formalities of all nations, it is the duty of an Envoy Extraordinary and Minister Plenipotentiary to personally present to the nation's sovereign the credentials of his own country on the day of arrival at his post. Because the coronation ceremony of His Majesty the Emperor of this esteemed country took place on the 22nd day of the previous month, I first presented the personal letter of His Majesty the King of my country and have not yet presented my credentials.

Esteemed Minister, please convey this information to His Imperial Majesty and decide upon a date on which I may present my credentials.

Now this envoy respectfully and in compliance with etiquette personally presents this dispatch for the attention of the emperor.

Let the above dispatch be given to the Minister of Foreign Affairs of Great Russia, Lobanov.

The fourth day of the six month of the founding year of Kŏnyang (1896).

[Envoy's *tojang* seal. Envoy's *injang* seal.]

[There was no dispatch in reply. Planson personally conveyed the date of presentation as the sixth.][4]

LOBANOV'S "POINTS IN REPLY TO THE KOREAN AMBASSADOR"

1. The king during his sojourn in the Russian Mission will be protected by a Russian guard. He may remain in the Mission as long as he himself shall deem needful and convenient; should a return of the king to his own palace ensue, the Russian government may assume moral guarantee of his safety. The Russian detachment now located at the Mission shall remain there at the orders of the Russian minister, and in event of need may even be reinforced.

2. For the settlement of the question of instructors, there shall be dispatched to Seoul very shortly an experienced Russian officer of high rank whom the Russian government will charge with entering into negotiations with the Koreans on this subject; the said officer shall, first of all, be charged to occupy himself with the question of setting up a king's bodyguard. An equally competent person shall be dispatched from Russia for the study of Korea's economic situation and to ascertain the financial measures necessary.

3. The question regarding the sending of Russian advisers to cooperate with the Korean government is answered by the previous point. The above-mentioned trustworthy persons will, obviously, under the direction of the Russian minister, serve as such advisers in the military and financial department.

4. The conclusion of a loan to the Korean government will be considered as soon as the economic situation of the country and the needs of the government shall have been ascertained.

5. The Russian government agrees to the amalgamation of its overland telegraph lines with the Korean and will supply the assistance requisite to this undertaking.[5]

MIN'S CREDENTIALS PRESENTED TO THE RUSSIAN COURT

His Majesty the King of Great Chosŏn sends His regards to His Most Imperial Majesty of Great Russia. We solemnly consider the treaty relations between our two countries, which have existed for several years, to be entirely satisfactory. To make our neighborly relationship even closer and especially to increase the amity that makes relations between nations firm, stable, and eternally unchanging, We have especially chosen our intimate and beloved Special Entry Officer of the First Rank in the Department of the Royal Household, Min Yŏng-hwan, to be our Envoy Extraordinary and Minister Plenipotentiary. He will proceed to the capital city of Your noble country and fulfill all the necessary requirements for satisfactory negotiations.

We know this minister to be loyal, diligent, and meticulous. By means of this specially prepared letter, We command this minister to present himself in person before the emperor. We sincerely hope that Your Majesty the Emperor will place your trust in him and receive him with kindness. Please grant him an audience whenever it is appropriate to convey as Our representative Our inner feelings so that the benevolence and harmony between us may increase and that we may enjoy tranquillity and peace together.

With kindest regards to Your Imperial Majesty and may You have great fortune without end.

Signed and sealed in the name of the King at the capital Hanyang on the 1st day of the 4th month of the founding year of Kŏnyang[6] in the 505th year since the national foundation of Great Chosŏn.[7]

THE PERSONAL LETTER OF KING KOJONG TO TSAR NICHOLAS II

We reverently inform Our good brother, Your Majesty the Emperor of Russia, of our two countries' generous friendship. Last year a distressful situation suddenly arose, and We moved Our residence to your noble country's legation. There I was grateful to be protected by your marines. This was managed by Minister Waeber, who employed a true heart and true strength. Everything was done in a most satisfactory way, so that We felt that We were under the protection of Your Majesty. This was the result of the bestowal of Your Majesty's deep friendship.

Because of Our people's frequent requests, We have returned to Our former royal palace. Once again We do not know how to completely express Our gratitude for all your kind assistance.

We are sending Minister Plenipotentiary Min Yŏng-hwan to participate in the congratulatory ceremonies and to convey on Our behalf Our special congratulations to your exalted relative.[8] This proves how the relations between our nations are becoming daily closer. What greater fortune could there be?

Therefore, We have commanded Minister Plenipotentiary Min Yŏng-hwan to take up residence and present this personal letter conveying Our intentions in Our stead.

May Your Majesty have matchless blessings and long life.

On the 22nd day of the 3rd month of the 2nd year of Kŏnyang and the 506th year since the foundation of Great Chosŏn, at Kyŏng'un Palace in Hanyang.

Your Majesty's good brother,

[royal seal][9]

THE PERSONAL LETTER OF KING KOJONG TO QUEEN VICTORIA

I congratulate Your Majesty on the joyful occasion of your sixtieth year since acceding to the Imperial throne. It is truly your bright virtue that has laid the foundations of your reign. Such luminous fortune was rare even in ancient times; therefore, I have ordered Minister Plenipotentiary and Envoy Extraordinary Min Yŏng-hwan to take up the post of Our ambassador in order to take and present this personal letter and to express Our sincere congratulations.

We wish Your Majesty long life, matchless happiness, eternal joy, health, and peace.

The 22nd day of the 3rd month of the 2nd year of Kŏnyang at Kyŏng'un Palace in Hanyang.

[royal seal][10]

MIN'S CREDENTIALS
PRESENTED TO THE BRITISH COURT

The sovereign of Great Chosŏn inquires after the health of Your Majesty the sovereign of Great Britain and great empress of India. Now that our two nations have already had sincere treaty relations for a long time, and your noble country's envoy has resided here for several years, Our country also should send an envoy in sincere and intimate friendship.

We have, therefore, selected a dearly beloved Minister of the Senior First Rank, State Councillor, and Minister of War, Min Yŏng-hwan, and have appointed him to be Minister Plenipotentiary and Envoy Extraordinary to proceed to your noble country, reside at the capital, and satisfactorily carry out affairs concerned with our mutual relations.

We know that this minister is loyal, diligent, and has a detailed understanding, qualifying him for this official post. We have ordered this envoy to proceed with specially prepared documents to be presented to you. In addition, We hope that there may be mutual trust between you and that you will generously condescend to permit him, at appropriate times, to have an audience, whereby he may convey Our inner feelings so that our friendship may increase and that together we may enjoy great prosperity.

I wish Your Majesty great joy without measure.

The 506th year since the foundation of Great Chosŏn and the 22nd day of the 3rd month of the 2nd year of Kŏnyang at Kyŏng'un Palace in Hanyang.

[royal seal][11]

APPENDIX 4.
Min's Telegrams to King Kojong on His Departure from Europe in 1897[1]

1. To the King of Corea, dispatched from London June 27, 1897; received at Seoul July 22, 1897.

[translation]

I have received your Majesty's telegram with reference to matters affecting the dynasty. It is not meet that your agent should violate existing Treaties. Will you put the law into operation against me or not? I humbly trust you will advise the Government to appoint an Envoy in my stead. It is impossible that I should not personally lay the facts before your Majesty. I am just about to return to my country in fear and trembling.

2. To the Corean Foreign Office, undated.

I have received your telegraphic instructions with reference to the secret treaties of guarantee with France and Germany. Corea is unlucky in her agent. You may put the law into operation against me; joyfully will I submit to the axe. I am returning home. Another Envoy should be sent to France, Germany, Italy, and Austria.

3. To the King of Corea, dispatched from Washington; received July 26, 1897.

I am on my way home in fear and trembling. If you are appointing an envoy in my stead to complete the objects of my Mission, it would be a convenient arrangement if the Minister to the United States and myself were to change places. In obedience to your Majesty's commands of the 24th instant, in fear and trembling I am delivering up to your Majesty my letters of credence.

Notes

INTRODUCTION

1. Japanese civilian residents of Seoul who were occasionally hired to do the "dirty work" of the Japanese legation.

2. Hwang Hyŏn, *Maech'ŏn yarok* [Unofficial records of Mae Ch'ŏn], p. 29. Hwang Hyŏn (pen name: Mae Ch'ŏn)(1855–1910) passed the Classics Licentiate Examination (*saeng-wŏnsi*) with the highest mark in 1888, but he chose to live in retirement. He was strongly critical of the ruling administration and the Min clan in particular. Many of his observations in *Maech'ŏn yarok* are clearly based on rumor and hearsay and lack chronological accuracy. Martina Deuchler, for example, criticizes the author of *Han'guksa, ch'oegŭnse-p'yŏn*, Yi Sŏn-gŭn, for his overreliance on *Maech'ŏn yarok* as a source for this period. See Martina Deuchler, *Confucian Gentlemen and Barbarian Envoys*, pp. 236–237. Nevertheless, Hwang provides an important, albeit subjective, perspective on the political scene of his day. Hwang committed suicide in 1910 in protest against Japan's annexation of Korea.

3. Annie Ellers Bunker, "My First Visit to Her Majesty, the Queen," p. 374.

4. See Lillias Horton Underwood, *Fifteen Years among the Top-knots or Life in Korea*, pp. 24–25; and Isabella Bird Bishop, *Korea and Her Neighbours*, pp. 252–260.

5. Queen Myŏngsŏng's adopted elder brother, Min Sŭng-ho, was killed in 1875 by a bomb disguised as a present. The Taewŏn'gun was considered the prime suspect at the time. See Hwang Hyŏn, *Maech'ŏn yarok*, p. 17.

6. Yun Ch'i-ho, *Yun Ch'i-ho ilgi* [Diary of Yun Ch'i-ho], vol. 4, pp. 299–300. It should be noted that in other entries in his diary Yun was scathingly critical of Queen Myŏngsŏng, King Kojong, and Min Yŏng-hwan himself.

    Yun started writing his diary in classical Chinese on 1 January 1883, changed to *han'gŭl* on 24 November 1887, and from 7 December 1889 wrote in English. Yun's diary entries are all solar dates. Lunar dates are given in the notes for convenience. Chosŏn officially adopted the solar calendar after the Kabo reforms.

7. Dalchoong Kim, "Korea's Quest for Reform and Diplomacy in the 1880's," p. 5.

8. F. V. Dickins and Stanley Lane-Poole, *The Life of Sir Harry Parkes*, vol. 2, p. 221.

9. Dalchoong Kim, "Korea's Quest," p. 5.

10. William Franklin Sands, *Undiplomatic Memories,* p. 127. See also p. 227 of the same work, in which Sands classes Min Yŏng-hwan as one of the "intelligent men and earnest patriots" at the Korean court. Both Min Sang-ho and Min Yong Ki (Min Yŏng-gi), however, were later to accept official posts under the Japanese colonial administration.

11. Chŏng Kyo, *Taehan kyenyŏnsa* [History of the last years of the Yi dynasty], p. 330.

12. Yi Kwang-nin, *Hanguksa kangjwa 5: kŭndae p'yŏn* [Korean history course, vol. 5: Modern period], p. 454.

13. Scott S. Burnett, ed., *Korean-American Relations, Documents Pertaining to the Far Eastern Diplomacy of the United States,* vol. 3: *The Period of Diminishing Influence, 1896–1905,* p. 53.

14. Gregory Henderson, *Korea: The Politics of the Vortex,* p. 209.

15. Tai-jin Kim, ed. and trans., *A Bibliographical Guide to Traditional Korean Sources,* p. 507. Min Pyŏng-gi, who was educated in the United States, played an important role both as a politician and an academic in Korea until his death in 1986.

16. Full bibliographic details of these books may be found in the Bibliography.

17. For a brief outline of the major works in English on this period of Korean history, see appendix 2.

CHAPTER I. EARLY LIFE AND POLITICAL CAREER

1. M. Frederick Nelson, *Korea and the Old Orders in Eastern Asia,* p. 14.

2. Key-hiuk Kim, *The Last Phase of the East Asian World Order,* p. 3.

3. Ibid.

4. In K. Hwang, *The Korean Reform Movement of the 1880s,* p. 49.

5. Key-hiuk Kim, *Last Phase,* p. 5.

6. Ibid., p. 6. For additional studies in English on the Sino-Korean tributary system, see Hae-jong Chun, "Sino-Korean Tributary Relations in the Ch'ing Period," pp. 90–111; and also Edwin O. Reischauer and John K. Fairbank, *East Asia: The Great Tradition,* p. 317.

7. Key-hiuk Kim, *Last Phase,* p. 6.

8. Ibid., p. 15.

9. Hilary Conroy, *The Japanese Seizure of Korea, 1868–1910,* p. 22.

10. For details of the role played by the island of Tsushima in the trade relations between Korea and Japan, see Key-hiuk Kim, *Last Phase,* pp. 17–20.

11. Nelson, *Korea and the Old Orders,* p. 87.

12. The most thorough account of the Taewŏn'gun's policies in English may be found in James Palais, *Politics and Policy in Traditional Korea.* Another valuable study is Ching Young Choe, *The Rule of the Taewŏn'gun, 1864–1873: Restoration in Yi Korea.* For a more partisan appreciation of his policies, which nevertheless acknowledges his ultimately pernicious influence on the politics of the period, see Lee Sun-

keun, "Some Lesser-Known Facts about Taewongun and His Foreign Policy," pp. 23–46.

13. See Lee Sun-keun, "Some Lesser Known Facts," pp. 27–32.

14. C. I. Eugene Kim and Han-kyo Kim, *Korea and the Politics of Imperialism, 1876–1910*, p. 14.

15. Deuchler, *Confucian Gentlemen*, p. 105.

16. Choe, *The Rule of the Taewŏn'gun*, pp. 111–112.

17. For detailed studies on the 1871 American expedition to Korea, see Kim Wŏn-mo, *Kŭndae Han-Mi kyosŏpsa* [A modern history of Korean-American relations]; and Robert R. Swartout, Jr., "Cultural Conflict and Gunboat Diplomacy," pp. 117–169.

18. Lak-Geoon G. Paik, *The History of Protestant Missions in Korea, 1832–1910*, p. 64.

19. Carter J. Eckert et al., *Korea Old and New*, p. 200.

20. Nelson, *Korea and the Old Orders*, p. 131.

21. Deuchler, *Confucian Gentlemen*, p. 49.

22. Ibid., p. 122.

23. George M. McCune and John A. Harrison, eds., *Korean-American Relations*, vol. 1: *The Initial Period, 1883–1886*, p. 25.

24. Spencer J. Palmer, ed., *Korean-American Relations*, vol. 2: *The Period of Growing Influence, 1887–1895*, p. 86.

25. For a full account of the 1884 Incident, see Harold F. Cook, *Korea's 1884 Incident*.

26. Young Ick Lew, "Yüan Shih-k'ai's Residency and the Korean Enlightenment Movement (1885–1894)," p. 70.

27. Ibid., p. 71. As Lew points out, the English title of "resident" appears to have been copied from the title given to the British governor-general's political agents residing at Indian courts.

28. Ibid., p. 104.

29. Ibid., p. 106.

30. Under article 3 of this convention, either of the signatories was permitted to dispatch troops to the peninsula in the case of uprisings or disturbances, on the condition that advance notice was provided to the other party.

31. Kim and Kim, *Korea and the Politics of Imperialism*, p. 83.

32. For compelling circumstantial evidence of the complicity of Inoue and the Japanese cabinet in the murder of Queen Myŏngsŏng, see Yi Min-wŏn, "A'gwan p'ach'ŏn chŏnhu ŭi hanno kwan'gye: 1895–1898" [Korean-Russian relations around the time of Kojong's flight to the Russian legation], pp. 24–54.

33. Nelson, *Korea and the Old Orders*, p. 257.

34. For a concise summary and analysis of the Taft-Katsura Memorandum, see Jong-suk Chay, *Diplomacy of Asymmetry: Korean American Relations to 1910*, pp. 143–144. A reproduction of the original text of this secret document may be found in Tyler Dennett, "Roosevelt's Secret Pact with Japan," pp. 16–17.

35. Fred Harvey Harrington, *God, Mammon, and the Japanese*, pp. 323–324.

36. Although "good offices" were tendered during the Sino-Japanese War (1894–1895),

the United States administration did not back them up with any further action. During the Russo-Japanese War (1904–1905), however, they were never even offered. For an objective discussion of the "good offices" clause and its significance for Korean-American relations during this period, see Chay, *Diplomacy of Asymmetry*, pp. 9–10, 61, 73, and 94–100.

37. Ki-baik Lee, *A New History of Korea*, p. 239.

38. For an introduction to the diversity of *sirhak* scholarship, see Mark Setton, *Chŏng Yagyong*, pp. 9–51.

39. Ki-baik Lee, *New History*, p. 241.

40. For an authoritative English translation of Hamel's journal, see Hendrik Hamel, *Hamel's Journal*. See also Gary Ledyard, *The Dutch Come to Korea*.

41. See Ki-baik Lee, *New History*, p. 255.

42. Deuchler, *Confucian Gentlemen*, pp. 101–102.

43. Young Ick Lew, "Yu Kil-chun," vol. 16, p. 924.

44. For a thorough examination of the Kabo-Ŭlmi period in English, see Young Ick Lew's articles listed in the bibliography.

45. *Independent*, 10 November 1896. For the complete interview, see chapter 4.

46. Yun, *Ilgi*, vol. 6, pp. 213–214.

47. Yŏhŭng: present-day Yŏju, Kyŏnggi-do.

48. See "Chŏn Pong-jun *kongch'o* (a)," p. 329, quoted in Young Ick Lew, "The Conservative Character of the 1894 Tonghak Uprising," p. 164.

49. Hwang Hyŏn, *Maech'ŏn yarok*, p. 27.

50. This outline of Min Yŏng-hwan's ancestry is based on the *Yŏhŭng Min-ssi chokpo* [Genealogical record of the Yŏhŭng Min clan] and *Yŏhŭng Min-ssi sambangp'a segye* [Genealogical table of the three-branch line of the Yŏhŭng Min clan], in Kang Sŏng-jo, "Kyejŏng Min Yŏng-hwan yŏn'gu" [Study on Kyejŏng Min Yŏng-hwan], pp. 39–41. Kang's biographical article provides a very useful overview and assessment of Min's life and career, although, as will be seen in this study, one or two of his conclusions appear to be incorrect. Kang was particularly fortunate in being able to interview Min Yŏng-hwan's grandson Min Pyŏng-gi (Kang was an assistant professor at Inch'ŏn University when Min Pyŏng-gi was the university president).

51. Yi Sang-ch'an, "1896 nyŏn ŭibyŏng undong ŭi chŏngch'ijŏk sŏnggyŏk" [The political characteristics of the "Righteous Army Movement" of 1896], p. 49.

52. Kang Sŏng-jo, "Kyejŏng," p. 39.

53. Dalchoong Kim, "Korea's Quest," p. 24.

54. Min Yu-jung's daughter was not the first Chosŏn queen to have come from the Yŏhŭng Min clan. Queen Wŏn'gyŏng (Wŏn'gyŏng wanghu), the consort of the third king of the Chosŏn dynasty, King T'aejong (r. 1400–1418), and the mother of the dynasty's most renowned sovereign, King Sejong (r. 1418–1450), was also a member of the Yŏhŭng Min clan. See Dalchoong Kim, "Korea's Quest," p. 25.

55. Queen Inhyŏn's turbulent life was recorded by a contemporary anonymous author, believed to have been a palace lady, in a work originally titled *Inhyŏn sŏnghu*

tŏkhaengnok [Record of the virtuous deeds of Queen Inhyŏn], but which is generally known as *Inhyŏn wanghu chŏn* [The story of Queen Inhyŏn].

56. King Sukchong, in fact, officially married three times. Queen Inhyŏn was his second consort *(kyebi),* whom he married after the death of his first consort *(ch'obi),* the daughter of Kim Man-gi.

57. Tan-hyŏn was the second son of Paek-yu and was adopted by Paek- sul, who had no sons. This practice of adoption of the son of a close relative of the same generation in order to continue the family line was common practice among *yangban* families during the Chosŏn era.

58. The Taewŏn'gun's mother was the daughter of Min Kyŏng-hyŏk (1746–1815) and consequently also a member of the Yŏhŭng Min clan. See Dalchoong Kim, "Korea's Quest," p. 28.

59. Min T'ae-ho (1828–1860), the son of Min Ch'i-gu, should not be confused with the son of Min Ch'i-o, who was also named Min T'ae-ho (1834–1884). The latter was the father of both Min Yŏng-ik and the consort of the crown prince, the future Emperor Sunjong. A powerful and influential figure in Kojong's court, he was assassinated during the Kapsin coup of 1884. See the Glossary for the Chinese character readings of all Korean, Chinese, and Japanese names as well as the adopted Chinese names of Westerners in Korea.

60. Present-day Kyŏnji-dong, 45 *bŏnji,* near Ch'ungjŏngno. The location of Min Yŏng-hwan's birthplace is based on the testimony of Min Pyŏng-gi in Kang Sŏng-jo, "Kyejŏng," p. 39.

61. Ibid. Min's date of birth according to the lunar calendar was the twelfth day of the seventh month of 1861. All dates in the text have been converted to solar dates for the sake of consistency. Because the dating of Min's memorials follow the lunar calendar, the lunar dates have been included in the footnotes for ease of reference.

62. This pen name may be a reference to Guigong (Kyekung), a palace built at Xi'an by the Han dynasty's martial emperor, Han Wudi (r. 140–87 B.C.).

63. Kang Sŏng-jo, "Kyejŏng," p. 41.

64. Ibid., p. 42.

65. Song Sang-do, comp., *Kiro sup'il* [Biographical essays], p. 61. The story concerning Min's mother's birth dream is also recounted in Hwang Hyŏn, *Maech'ŏn yarok,* p. 183.

66. Cho Yong-man, *Aegukcha Min Ch'ungjŏnggong* [Patriot Min Yŏng-hwan], p. 23.

67. Ibid., p. 24.

68. Lillias Horton Underwood, *Underwood of Korea,* p. 221. Although Min was not a prince of the royal line, as a close relative of the king and queen, he was commonly referred to as Prince Min in nineteenth-century Western writings.

69. *Kojong sidaesa* [History of the Kojong era], vol. 6, p. 33.

70. See *Min Ch'ungjŏnggong sillok* (an anonymous contemporary account of Min's protest, death, and funeral; it forms part of the fifth volume [pp. 195–207] of *Min Ch'ungjŏnggong yugo),* p. 195; Min's memorial of 1. 2 .1879 in *Soch'a,* p. 2; and Kang Sŏng-jo, "Kyejŏng," p. 42.

71. Kang Sŏng-jo, "Kyejŏng," p. 42.

72. According to the appendix of *Min Ch'ungjŏnggongyugo,* titled "Haengjŏk," but in Kang Sŏng-jo, "Kyejŏng," 1899 is given.

73. Kang Sŏng-jo, "Kyejŏng," p. 42. The names and dates of birth of Min's two daughters are not recorded in any of the available biographical records, but from a surviving photograph, the eldest daughter appears to have been about one year younger than Pŏm-sik, and the second daughter appears to have been about one year older than Chang-sik.

74. Han'gŭl hakhoe, ed., *Urimal k'ŭn sajŏn* [Dictionary of the Korean language], vol. 1, p. 1108.

75. *Kojong sidaesa,* vol. 2, pp. 3, 17. Kang Sŏng-jo, "Kyejŏng," p. 44. *Min Ch'ungjŏnggong yugo,* "Haesŏl" [Commentary], p. 1. The final stage of the Erudite Examination was the *chŏnsi,* which was taken in the presence of the king. For a concise description of the Chosŏn administrative and examination systems in English, see Han Woo-keun, *The History of Korea,* pp. 229–239.

76. *Soch'a,* p. 1. There were nine ranks *(p'um)* altogether in the Chosŏn administration, with the first rank being the highest. These ranks were further subdivided into senior *(chŏng)* and junior *(chong).* The senior third rank, however, was further divided into an upper *(tangsang)* and a lower *(tangha)* rank. For a useful overview of the Chosŏn administrative ranks in tabular form, see Yi Hyŏn-chong, *Tongyang yŏnp'yo: kaejŏng chŭngbop'an* [East Asian chronology: Revised and enlarged edition], pp. 168–187.

77. See Harold F. Cook, "Kim Ok-kyun and the Background of the 1884 Émeute," p. 44; Dalchoong Kim, "Korea's Quest," p. 38; and Deuchler, *Confucian Gentlemen,* pp. 152–158.

78. *Soch'a,* pp. 1–2.

79. For evidence of all these aspects of Min's personality, see *Soch'a,* pp. 1–43.

80. 4.1.1879 lunar. *Kojong sidaesa,* vol. 2, p. 70.

81. *Soch'a,* p. 2.

82. Kang Sŏng-jo, "Kyejŏng," p. 44.

83. 7.2.1879 lunar. *Kojong sidaesa,* vol. 2, p. 74; *Soch'a,* p. 2.

84. Hwang Hyŏn, *Maech'ŏn yarok,* p. 52.

85. Ibid.

86. *Soch'a,* pp. 2–3.

87. *Kojong sidaesa,* vol. 2, pp. 84, 86, 93, 94, 122, 124, and 133. Min was appointed to the posts of third inspector and junior fourth counsellor twice in the same year.

88. 26.4.1880 lunar. *Kojong sidaesa,* vol. 2, pp. 162 and 168.

89. 22.6.1880 lunar. *Soch'a,* pp. 3–4.

90. 19.9.1880 lunar. Ibid., p. 4; *Kojong sidaesa,* vol. 2, p. 189.

91. For a highly appreciative assessment of Pak's integrity and good sense, see Horace N. Allen, *Things Korean,* pp. 164–166.

92. *Soch'a,* p. 5.

93. Ibid., pp. 5–6.

94. John K. Fairbank, *China: A New History*, p. 66.

95. 19.2.1881 lunar. *Kojong sidaesa*, vol. 2, p. 223; Kang Sŏng-jo, "Kyejŏng," p. 45.

96. Kang Sŏng-jo, "Kyejŏng," p. 45.

97. *Soch'a*, p. 6.

98. *Kojong sidaesa*, vol. 2, p. 298.

99. *Soch'a*, pp. 6–7. One *kŭn* is equal to 601.04 grams.

100. *Kojong sidaesa*, vol. 2, pp. 298, 321.

101. Dalchoong Kim, "Korea's Quest," p. 6.

102. One of the best accounts of the origins, course, and outcome of the rebellion in English is Deuchler, *Confucian Gentlemen*, pp. 129–147.

103. Hwang Hyŏn, *Maech'ŏn yarok*, p. 27.

104. Ibid., p. 33.

105. 6.9.1884 lunar. *Kojong sidaesa*, vol. 2, p. 654.

106. The exact length of the mourning period for both parents in Chosŏn Korea was, in fact, twenty-seven months. See Martina Deuchler, *The Confucian Transformation of Korea*, p. 183.

107. *Soch'a*, pp. 7–9.

108. The coup d'état of 1884 took place on the seventeenth day of the tenth month according to the lunar calendar (4 December 1884 according to the solar calendar).

109. 6.12.1884 lunar. *Soch'a*, p. 9.

110. *Min Ch'ungjŏnggong sillok*, p. 200, quoted in Kang Sŏng-jo, "Kyejŏng," p. 45. See chapter 5 for the full text of Kojong's proclamation.

111. Sands, *Undiplomatic Memories*, p. 128.

112. *Kojong sidaesa*, vol. 2, pp. 717, 724, 727, 729, and 734.

113. Ibid., pp. 769, 770, 771, and 773. For an account of the establishment of the mint, see Deuchler, *Confucian Gentlemen*, pp. 155–156.

114. 2.2.1886 lunar. *Kojong sidaesa*, vol. 2, p. 817.

115. *Soch'a*, p. 12.

116. Ibid., p. 13.

117. 13.5.1887 lunar. Ibid., pp. 13–14.

118. *Kojong sidaesa*, vol. 2, pp. 818, 826, 853, and 873.

119. Cook, *Korea's 1884 Incident*, p. 247.

120. 27.2.1887 lunar. *Kojong sidaesa*, vol. 2, p. 897.

121. *Kojong sidaesa*, vol. 2, pp. 897, 900, 919, 930, and 946.

122. An honorific title for officials of senior second rank. *"Chahŏn"* has the literal meaning of "signally helpful."

123. Kang Sŏng-jo, "Kyejŏng," p. 47.

124. 4.4.1888 lunar. *Kojong sidaesa*, vol. 3, pp. 15–16.

125. *Soch'a*, pp. 15–16.

126. *Kojong sidaesa*, vol. 3, pp. 23 and 31.

127. Yun, *Ilgi*, vol. 4, p. 166.

128. 8.11.1890 lunar. *Kojong sidaesa*, vol. 3, pp. 106, 123, and 195.

129. *Soch'a*, pp. 16–23.

130. 22.8.1890 lunar. Ibid., p. 23.
131. Ibid., p. 24.
132. Ibid., pp. 24–28.
133. 27.2.1891 lunar. Ibid., p. 28.
134. One of four or five. See Deuchler, *Confucian Gentlemen*, p. 154.
135. 28.10.1893 lunar. *Kojong sidaesa*, vol. 3, pp. 394, 397, and 400.
136. Ibid., pp. 405, 413, 414, 468, and 473.

CHAPTER 2. PROPOSALS FOR REFORM

1. The title *Ch'ŏnilch'aek* is an allusion to the Chinese phrase "*yu zhe qian lu bi you yi de,*" meaning "Out of a thousand ideas of a fool there is bound to be one that is useful." See Tai-jin Kim, *Bibliographical Guide*, p. 509.
2. Kang Sŏng-jo, "Kyejŏng," p. 58.
3. *Ch'ŏnilch'aek*, p. 66.
4. Ibid., p. 67.
5. Ibid., p. 47.
6. Ibid., p. 52.
7. Ibid., p. 65.
8. Ibid., p. 48.
9. Ibid., p. 49.
10. Yi Kwang-nin, *Han'guksa*, p. 278.
11. *Ch'ŏnilch'aek*, p. 49.
12. Yi Kwang-nin, *Han'guksa*, p. 287.
13. Another name for Kŭmsŏng (present-day Kyŏngju), the capital of the ancient Korean kingdom Silla.
14. *Ch'ŏnilch'aek*, p. 47. The years Kabo and Ŭlmi, of course, occur every sixty years, but in this context Min could only be referring to 1894 and 1895, the years of the Sino-Japanese War and the so-called Kabo-Ŭlmi reform movement.
15. *Ch'ŏnilch'aek*, p. 46.
16. Kang Sŏng-jo, "Kyejŏng," p. 69.
17. *Ch'ŏnilch'aek*, p. 45.
18. Again it is unlikely that Min would have put forward a policy so hostile to Russia at a time when Kojong was under the protection of the Russian legation from 1896 to 1897.
19. *Ch'ŏnilch'aek*, p. 45.
20. Ibid.
21. Ibid.
22. Ibid.
23. S. I. Witte, *The Memoirs of Count Witte*, p. 83.
24. George A. Lensen, *Balance of Intrigue*, vol. 2, pp. 835–854.
25. M. N. Pak with Wayne Patterson, "Russian Policy toward Korea before and during the Sino-Japanese War of 1894–1895," p. 110.

26. Andrew C. Nahm, "Korea and Tsarist Russia, pp. 4–5. For an illuminating contemporary account of the "Russian enigma" in relation to Korea, see Sands, *Undiplomatic Memories*, pp. 215–218.

27. *Ch'ŏnilch'aek*, p. 46.

28. Ibid.

29. Ibid.

30. For detailed discussions of the *sei-Kan-ron*, which split the Japanese government's leadership circa 1873, see Key-Hiuk Kim, *Last Phase*, pp. 169–187; and Conroy, *Japanese Seizure of Korea*, pp. 18–71.

31. *Ch'ŏnilch'aek*, p. 46.

32. Ibid.

33. Ibid., pp. 46–47.

34. For an in-depth discussion of Fukuzawa's influence on Kim Ok-kyun, see Cook, *Korea's 1884 Incident*.

35. See Conroy, *Japanese Seizure of Korea*, p. 202.

36. Sands, *Undiplomatic Memories*, pp. 219–220.

37. Ibid., pp. 220–223.

38. Kang Sŏng-jo, "Kyejŏng," p. 58, n. 65.

39. *Ch'ŏnilch'aek*, p. 47.

40. For Ernest Satow's translation of this important document, see Foreign Office (FO) Confidential Print, 1881: Correspondence respecting the Russo-Chinese Treaty (Kuldja Territory), No. 47, Kennedy to Granville, 8 June 1881, inclosure no. 2, "The True Policy for Corea: A Private Memorandum by Huan Tsun-hsien, Secretary of the Chinese Legation in Japan," in Park Il-Keun, *Anglo-American Diplomatic Materials relating to Korea, 1866–1886*, pp. 105–115. For a discussion of the effect this document had on the Chosŏn court, see Deuchler, *Confucian Gentlemen*, pp. 88–92.

41. Young Ick Lew, "Yüan Shih-k'ai's Residency."

42. *Ch'ŏnilch'aek*, p. 47.

43. Ibid., p. 48.

44. For critical assessments of Qing policy in Korea during the 1880s, see Key-Hiuk Kim, *Last Phase;* Dalchoong Kim, "Korea's Quest"; and Robert R. Swartout, Jr., *Mandarins, Gunboats, and Power Politics.*

45. The two most detailed studies on Korean-American relations in the 1880s are Chay, *Diplomacy of Asymmetry;* and Swartout, *Mandarins, Gunboats, and Power Politics.*

46. See Sands, *Undiplomatic Memories*, pp. 120–124.

47. Frederick A. McKenzie, *Korea's Fight for Freedom*, p. 42.

48. See FO Confidential Print: Further Correspondence respecting the Affairs of Corea, no. 13, Sir H. Parkes to Earl Granville, 7 December 1883, inclosure, "Memorandum of Interview with Grand Secretary Li," in Park, *Anglo-American Diplomatic Materials*, pp. 397–401.

49. Hosea B. Morse, *The International Relations of the Chinese Empire*, vol. 3, pp. 15–16 n.

50. *Ch'ŏnilch'aek*, p. 48.

51. Ibid., p. 49.
52. A useful overview of Korean and Japanese studies of the Tonghak rebellion may be found in Han Woo-keun, "Tonghak and the Tonghak Revolt," pp. 213–246.
53. *Ch'ŏnilch'aek*, p. 50.
54. See Min's memorial to the throne of 19.9.1880 (22 October 1880), *Soch'a*, p. 4, in which he demanded the strict punishment of Pak Chŏng-yang and others for their involvement in irregularities in the state examination *(kwagŏ)*.
55. *Ch'ŏnilch'aek*, p. 50.
56. Ibid.
57. Ibid., p. 51. There are five Chinese classics: the *Yi jing* [Classic of changes], the *Shu jing* [Classic of documents], the *Shi jing* [Classic of songs], the *Chun qiu* [Spring and autumn annals], and the *Li ji* [Record of ceremonies and proper conduct].
58. *Ch'ŏnilch'aek*, p. 51.
59. A veiled reference to Russia, already referred to as a "modern-day Qin," and Japan. Ibid., pp. 51–52.
60. See Min's interview in the *Independent* in chapter 4.
61. *Ch'ŏnilch'aek*, p. 52.
62. Ibid.
63. Ibid.
64. Ibid., p. 53.
65. Ibid.
66. Ibid.
67. Sands, *Undiplomatic Memories*, pp. 120–121.
68. *Ch'ŏnilch'aek*, p. 54.
69. Ibid.
70. Ibid.
71. Ibid.
72. Ibid., p. 55.
73. Ibid.
74. Ibid.
75. For a highly critical account of the activities of the American military instructors employed by the Chosŏn administration in the late 1880s and early 1890s under the command of William McEntyre Dye, see Young Ick Lew, "American Advisers in Korea, 1885–1894, pp. 64–90.
76. *Ch'ŏnilch'aek*, p. 55.
77. Ibid., p. 56.
78. Ibid.
79. Ibid.
80. Ibid., p. 57.
81. A standard straw sack of rice, also known as a *sŏm*.
82. Inclosure in no. 205 in Trench to Earl Granville, 5 November 1883, in Park, *Anglo-American Diplomatic Materials*, p. 365.

83. See Kim and Kim, *Korea and the Politics of Imperialism,* pp. 71–73; and Yi Kwang-nin, *Han'guksa,* pp. 262–265.

84. *Ch'ŏnilch'aek,* p. 57.

85. Ibid.

86. Ibid.

87. Ibid., p. 58.

88. Ibid. According to the U.S. naval attaché George C. Foulk, by 1885 the Korean army was in possession of three thousand Remington and one thousand Peabody-Martini rifles and had on order six Gatling guns to be supplied with seventy-five thousand cartridges. See Foulk to Bayard, 2 September 1885, in Park, *Anglo-American Diplomatic Materials,* p. 1008.

89. Approximately 600 grams.

90. *Ch'ŏnilch'aek,* pp. 58–59.

91. The Kigiguk had been established on 15 June 1883 for the repair and manufacture of military equipment. See Deuchler, *Confucian Gentlemen,* p. 156.

92. *Ch'ŏnilch'aek,* p. 59.

93. Hwang, *Maech'ŏn yarok,* p. 10.

94. Robert T. Oliver, *Syngman Rhee,* p. 32.

95. See Underwood, *Fifteen Years,* p. 29; and Allen, *Things Korean,* pp. 128–129.

96. *Ch'ŏnilch'aek,* p. 59.

97. Ibid., pp. 59–60.

98. Ibid., p. 60.

99. Ibid.

100. Later Liang, Later Tang, Later Jin, Later Han, and Later Zhou. This period lasted A.D. 907–960.

101. *Ch'ŏnilch'aek,* p. 61.

102. A book written during the Five Dynasties period.

103. *Ch'ŏnilch'aek,* p. 61.

104. Ibid.

105. For an account of the development of Western medical missions in Korea until 1910, see Lak-Geoon George Paik, *The History of Protestant Missions in Korea.*

106. *Ch'ŏnilch'aek,* p. 61.

107. Ibid., pp. 61–62.

108. Yi Kwang-nin, *Han'guksa,* pp. 25–27.

109. *Ch'ŏnilch'aek,* p. 62.

110. Ibid.

111. The three ancient dynasties, Xia, Shang, and Zhou.

112. One ounce of silver, a *tael.*

113. *Ch'ŏnilch'aek,* p. 63.

114. Ibid.

115. A measurement of land, based on its productivity, used for taxation purposes in the Chosŏn period.

116. *Ch'ŏnilch'aek*, p. 63.
117. A string of cash.
118. *Ch'ŏnilch'aek*, p. 63.
119. Yi I (Yi Yul-gok), a Chosŏn neo-Confucian scholar who lived from 1536 to 1584.
120. *Ch'ŏnilch'aek*, p. 63.
121. Ibid., pp. 63–64.
122. Ibid.
123. Ibid.
124. Ibid.
125. Ibid.
126. Ibid.
127. Ibid., p. 65.
128. When Min mentioned Sŏhak, he was referring to Roman Catholic believers. See Yi Kwang-nin, *Han'guksa*, p. 14.
129. *Ch'ŏnilch'aek*, p. 65.
130. Ibid.
131. Ibid.
132. Ibid.
133. Ibid., pp. 65–66.
134. Ibid., p. 66.
135. Ibid.
136. Ibid.
137. Ibid., pp. 66–67.
138. Ibid., p. 67.
139. Quoted in Dalchoong Kim, "Korea's Quest," pp. 394–395 and 397–399.
140. See ibid., pp. 335 and 383; and Yi Kwang-nin, *Han'guksa*, p. 208.
141. *Ch'ŏnilch'aek*, p. 67.
142. Dong Zhongshu (Han Confucianist).
143. *Ch'ŏnilch'aek*, p. 68.

CHAPTER 3. MISSION TO RUSSIA

1. Nahm, "Korea and Tsarist Russia," p. 4. I am indebted to Nahm's concise account of this period in this article. For a more detailed discussion of the same subject, see Seung Kwon Synn, "The Russo-Korean Relations in the 1880s," pp. 26–39. The most comprehensive study of Korean-Russian relations at the close of the nineteenth century, however, remains Lensen, *Balance of Intrigue*.
2. Foulk to Bayard, 14 October 1885, in McCune and Harrison, eds., *Korean-American Relations*, pp. 85–86.
3. For the best study on "the first 'official' Western adviser to the Korean government," Paul Georg von Möllendorff, see Yur-Bok Lee, *West Goes East*.
4. For a concise and lucid account of this affair see Andrew W. Hamilton, "The

Kŏmundo Affair." For an in-depth study of Anglo-Korean relations in this period, see Yung Chung Kim, "Great Britain and Korea, 1883–1887."

5. Nahm, "Korea and Tsarist Russia," p. 8.

6. Ibid.

7. Yi Min-wŏn, "A'gwan p'achŏn, pp. 24–42 and 188–189.

8. For details of the correspondence in *Ku Han'guk oegyo munsŏ: A-an* [Diplomatic documents of the late Yi dynasty: Russian archives], compiled by the Asiatic Research Center, Korea University (Seoul: Asiatic Research Center of Korea University, 1965–1970), see Ko Pyŏng-ik, "Nohwang taegwansike ŭi sahaenggwa hanno kyosŏp" [The Russo-Korean negotiations on the occasion of the coronation of Nicholas II in 1896], p. 42.

9. Min Yŏng-hwan, *Haech'ŏn ch'ubŏm* [Sea, sky, autumn voyage]; *Min Ch'ungjŏng-gong yugo,* vol. 3, p. 69; *Kojong sidaesa,* vol. 4, p. 61.

10. Ko Pyŏng-ik, "Nohwang taegwansike ŭi sahaenggwa hanno kyosŏp," p. 42.

11. *Kojong sidaesa,* vol. 3, pp. 798 and 985.

12. Yun Ch'i-ho, *Ilgi,* vol. 4, p. 153.

13. Ibid., p. 162.

14. Witte, *Memoirs,* p. 82.

15. For a detailed account of Li Hong-zhang's negotiations with Witte, see Lensen, *Balance of Intrigue,* vol. 2, pp. 477–513.

16. Ibid., p. 512. Incidentally, Witte emphatically denied the existence of the bribe. See Witte, *Memoirs,* p. 95.

17. For a more detailed account of this agreement, also known as the Protocol of Moscow, see Kim and Kim, *Korea and the Politics of Imperialism,* pp. 91–92.

18. Andrew Malozemoff, *Russian Far Eastern Policy 1881–1904,* 107 ff.

19. *Haech'ŏn ch'ubŏm,* pp. 135 and 137.

20. Ibid., p. 137.

21. The first unofficial visit to Europe by a high-ranking Korean official was made in 1884 by Min Yŏng-hwan's cousin Min Yŏng-ik and Sŏ Kwang-bŏm on their return from an official visit to the United States on the U.S. naval vessel *Trenton* in 1883. See Ko, "Nohwang taegwansike ŭi sahaenggwa hanno kyosŏp," p. 64. A mention of their arrival in England at that time may be found in "Prince Min Yong in England," *Times* (London) 17 January 1884, p. 9, col. e.

22. *Kojong sidaesa,* vol. 4, p. 64; *Haech'ŏn ch'ubŏm,* p. 70.

23. *Haech'ŏn ch'ubŏm,* pp. 70, 71.

24. Ko, "Nohwang taegwansike ŭi sahaenggwa hanno kyosŏp," pp. 41–69.

25. A manuscript attributed to Min Yŏng-hwan, titled *Ayŏng kijŏng* [Record of a journey to Russia and Britain] and dated 1897 is in Sŏgang University library.

26. *"Hwan"* means "to encircle; *"gu"* is a traditional percussion musical instrument (composed of slabs of jade suspended on a frame) or the sound that such an instrument makes. The title refers to the round-the-world journey made by Min Yŏng-hwan and his entourage.

27. *Haech'ŏn ch'ubŏm,* p. 137.

28. For an introduction to the life and thought of Yun Ch'i-ho (1865–1945), see Kenneth M. Wells, *New God, New Nation*, pp. 47–70.

29. The Russian secretary Stein originally gave this appellation to Kim Tŭng-nyŏn because of the latter's hard drinking.

30. Yun, *Ilgi*, vol. 4, pp. 266–267. At the time that Ko wrote his article (1965), he did not have access to Yun's diary, which was first published from 1973 to 1976.

31. *Haech'ŏn ch'ubŏm*, p. 140.

32. Seoul's west gate, destroyed in 1915.

33. *Haech'ŏn ch'ubŏm*, p. 73.

34. The most extensive account of von Möllendorff's activities at the Chosŏn court, which included an attempt to secure Russian protection for the Korean peninsula in 1884–1885, is in Yur-Bok Lee, *West Goes East*.

35. Dmitrii Dmitrievich Pokotilov, formerly a Chinese language student at Beijing (1891–1893) and subsequently minister to China (1906–1907), was sent to Korea as a temporary representative of the Russian Finance Ministry to assess Korea's financial condition in response to Min Yŏng-hwan's request for a Russian loan made during his negotiations with Lobanov and Witte in Moscow and St. Petersburg. See Lensen, *Balance of Intrigue*, vol. 2, p. 652.

36. I. A. Reding, Russian consul at Shanghai, 1885–1896.

37. It is interesting to note that before traveling to Washington as minister plenipotentiary to the United States in November and December 1887, Pak Chŏng-yang also briefly visited Min Yŏng-ik, who was staying in Hong Kong at that time. See Dalchoong Kim, "Korea's Quest," p. 421.

38. Yun Ch'i-ho, on the other hand, often provides verbatim records of such conversations. See Yun, *Ilgi*, vol. 4, passim.

39. Ibid., p. 166.

40. *Haech'ŏn ch'ubŏm*, p. 73.

41. Concerning Alekseev and his squadron, Lensen writes, "The Pacific squadron of Russia was weaker than outsiders realized. The arbitrary rule of Rear Admiral Alekseev, the illegitimate son of Alexander II, and of the ships' commanders had thoroughly demoralized the officers, some of whom had been at sea for over five years without relief. Lack of discipline, improper training and assignment, and general disorder characterized the squadron while Alekseev was in command from 1895–1897." Lensen, *Balance of Intrigue*, vol. 2, p. 839.

42. V. I. Kostylev, Russian consul at Nagasaki 1885–1900. In 1885 Kostylev had been involved in von Möllendorff's attempt to acquire Russian military instructors for Korea. See Lensen, *Balance of Intrigue*, vol. 1, p. 37.

43. According to Yun, the prince was a notorious womanizer and heavily in debt. For a more sympathetic, albeit brief, portrayal of the prince and his life in Japan and the United States in the late 1890s, see James S. Gale, *Korean Sketches*, pp. 222–226.

44. *Haech'ŏn ch'ubŏm*, p. 76.

45. Ibid.

46. Ibid.

47. Ibid., p. 77.

48. Donald Baker, "Sirhak Medicine: Measles, Smallpox, and Chŏng Tasan," pp. 157–158.

49. *Haech'ŏn ch'ubŏm*, p. 78. Compare this account of an encounter with an elevator with that of the Korean envoy to the United States, Pak Chŏng-yang, and his aides nearly a decade earlier in 1888: "Certainly Pak and his aides were out of place in the United States, unprepared for the wonders of industrial civilization. . . . Arriving at the Palace Hotel in San Francisco, they were crowded into a tiny room. Small, they thought, for so considerable a party; and then, to their amazement and horror, the room began to move. They trembled and cried that it was an earthquake, come to plague them in a foreign land. Allen explained how elevators worked; but after that the Koreans used the stairs." This account of Korean officials abroad is attributed to Horace N. Allen in Harrington, *God, Mammon, and the Japanese*, pp. 238–239.

50. *Haech'ŏn ch'ubŏm*, p. 78.

51. Ibid., p. 79.

52. Qi and Chu were kingdoms during the period of Warring States that were overthrown by Qin in 221 B.C.

53. *Haech'ŏn ch'ubŏm*, p. 79.

54. Ibid.

55. Yun, *Ilgi*, vol. 4, p. 175. Min, however, gives his name in *han'gŭl* as "Olnarobŭsŭgi [Olnarovsky]." Min generally gives the names of Western places and persons in *han'gŭl* (except for places with an established Chinese-character version of their name such as London and Berlin), whereas Yun provides the names as they would be written in English. Yun's versions of Western proper names, therefore, have been preferred over Min's. Unfortunately, neither Yun nor Min provides given names for the people they mention. Where Western names appear in the text without given names, it has not been possible to identify that person.

56. Yun, *Ilgi*, vol. 4, p. 175. Unlike Sŏ Kwang-bŏm, Min and his party, including Yun, wore traditional Korean clothes, attracting unwelcome attention from some New Yorkers. "If laughing and smiling are a sign of happiness, certainly we, in our strange dress, were an innocent cause of making many a person happy in N.Y.," Yun wrote with some chagrin. See ibid., pp. 175–176.

57. *Haech'ŏn ch'ubŏm*, p. 80.

58. Ibid., p. 81.

59. Ibid., p. 82.

60. Ibid.

61. Ibid.

62. Yun, *Ilgi*, vol. 4, p. 179. Min gives the name as the Europa Hotel.

63. *Haech'ŏn ch'ubŏm*, p. 83.

64. Ibid.

65. *Kojong sidaesa*, vol. 4, p. 135; *Haech'ŏn ch'ubŏm*, p. 83.

66. Yun, *Ilgi*, vol. 4, p. 206; *Haech'ŏn ch'ubŏm*, p. 83.

67. *Haech'ŏn ch'ubŏm*, p. 83.

68. Grand Duke Sergei Alexandrovich (1857–1905) was the fifth son of Tsar Alexander II.

69. Alexandra Feodorovna was the former Princess Alix of Hesse-Darmstadt and a granddaughter of Queen Victoria. Maria Dagmar was a sister of Queen Alexandria, the wife of King Edward VII of Great Britain.

70. Yun, *Ilgi*, vol. 4, pp. 202–203.

71. Ibid., p. 173.

72. Ibid.

73. Ibid., p. 181.

74. Ibid., vol. 5, p. 6.

75. Ibid., vol. 4, p. 182.

76. For the full text of Kojong's personal letter, see appendix 3.

77. *Haech'ŏn ch'ubŏm*, p. 137.

78. Yun, *Ilgi*, vol. 4, p. 197.

79. Ibid., p. 182.

80. Ibid., p. 183.

81. Ibid., pp. 185–186.

82. Ibid., p. 189.

83. Ibid., vol. 5, p. 36.

84. *Haech'ŏn ch'ubŏm*, p. 90.

85. Ibid.

86. Ban Byung-yool, "Korean Emigration to the Russian Far East, 1860s-1910s," p. 129.

87. *Haech'ŏn ch'ubŏm*, p. 133.

88. See appendix 3.

89. Yun, *Ilgi*, vol. 4, p. 201.

90. According to Yun this treaty was signed by Chŏng Pyŏng-ha circa 1886.

91. The assassination of Queen Myŏngsŏng.

92. Yun, *Ilgi*, vol. 4, p. 202.

93. For the text of Min's credentials, see appendix 3.

94. Yun, *Ilgi*, vol. 4, p. 203.

95. Ibid.

96. Ibid., pp. 203–204.

97. *Haech'ŏn ch'ubŏm*, p. 91.

98. Kŏnyang (Lustrous inauguration) was the year appellation given to the period 1896–1897 in the reign of King Kojong.

99. Yun, *Ilgi*, vol. 4, p. 205.

100. Ibid.

101. Ibid., p. 213.

102. Ibid., p. 214.

103. English text from William W. Rockhill, ed., *Treaties and Conventions with or concerning China and Korea, 1894–1904*, pp. 430–431.

104. Malozemoff, *Russian Far Eastern Policy*, p. 88.

105. Yun, *Ilgi*, vol. 4, p. 214.
106. Ibid.
107. Ibid., p. 215.
108. Ibid.
109. Ibid.
110. Ibid., pp. 216–217.
111. Ibid., p. 219.
112. Ibid., p. 220.
113. Ibid., p. 221.
114. Ibid.
115. *Haech'ŏn ch'ubŏm*, p. 96.
116. Yun, *Ilgi*, vol. 4, p. 233. To compare Yun's version with Lobanov's "points in reply to the Korean ambassador," which was approved by Tsar Nicholas II, see appendix 3.
117. Lensen, *Balance of Intrigue*, p. 652.
118. Tschirschky to Hohenlohe-Schillingsfürst, no. A 8670, St. Petersburg, 10 August 1896, Auswärtiges Amt, in Lensen, *Balance of Intrigue*, pp. 650–651.
119. Yun, *Ilgi*, vol. 4, p. 224.
120. There appears to be some disagreement, however, about Yun's ancestral seat. *Han'guk inmyŏng taesajŏn* [Korean biographical dictionary] gives P'ap'yŏng, while the more recently published Yu Yŏng-nyŏl, "Yun Ch'i-ho," vol. 17, p. 328, and Wells, *New God, New Nation*, p. 48, give Haep'yŏng.
121. Wells, *New God, New Nation*, p. 48.
122. For an account of the Andong Kim clan and its political rivalry with the Yŏhŭng Min clan, see Cook, *Korea's 1884 Incident*, pp. 13–17.
123. *Haech'ŏn ch'ubŏm*, p. 137.
124. Yun, *Ilgi*, vol. 4, p. 230.
125. *Haech'ŏn ch'ubŏm*, p. 138.
126. Yun, *Ilgi*, vol. 4, p. 231.
127. Ibid., pp. 268, 270, and 275.
128. Ibid., vol. 6, pp. 213–214.
129. *Haech'ŏn ch'ubŏm*, pp. 93–94.
130. Ibid., p. 95.
131. Ibid., p. 96.
132. Ibid.
133. Ibid.
134. Ibid., pp. 105–106. The biblical echo in this comment may derive from the fact that Min's paternal aunt, the wife of the Taewŏn'gun, was reputedly a Christian.
135. Envoy extraordinary and minister plenipotentiary.
136. Yun, *Ilgi*, vol. 4, p. 268.
137. *Haech'ŏn ch'ubŏm*, p. 115.
138. Yun, *Ilgi*, vol. 4, p. 274.
139. *Haech'ŏn ch'ubŏm*, p. 141.

140. Kim and Kim, *Korea and the Politics of Imperialism,* pp. 95–96.

141. *Haech'ŏn ch'ubŏm,* p. 117.

142. Ibid., pp. 117–118.

143. Ibid., p. 120.

144. Ibid., p. 121.

145. Ibid., p. 123.

146. According to Wayne Patterson, *Korean Frontier,* p. 2, 23,000 Koreans were living in the Russian Maritime Provinces by the end of the nineteenth century.

147. *Haech'ŏn ch'ubŏm,* p. 124.

148. Ibid.

149. Ibid., p. 126.

150. Patterson, *Korean Frontier,* p. 2.

151. Ibid.

152. *Haech'ŏn ch'ubŏm,* p. 127.

153. Ban, "Korean Emigration," p. 121.

154. *Haech'ŏn ch'ubŏm,* p. 128.

155. Ibid., p. 129.

156. Ibid.

157. Lensen, *Balance of Intrigue,* vol. 2, p. 652.

158. *Independent,* 24 October 1896.

159. *Haech'ŏn ch'ubŏm,* p. 130.

160. Ibid., pp. 132–133.

161. Bishop, *Korea and Her Neighbours,* pp. 447–448.

162. Ki-baik Lee, *New History,* pp. 301 and 310.

163. *Haech'ŏn ch'ubŏm,* p. 133.

164. *Kojong sidaesa,* vol. 4, p. 288; *Haech'ŏn ch'ubŏm,* p. 135. For the text of the Tsar's personal letter, see appendix 2.

165. *Chosŏn wangjo sillok: Kojong p'yŏn* (21 October 1896).

CHAPTER 4. EMBASSY TO QUEEN VICTORIA'S DIAMOND JUBILEE

1. *Kojong sidaesa,* vol. 4, p. 273.

2. Ibid., p. 293.

3. Plancy to Hanotaux, DP, no. 50, Seoul, 17 January 1897, French Archives, Korea, PE, 8:2–4; Jordan to MacDonald, no. 3, Seoul, 14 January 1897, FO 404/73, pp. 22–23, quoted in Lensen, *Balance of Intrigue,* p. 890, n. 18.

4. Lensen, *Balance of Intrigue,* p. 654.

5. FO 405, part 10, Jordan to MacDonald, 14 November 1896.

6. Yun, *Ilgi,* vol. 4, p. 263.

7. Vipan Chandra, *Imperialism, Resistance, and Reform in Late Nineteenth-Century Korea,* p. 108.

8. *Independent,* 10 November 1896.

9. Ibid., 28 November 1896.

10. The rebels referred to here must have been either members of a "righteous army" (*ŭibyŏng*) or remnants of the Tonghak.

11. *Independent,* 1 December 1896.

12. Ibid.

13. Ibid., 5 December 1896.

14. Ibid., 9 February 1897.

15. Ibid.

16. Yun, *Ilgi,* vol. 5, p. 19.

17. *Independent,* 4 February 1897.

18. Sŏ married Muriel Josephine Armstrong in 1892. She was the daughter of the founder of the U.S. Railway Mail Service, Colonel George Buchanan Armstrong, a cousin of President James Buchanan. See Chandra, *Imperialism, Resistance, and Reform,* p. 87.

19. Yun, *Ilgi,* vol. 5, p. 20. The Reids must have been Dr. C. F. Reid and his wife, who had moved from Shanghai to Korea in 1896 to found the Southern Methodist Mission in Korea at the invitation of Yun Ch'i-ho. See Paik, *History of Protestant Missions,* pp. 197–199.

20. Yun, *Ilgi,* vol. 5, p. 21.

21. Ibid., p. 24.

22. Ibid.

23. Yi Sŏn-gŭn, *Taehan'guksa* [History of Korea], vol. 8, p. 60.

24. See *Ku han'guk oegyo munsŏ* [Diplomatic documents of the late Yi dynasty], vol. 10: *Mian* [U.S. records], p. 582.

25. FO 228/1259, Jordan to MacDonald, 20 March 1897.

26. *Independent,* 7 April 1896.

27. *Sagu sokch'o,* p. 143.

28. Dalchoong Kim, "Korea's Quest," pp. 407, 427–428.

29. *Sagu sokch'o,* p. 143. *Kojong sidaesa,* vol. 4, p. 313. *Independent,* 12 January 1897, p. 134.

30. Willis, the Chinese translator at the British legation in Seoul, explained the difference between "*taesa*" and "*kongsa*" as follows: "The term used for Ambassador is not the usual Chinese expression: the phrase, however, literally "Great Envoy" is used in Corean-Chinese to signify an Envoy of higher rank than Envoy Extraordinary." FO 228/1259, inclosure in Jordan to MacDonald, 6 March 1897.

31. Ibid.

32. See appendix 3.

33. FO 228/1259, Jordan to MacDonald, 6 March 1897.

34. For a detailed account of the circumstances surrounding the publication of these two agreements by the Japanese and Russian governments and the Korean government's official response, see Lensen, *Balance of Intrigue,* vol. 2, pp. 635–637.

35. FO 228/1259, Jordan to MacDonald, 6 March 1897.

36. Plancy to Hanotaux, DP, no. 50, Seoul, 17 January 1897, Korea, PE, 8:2–4, quoted in Lensen, *Balance of Intrigue,* vol. 2, p. 890.

37. Yun, *Ilgi*, vol. 4, p. 213.
38. FO 405/73, part 10, Jordan to MacDonald, no. 3, Seoul, 14 January 1897, pp. 22–23.
39. *Sagu sokch'o*, p. 144.
40. *Independent*, 25 February 1897.
41. Sands, *Undiplomatic Memories*, p. 127. According to Sands, a portrait of Min Sang-ho may be found in a collection of portraits of Korea, China, and India by Hubert Vos.
42. FO 405/73, part 10, Jordan to MacDonald, 11 February 1897.
43. *Sagu sokch'o*, p. 144. See also FO 405/73, part 10, Jordan to Salisbury, 13 February 1897.
44. *Sagu sokch'o*, p. 145.
45. Ibid.
46. FO 405/73, Jordan to MacDonald, no. 4, Seoul, 18 January 1897, "Very Confidential," 23–24, quoted in Lensen, *Balance of Intrigue*, p. 890.
47. FO 405/73, part 10, Jordan to MacDonald, 11 February 1897.
48. *Kojong sidaesa*, vol. 4, p. 330.
49. *Sagu sokch'o*, p. 193.
50. Ibid., p. 146.
51. Tŏksu Palace.
52. *Sagu sokch'o*, p. 146; *Independent*, 18 March 1897.
53. *Sagu sokch'o*, p. 146.
54. FO 228/1259, Jordan to MacDonald, 20 March 1897.
55. *Independent*, 26 December 1896.
56. The China correspondent for the *Times*, G. E. Morrison, who held a high opinion of Jordan, was contemptuous of MacDonald, describing him as "an ill-read half educated infantry major, without brains, memory or judgment for this most difficult post [i.e., British minister to China and Korea]." See G. E. Morrison, *The Correspondence of G. E. Morrison*, vol. 1, p. 118.
57. Min Yŏng-ch'an later confided to Yun Ch'i-ho the following unflattering account of Mrs. Waeber: "During our journey from Nagasaki to Odessa we found Mrs. Waeber a most perverse person, fickle, arrogant and patronizing." See Yun, *Ilgi*, vol. 5, p. 97.
58. *Independent*, 23 March 1897.
59. Yun, *Ilgi*, vol. 5, p. 36.
60. Ibid., vol. 4, pp. 175–176.
61. The firm's Sino-Korean name was Sech'ang yanghaeng. Its headquarters were in Hamburg, and its main office in the Far East was in Hong Kong. The Inch'ŏn branch office was opened in 1884 with Carl Wolter as manager. See Dalchoong Kim, "Korea's Quest," p. 464.
62. *Sagu sokch'o*, p. 149.
63. *Independent*, 22 April 1897.
64. *Sagu sokch'o*, pp. 149–150. The fleet of ships that sailed between Odessa and Vladivostok was known as the Volunteer Fleet.

65. *Sagu sokch'o*, p. 150.
66. Ibid., p. 151.
67. Ibid.
68. Ibid.
69. Ibid.
70. Ibid., p. 152.
71. Ibid.
72. See Choe, *Rule of the Taewŏn'gun*, p. 95.
73. Underwood, *Underwood of Korea*, p. 236.
74. *Sagu sokch'o*, p. 152.
75. Ibid., p. 153.
76. Ibid.
77. Ibid.
78. Ibid.
79. Ibid., p. 154.
80. Ibid.
81. Ibid.
82. Ibid., p. 155.
83. Ibid., p. 156.
84. Ibid., p. 157.
85. Ibid.
86. Ibid., p. 158.
87. Ibid.
88. The Brothers is a small island group at the northern end of the Red Sea.
89. *Sagu sokch'o*, p. 160. The French engineer Ferdinand de Lesseps was responsible for the construction of the Suez Canal, which was opened on 17 November 1869.
90. Ibid., p. 161.
91. Ibid.
92. Ibid., p. 162.
93. Ibid.
94. Ibid.
95. Ibid., pp. 163–164. Min Kyŏng-sik had arrived in St. Petersburg on 15 July 1896, while Min was concluding his negotiations with Lobanov, and appears to have remained there since that time in an unofficial capacity.
96. This is an approximation of the hotel's name derived from variant *han'gŭl* versions in the text.
97. *Independent*, 29 May 1897.
98. *Sagu sokch'o*, p. 165.
99. Ibid., p. 166.
100. For the translated text of Kojong's personal letter, see appendix 3.
101. *Sagu sokch'o*, p. 167.
102. FO 228/1259, MacDonald to Jordan, 3 May 1897.
103. *Sagu sokch'o*, pp. 168–169.

104. Ibid., p. 171.
105. Ibid., p. 172.
106. Ibid., p. 173.
107. Admiral Michiel Adriaanszoon de Ruyter fought under Admiral Maarten Tromp in the Anglo-Dutch war of 1652–1654.
108. For the exact location of the Cecil Hotel, which now appears to have been incorporated into the Savoy Hotel, see K. Baedeker, *London und Umgebungen.*
109. *Sagu sokch'o,* p. 174.
110. Ibid., p. 175.
111. Ibid.
112. For the texts of Kojong's personal letter to Queen Victoria and Min's credential letter, see appendix 3.
113. Lord Robert Gascoyne-Cecil Salisbury was also the prime minister at this time.
114. *Sagu sokch'o,* p. 176.
115. Ibid.
116. Ibid., pp. 176–177.
117. *Independent,* 17 August 1897; and the *Times* (London), "Diamond Jubilee: The Jubilee Guests," 17 June 1897, p. 12, col. b.
118. *Sagu sokch'o,* p. 178.
119. Alfred Edward J. Cavendish, *Korea and the Sacred White Mountain.*
120. See Cavendish's correspondence with Lord Kimberley in MS Eng. c. 4396, fol. 16–21, 29–35, 42–56, and 77–78, held at the Department of Western Manuscripts in the Bodleian Library, Oxford.
121. *Sagu sokch'o,* p. 179.
122. Ibid.
123. Ibid.
124. Ibid., p. 180.
125. As a matter of interest, early films of this procession are held at the National Film and Television Archive, British Film Institute, London.
126. *Sagu sokch'o,* p. 180.
127. Ibid., p. 181.
128. Ibid.
129. Ibid., p. 182.
130. Ibid.
131. Ibid. Sadly, these gifts appear to have been lost as there is no record of their existence either in the Royal Collection at Buckingham Palace or at the Victoria and Albert Museum, where many such gifts were sent.
132. Ibid., p. 183.
133. Ibid., p. 184.
134. Ibid.
135. Yun, *Ilgi,* vol. 5, p. 92.
136. *Sagu sokch'o,* p. 189.
137. Yun, *Ilgi,* vol. 5, p. 77.

138. Ibid.
139. Ibid., p. 78.
140. Ibid., p. 98.
141. Boris A. Romanov, *Russia in Manchuria, 1892–1906*, p. 113.
142. *Independent*, 3 August 1897. See also *Kojong sidaesa*, vol. 4, p. 398.
143. *Independent*, 3 August 1897.
144. Yun, *Ilgi*, vol. 5, p. 79.
145. FO 405/73, part 10, Jordan to Salisbury, 4 August 1897, p. 116.
146. Yun, *Ilgi*, vol. 4, pp. 268–269.
147. For the translated texts of the three telegrams in the possession of Jordan, see appendix 4.
148. Ibid.
149. *Independent*, 16 October 1897.
150. Ibid., 13 January 1898.
151. Hwang Hyŏn, *Maech'ŏn yarok*, p. 111.
152. FO 350/3, Jordan to Bertie, 16 April 1902. The same dispatch also mentions that Min Yŏng-hwan had "been working steadily at English with a teacher for many months in the hope of going as Representative to the Coronation. Not being a member of the Imperial family, he was ineligible."
153. Bishop, *Korea and Her Neighbours*, p. 259.
154. FO 350/3, Jordan to Bertie, 16 April 1902.
155. *Parliamentary Debates*, 4th ser., vol. 51 (1897), pp. 437–438; *Times* (London), 20 July 1897, p. 6, col. f.
156. Morrison, *Correspondence*, vol. 1, p. 53, n. 2.
157. Bishop, *Korea and Her Neighbours*, p. 457.

CHAPTER 5. THE FINAL PHASE

1. *Independent*, 14 September 1897.
2. "Letter from Washington" (dated 3 August 1898) in the *Independent*, 13 September 1898.
3. *Kojong sidaesa*, vol. 4, p. 570.
4. According to Wayne Patterson, Min Yŏng-hwan had visited Hawai'i on his "way to the mainland United States," but this visit must have occurred around this time when Min was returning to Seoul from Washington. See Patterson, *Korean Frontier*, p. 9.
5. Yun, *Ilgi*, vol. 5, pp. 97–98. In this diary entry Yun relates a conversation that he had had with Min Yŏng-ch'an, who told him, "From Russia we went to London where we had a fine time. While there we received telegrams from the Seoul Court instructing my brother to work for the emperor business."
6. *Independent*, 5 October 1897.
7. *Kojong sidaesa*, vol. 4, p. 664.
8. "A New Broom Sweeps Clean (?)," *Independent*, 15 October 1898.

9. Ibid., 20 October 1898.

10. Ibid., 25 October 1898. *Kojong sidaesa,* vol. 4, p. 717.

11. Chŏng, *Taehan kyenyŏnsa,* vol. 1, p. 341.

12. *Kojong sidaesa,* vol. 4, p. 721; Kang Sŏng-jo, "Kyejŏng," p. 66.

13. Eckert et al., *Korea Old and New,* pp. 265–266. Several years earlier Min Yŏng-hwan had pointed out the serious loss of government revenue as a result of tax avoidance in his policy essay *Ch'ŏnilch'aek.*

14. See Kang Chae-ŏn, *Han'guk ŭi kŭndae sasang* [Korea's modern thought], p. 242.

15. Son In-su, "Hŭnghwa hakkyo" [Promoting reform school], vol. 25, pp. 766–767.

16. *Independent,* 26 November 1898; *Kojong sidaesa,* vol. 4, p. 724.

17. *Kojong sidaesa,* vol. 4, p. 728.

18. *Independent,* 13 December 1898.

19. Ibid., 20 December, 1998.

20. Ibid.; *Kojong sidaesa,* vol. 4, p. 740.

21. FO 350/3, Jordan to Satow, 17 January 1904. The American minister Horace N. Allen also made the comparison between Kojong and Nero. See Harrington, *God, Mammon, and the Japanese,* p. 326.

22. Yun, *Ilgi,* vol. 5, p. 193.

23. *Kojong sidaesa,* vol. 4, p. 752.

24. Ibid., p. 767.

25. At this time Min was active in the Independence Club (Tongnip hyŏphoe) and was eventually forced out of his government posts by threats from the Imperial Association (Hwangguk hyŏphoe), an association of peddlers controlled by conservative forces in the government.

26. During this period Min was awarded two medals, the *huniltŭng t'aegŭkchang* and the *taehunwi ŭihwajang.*

27. The full title is *poguk sŭngnok taebu.* It is an honorific phrase for officials of senior first rank and literally means "His Eminence Defender of the State."

28. *Soch'a,* p. 30.

29. Ibid., pp. 30–33. The nature of Min's illness is not entirely clear. From the vague references that appear in the memorials, however, Min may have suffered from some form of chronic bowel disease. According to Hwang-hyŏn, Min was also suffering from diarrhea on the night of his suicide. See Hwang Hyŏn, *Maech'ŏn yarok,* pp. 182–183.

30. *Soch'a,* p. 34.

31. Ibid., pp. 34–35.

32. Sands, *Undiplomatic Memories,* p. 229.

33. See Cho Ki-jun, "Yi Yong-ik," in *Han'guk minjok munhwa taebaekkwa sajŏn* [Encyclopedia of the culture of the Korean people], vol. 18, pp. 108–109.

34. See *Han'guk inmyŏng taesajŏn,* p. 686.

35. Hawaiian Sugar Planters' Association, Trustees, Minutes, 5 September 1902, quoted in Patterson, *Korean Frontier,* p. 31.

36. Ibid., p. 81.

37. Patterson, *Korean Frontier in America*, pp. 158–159.
38. Ibid., p. 23.
39. *Soch'a*, pp. 35–36.
40. Ibid., pp. 36–37.
41. *Ku Han'guk oegyo munsŏ*, vol. 16: *Tŏg-an* [German records], part 2, pp. 117 and 539. For an unflattering account of Prince Heinrich's visit, see Sands, *Undiplomatic Memories*, pp. 106–111.
42. *Kojong sidaesa*, vol. 6, pp. 27, 33, 44, 66, 106, and 138.
43. FO 405/148, part 5, Jordan to Lansdowne, 31 March 1904, p. 30.
44. Yun, *Ilgi*, vol. 6, p. 17.
45. Lew Young Ick, *Yi Sŭng-man ŭi samgwa kkum*, p. 30.
46. Oliver, *Syngman Rhee*, p. 75. Oliver was a long-time associate of Syngman Rhee and was one of his closest advisers during Rhee's presidency of the Republic of Korea (1948–1960). See Bruce Cumings, *Korea's Place in the Sun*, p. 214.
47. Park Il-Keun, *Anglo-American Diplomatic Materials*, p. 925.
48. Allen, *Things Korean*, p. 214.
49. Oliver, *Syngman Rhee*, p. 79.
50. Ibid., p. 81.
51. Ibid., p. 83.
52. Ibid., p. 90. For the report of the Japanese chargé d'affaires in Washington to the Japanese foreign secretary concerning the activities of Yun Pyŏng-gu and "Min Yŏng-hwan's underling *(puha)*" Syngman Rhee in Washington, see *Kojong sidaesa*, vol. 6, pp. 296–297.
53. For a concise analysis of this contentious "memorandum of agreement," see Chay, *Diplomacy of Asymmetry*, pp. 143–144.
54. *Kojong sidaesa*, vol. 6, pp. 213–331.
55. Ibid., p. 231.
56. Yun, *Ilgi*, vol. 6, pp. 135–136. Yun is referring here to Hayashi Gonsuke, the Japanese minister to Seoul, who was later to assist Itō Hirobumi in "persuading" the Korean cabinet to accept the 1905 protectorate treaty.
57. G. P. Gooch and Harold Temperley, *British Documents on the Origins of the War, 1898–1914*, vol. 4: *The Anglo-Russian Rapprochement, 1903–1907*, p. 166.
58. Quoted by MacDonald in a telegram to the Marquess of Lansdowne (FO Japan 673), ibid., p. 146.
59. Ku Dae Yeol, "A Korean Diplomat in London: Yi Haneung [Yi Han-ŭng] and Anglo-Korean Relations," p. 69.
60. "Suicide of the Korean Chargé d'Affaires," *Times* (London), 13 May 1905, p. 13, col. d.
61. See, for example, Yi T'ae-jin, ed., *Ilbon ŭi Taehan Cheguk kangjŏm: "poho choyak" esŏ "pyŏnghap choyak" kkaji* [Japan's forcible occupation of the Taehan Empire: From the "protectorate treaty" to the "annexation treaty"].
62. Translated extract from a copy of a report from von Saldern to von Bülow dated 20 November 1905 and reprinted as "Dokument Nr. 1" in *Koreana* 25 (1993): 11.

See also Michael Finch, "German Diplomatic Documents on the 1905 Japan-Korea Protectorate Treaty."

63. Finch, "German Diplomatic Documents," p. 61.

64. Burnett, ed., *Korean-American Relations,* p. 193.

65. Root to Eki Hioki, 21 December 1905, *Foreign Relations of the United States, 1905,* p. 616, in U.S. Department of State, Division of Historical Policy Research, *United States Policy regarding Korea,* p. 35. Although the Korean-American treaty was signed on 22 May 1882, it was not ratified by the U.S. president, Chester A. Arthur, until 13 February 1883, with the exchange of ratifications finally taking place at Inch'ŏn on 19 May of the same year. See Chay, *Diplomacy of Asymmetry,* pp. 54–55.

66. This account is based mainly on the *Min Ch'ungjŏnggong sillok,* pp. 195–207. In addition reference has been made to Hwang Hyŏn's account in *Maech'ŏn yarok,* pp. 182–183, and Chŏng-Kyo's account in *Taehan kyenyŏnsa,* vol. 2, pp. 198–199.

67. *Min Ch'ungjŏnggong sillok,* p. 195.

68. *Kojong sidaesa,* p. 389; *Min Ch'ungjŏnggong sillok,* pp. 195–196.

69. For the full text of these memorials, see *Soch'a,* pp. 42–43.

70. *Min Ch'ungjŏnggong sillok,* p. 196.

71. Ibid.

72. Ibid., p. 197.

73. Ibid., p. 198. See also Hwang Hyŏn, *Maech'ŏn yarok,* pp. 626–627.

74. *Min Ch'ungjŏnggong sillok,* p. 198.

75. Ibid.

76. "Japan and Korea," *Times* (London), 5 December 1905, p. 5, col. d.

77. See *Taehan maeil sinbo,* 1 December 1905, 3 December 1905, 6 December 1905, and 19 December 1905.

78. FO 371/179, Cockburn to Lansdowne, 1 December 1905.

79. Supplementary report dated 1 December 1905, in Finch, "German Diplomatic Documents," p. 59.

80. FO 371/179 Cockburn to Lansdowne 1 December 1905.

81. For evidence of the effect of Min Yŏng-hwan's suicide on the *ŭibyŏng* leadership, see Tongnip undongsa p'yŏnch'an wiwŏnhoe [Compilation committee of the history of the independence movement], ed., *Tongnip undongsa charyojip* [Collected materials on the history of the independence movement], vols. 1–3.

82. *Min Ch'ungjŏnggong sillok,* pp. 198–199.

83. Ibid., p. 199.

84. Ibid., p. 200.

85. Ibid., p. 201.

86. An official title of Silla, Koryŏ, and Chosŏn.

87. A senior fifth-rank official in the Six Ministries.

88. A four-line verse with five or seven characters in each line.

89. *Min Ch'ungjŏnggong sillok,* p. 203.

90. This account of Min's funeral is based on *Min Ch'ungjŏnggong sillok,* pp. 205–207.

Also see Michael Finch, "The Role of Min Yŏng-hwan in Korea's Protest against the Ŭlsa Treaty of Protection (1905)," pp. 70–71.

91. FO 371/179 Cockburn to Lansdowne, 28 December 1905. See also Hwang Hyŏn, *Maech'ŏn yarok*, p. 188.

92. *Taehan maeil sinbo*, 5 July 1906.

93. The approximate date provided by Hwang Hyŏn here as in many other instances in *Maech'ŏn yarok* is incorrect.

94. Hwang Hyŏn, *Maech'ŏn yarok*, p. 198. Additional accounts of the discovery of bamboo growing from Min's bloodstained clothes and the reaction of the Korean people to it, including patriotic poems, may be found in the *Taehan maeil sinbo*, 5 July 1906, 6 July 1906, 12 July 1906, 17 July 1906, 21 July 1906, 8 August 1906, and 15 August 1906.

95. *Sedo* politics refers to the dominant influence of powerful *yangban* families at court. In Kojong's reign the Min clan held that dominant position.

96. For evidence of the inspiration Min's example gave to the Righteous Army Movement (*ŭibyŏng undong*) in the wake of the protectorate treaty, see Yi Se-yŏng's testimony in Tongnip undongsa p'yŏnch'an wiwŏnhoe, ed., *Tongnip undongsa*, vol. 1: *Ŭibyŏng hangjaengsa* [The history of the resistance struggle of the righteous armies], p. 361.

APPENDIX 2. ENGLISH-LANGUAGE WORKS ON THE LATE CHOSŎN ERA

1. For a more detailed and extensive survey of both published and unpublished works of value in the study of this period, see Young Ick Lew, "The Late Yi (Chosŏn) Dynasty: 1876–1910."

2. Full citations for all the works discussed in this survey are in the Bibliography.

3. For Lee's views on Japanese "economic aggression," see Ki-baik Lee, *New History*, pp. 317–327.

APPENDIX 3. DIPLOMATIC CORRESPONDENCE AND DISPATCHES

1. All the documents in appendix 3, except Lobanov's "points in reply," have been translated from Chinese, the official written language of Korea during this period, from *Haech'ŏn ch'ubŏm*.

2. *Haech'ŏn ch'ubŏm*, pp. 135–136.

3. *Haech'ŏn ch'ubŏm*, p. 138. For the Russian text of this letter, see *Ku Han'guk oegyo munsŏ*, vol. 17: *A-an* [Russian records], part 1, p. 367.

4. *Haech'ŏn ch'ubŏm*, pp. 137–138.

5. Doc. no. 20 of the Foreign Ministry archive at St. Petersburg with Lobanov's covering letter to Witte, dated June 1896, stating that the five "points" had been "approved by his majesty," in Romanov, *Russia in Manchuria*, p. 106, n. 406.

6. "Lustrous inauguration" (1896–1897).
7. *Haech'ŏn ch'ubŏm*, p. 135.
8. Tsar Nicholas II was married to Queen Victoria's granddaughter, Alexandra.
9. *Sagu sokch'o*, p. 192.
10. Ibid.
11. Ibid., p. 193. The credential letters to the Russian and other European courts are essentially the same as this letter.

APPENDIX 4. MIN'S TELEGRAMS TO KING KOJONG ON HIS DEPARTURE FROM EUROPE IN 1897

1. FO 405/73, part 10, Jordan to Salisbury, p. 116.

Glossary

Where Chinese characters *(hancha)* for Korean personal names have not been given in the original documents, the names have been given in *han'gŭl*. Other Sino-Korean terms rendered in *han'gŭl* were originally written in *han'gŭl* rather than *hancha*.

Aegukcha Min Ch'ungjŏnggong　愛國者 閔忠正公
Ajŏng: Aden　亞丁
Amur River　黑龍江
Andong Kim clan　安東金氏
Anhyŏn　鞍峴
Annam: Vietnam　安南
An Se-jŏng　安世鼎
An T'ae-hyŏng　安台衡
Asan Bay　牙山灣
Ayŏng kijŏng　俄英記程

Beijing　北京
Bi yun ri ji　薜耘日記
bŏnji　番地

chaejŏng komun'gwan　財政顧問官
chahŏn taebu　資憲大夫
ch'amjŏng taesin　參政大臣
ch'amp'an　參判
ch'amŭi　參議
chang　丈
Chang hŭibin: Lady Chang　張禧嬪
changnye　掌禮
changnyŏng　掌令
chang ping cang　常平倉

Changsŏng　長城
Chang Sunping　長孫平
changwŏn kŭpche　壯元及第
Chang'yewŏn　掌隸院
Chang'yewŏn kyŏng　掌隸院卿
ch'anjŏng　贊政
chech'ŏng　祭廳
chehak　提學
Chemulp'o　濟物浦
chemun　祭文
chikchehak　直提學
ch'imjŏn sangnyangmun chesulgwan　寢殿上樑文製述官
Chinese Empress　清皇后
Ch'in'gunyŏng　親軍營
Ch'in'gun yŏnhaebang ŏsa　親軍沿海防御史
ch'insŏ　親書
chisa　知事
ch'obi　初妃
Cho Chung-sŏk　趙중석
Cho Chun-yŏng　趙準永
Ch'oe Che-u　崔濟愚
Ch'oe Chŏng-gŭn　崔정근
Ch'oe Ik-hyŏn　崔益鉉
Ch'oe Sŏg-in　崔錫仁

Cho Han-wŏn　趙漢遠

chohoemun　照會文

Ch'ŏlchong　哲宗

chŏlgu　絶句

Chŏlla Province　全羅道

chŏn　錢

Chŏndong　典洞

chŏng ch'ilp'um　正七品

Chŏng Chu-yŏng　鄭柱永

Chŏngdong　貞洞

Chŏngdongp'a　貞洞派

ch'onggwan　摠管

chŏnghae　丁亥

Chŏng Hang-mo　鄭학모

chong ip'um　從二品

chŏngja　正字

ch'ongjae　總裁

ch'ongjang　總長

chŏng kup'um　正九品

Chŏng Kyo　鄭喬

chŏngmun　旌門

Chongno　鐘路

ch'ongp'an　總辦

chŏng samp'um　正三品

Chong Shiheng　种世衡

Ch'ŏngsong Sim clan　靑松沈氏

Chŏng Tu-wŏn　鄭斗源

chŏn'gwŏn kongsa　全權公使

chŏn'gwŏn taesa　全權大使

Chŏng Yag-yong　丁若鏞

Chŏng'yu　丁酉

chŏnhu　前後

Chŏnhwan'guk　典圜局

Ch'ŏnilch'aek　千一策

Ch'ŏnju sirŭi　天主實義

Chŏn Pong-jun　全琫準

chŏnyŏngsa　前營使

Cho Pŏm-gu　趙範九

Cho Pyŏng-se　趙秉世

Cho Sin-hŭi　趙臣熙

Chosŏn　朝鮮

Chosŏn wangguk　朝鮮王國

ch'ot'osa　招討使

Cho Yong-man　趙容萬

Chu　楚

chuk　竹

Chungch'uwŏn　中樞院

Ch'ungjŏng　忠正

Ch'ungjŏngno　忠正路

Ch'ungju　忠州

Chŭng kwangsi　增廣試

ch'ungmun　忠文

chungsa　中使

Ch'ung Se-hyŏng　种世衡

Chun qiu　春秋

chusa　主事

Chu Sŏng-myŏn　朱錫冕

Ch'uyesa　秋禮社

Chu Yi-jŏn: John Jordan　朱邇典

chwach'amp'an　左參判

chwarang　佐郎

Dong Zhongshu　董仲舒

Dongzi　董子

Dou Nale: Sir Claude MacDonald
　竇納樂

Empress of China　清皇后

Fujian　福進

Fukuzawa Yukichi　福澤諭吉

Geng Shouchang　耿壽昌

Guan Zhong　管仲

Guigong　桂宮

haebang yŏngsa　海防營使

Haech'ŏn ch'ubŏm　海天秋帆

Haengjŏk　行蹟

Haep'yŏng Yun clan　海平尹氏

Hagiwara Moriichi　荻原森一

Haian　海岸 (海晏)

hakpu taesin　學部大臣

Hamgyŏng　咸鏡

Hamgyŏng Province　咸鏡道

Han　漢

Han Gaodi　漢高帝

han'gŭl　한글

Han Kyu-sŏl　韓圭卨

Han River　漢江

Hansŏng: Seoul　漢城

Hansŏng uyun　漢城右尹

Han Wudi　漢武帝

Hayashi Gonsuke　林權助

Hebei (Hopei)　河北

Hideyoshi Toyotomi　豊臣秀吉

Hoegyeguk　會計局

Hoemoktong　檜木洞

Hojo　戶曹

hŏnbyŏngsa ryŏnggwan　憲兵司令官

Hong Ch'ŏl-su　洪철수

Hong Kong　香港

Hong Kye-hun　洪啓薰

Hong Man-sik　洪萬植

Hongmun'gwan　弘文館

Hong Yŏng-sik　洪英植

Horimoto Reizō　堀本禮造

Hu Anding　胡安定

huang jai aimi (hwangje ŭi ŏmŏni)　皇帝 애미(皇帝의 어머니)

Huang Zunxian　黃遵憲

Hŭnghwamun　興化門

Hŭnghwa sarip hakkyo　興化私立學校

huniltŭng t'aegŭkchang　勳一等太極章

hunyu　訓諭

Hwangguk hyŏphoe　皇國協會

Hwanghae　黃海

Hwang Hyŏn　黃玹

Hwang Nam-su　黃南壽

Hwangsŏng sinmun　皇城新聞

Hwan'gu ilgi　環珎日記

Hwan'gu kŭmch'o　環珎唅艸

Hwanju　環州

Hyŏn Ch'an-bong　玄찬봉

Hyŏngjo　形曹

hyŏpp'an　協辦

Ijo　吏曹

ilbon t'ŭkp'a taesa yŏngjŏp wiwŏnjang　日本特派大使 迎接 委員長

Iltong kiyu　日東紀遊

Imjin　壬辰

Imo kullan　壬午軍亂

Imsi sŏri p'yohunwŏn　臨時署理表勳院

Im Tŏk-ki　林德基

Im Pyŏng-gwi　林炳龜

Inch'ŏn　仁川

Inhyŏn wanghu: Queen Inhyŏn　仁顯王后

Inhyŏn sŏnghu tŏkhaengnok　仁顯聖后德行錄

Inhyŏn wanghu chŏn　仁顯王后傳

injang　印章

Inoue Kaoru　井上馨

ip'um　二品

Itō Hirobumi　伊藤博文

Jiaqing　嘉慶

Jin　金

Jin　晉

jun shi　俊士

Kabinnisi: Alfred Cavendish　갑인니시

Kabo kyŏngjang　甲午更張

Kabo-Ŭlmi　甲午乙未

Kaehwadang　開化黨

kaehwa sasang　開化思想

Kaehyŏktang　改革黨

Kaesŏng　開城

kamni　監理

kamsa　監司

Kang gao　康誥

Kanghwa Island　江華島

Kang Sa-son　姜四孫

Kang Sŏng-jo　姜聖祚

Kangwŏn Province   江原道

Kangxi   康熙

Kapsin chŏngbyŏn   甲申政變

kasŏn taebu   嘉善大夫

Katsura Tarō   桂太郎

Keiō Gijyuku   慶應義塾

ki: qi   氣

Kigiguk   器機局

Kigyeguk   機械局

Kim Cho-hyŏn   金祚鉉

Kim Chung-hwan   金중환

Kim Chu-sin   金柱臣

Kim Han-jŏng   金한정

Kim Hong-jip   金弘集

Kim Hong-nyuk   金鴻陸

Kim Ki-su   金綺秀

Kim Kyu-hong   金奎弘

Kim Man-gi   金萬基

Kim Myŏng-jin   金明鎭

Kim Ok-kyun   金玉均

Kim Po-hyŏn   金輔鉉

Kim Pong-hak   金奉學

Kim Pyŏng-ok   金秉玉

Kim Sang-t'ae   金상태

Kim Sin-yŏng   金信榮

Kim T'ae-jin   金태진

Kim To-il   金道一

Kim Tŭng-nyŏn   金得鍊

Kim Yŏng-jŏk   金永迪

Kim Yong-wŏn   金鏞元

Kim Yun-hu   金允侯

Kim Yun-jŏng   金潤晶

Kim Yun-sik   金允植

King Wen   文王

Kiro sup'il   騎驢隨筆

kisa   騎士

kisaeng   妓生

Ko Ak-si (Russian official)   古樂詩

Kŏballyop'u (Russian official)   거발
   료푸

Kobu   古阜

kodosŏ   古圖書

Koguryŏ   高句麗

Kojong   高宗

Kojong sidaesa   高宗時代史

kŏmsa   檢事

kŏmsang   檢詳

Kŏmundo: Port Hamilton   巨文島

komungwan   顧問官

kŏmyŏl   檢閱

Kongjo   工曹

Kong Ming   孔明

Kŏn'guk   建國

Kŏnyang   建陽

Kŏnyang wŏnnyŏn   건양원년

Koryŏ   高麗

Ko Yŏng-gŭn   高영근

kukku   國舅

Kuksa p'yŏnch'an wiwŏnhoe   國史
   編纂委員會

kuksŏ   國書

Kŭmwiyŏng kisa   禁衛營 騎士

kŭn   斤

kunbŏp kyojŏng ch'ongjae   軍法校正
   總裁

kunbu taesin   軍部大臣

Kungnaebu   宮內府

kunjang   君長

kunjŏn   軍田

kunsu   郡守

Kuroda Kiyotaka   黑田淸隆

Kwach'ŏn   果川

kwagŏ   科擧

Kwak Ch'am-bong   郭참봉

Kwak Myŏng-jae   郭明哉

Kwanak Mountain   冠岳山

Kwangmu   光武

kwanjang   官長

kwŏn   卷

Kwŏn Chung-hyŏn   權重顯

kyebi   繼妃

Kyejŏng   桂庭

Kyerim (Silla)   鷄林

kyogwan   教官

kyŏl 結
kyŏlchŏn 結錢
kyŏm 兼
kyŏng 卿
Kyŏngbokkung 景福宮
Kyŏnggi-do 京畿道
Kyŏnghŭng 慶興
Kyŏngjong 景宗
Kyŏngju 慶州
kyŏngmusa 警務使
kyŏngni tangsang 經理堂上
Kyŏngun'gung 慶運宮
Kyŏngyŏn 經筵
Kyŏnjidong 堅志洞
kyŏnjŏn 遣尊
kyorin 交鄰
"Kyorin'guk" 『交鄰國』
Kyujanggak 奎章閣

Lei huan zhi lyue 瀛環誌略
li 理
Liao 遼
Liaodong Peninsula 遼東半島
Li Baozhen 李抱眞
Li Hongzhang 李鴻章
Li ji 禮記
li min (tax) 吏民
Liu Bei 劉備
Liuqiu (Ryūkyū) Islands 琉球
Lyu An 劉晏
Lyu xing 呂刑

Maech'ŏn yarok 梅泉野錄
manggŏn 網巾
man'guk pangmulwŏn 萬國博物院
manjang 輓章
Manminhoe 萬民會
Map'o 麻浦
Ma Xiuzhen 馬秀珍
Megata Tanetarō 目賀田種太郎
Meiji 明治
Mencius 孟子

min 緡
Min Ch'i-gu 閔致久
Min Ch'ing-do 閔稱道
Min Ch'i-rok 閔致祿
Min Chang-sik 閔章植
Min Chin-hu 閔鎭厚
Min Chin-wŏn 閔鎭遠
Min Chin-yŏng 閔鎭永
Min Chŏng-jung 閔鼎重
Min Chong-muk 閔種默
Min Ch'ung jŏnggong chinch'ungnok
 閔忠正公盡忠錄
Min Ch'ung jŏnggong sillok 閔忠正公
 實錄
Min Ch'ung jŏnggong yugo 閔忠正公
 遺稿
Ming 明
Min Kwang-hun 閔光勳
Min Kwang-sik 閔匡植
Min Kyŏm-ho 閔謙鎬
Min Kyŏng-sik 閔景植
Min Paek-sul 閔百述
Min Paek-yu 閔百裕
Min Pŏm-sik 閔範植
Min Pyŏng-gi 閔丙岐
Min Pyŏng-sŏk 閔丙奭
Min Sang-ho 閔商鎬
Min Si-jung 閔著重
Min Sim-ŏn 閔審言
Min Sŭng-ho 閔升鎬
Min T'ae-ho 閔泰鎬 (eldest son
 of Min Ch'i-gu)
Min T'ae-ho 閔台鎬 (eldest son
 of Min Ch'i-o)
Min Tan-hyŏn 閔端顯
Min Yo-su 閔樂洙
Min Yŏng-ch'an 閔泳瓚
Min Yŏng-gi 閔泳琦
Min Yŏng-hwan 閔泳煥
Min Yŏng-ik 閔泳翊
Min Yŏng-jun 閔泳駿
Min Yŏng-mok 閔泳穆

Min Yu-jung　閔維重

Miryang Pak clan　密陽朴氏

Miura Gorō　三浦梧樓

Mok Ha-jŏn: Megata (Tanetarō)
　目賀田 (種太郎)

Mok In-dŏk: P. G. von Möllendorff
　穆麟德

Mongmyŏk　木覓

mugwan　武官

mugwanjang　武官長

mudang　巫堂

Munkwa　文科

munhak　文學

Munyak　文若

Mutsuhito　睦仁

muwiyŏng　武衛營

myŏngjŏn ch'ŏngsa ch'unggwan paeg'il
　名傳青史忠貫白日

Myŏngsŏng hwanghu　明成皇后

Naemubu　內務府

Naemubusa　內務府事

naemu taesin　內務大臣

Nagasaki　長崎

Namdaemun　南大門

Namgung Ŏk　南宮檍

Nanjing　南京

Nishi Tokujirō　西德二郎

Noron (Old Doctrine)　老論

Northern Qi　北齊

No Tŭng-bi: Paul von Rauthenfeldt
　露騰飛

Ŏ Chae-yŏn　魚在淵

O Chin-sŏp　吳晋變

oemu taesin　外務大臣

Ojesa: Odessa　烏啼社

Ok Hŭi　玉姬

op'um　五品

Oryudong　梧柳洞

Owi toch'ongbu tosa　五衛都摠府
　都事

Ŏ Yun-jung　魚允中

Paekche　百濟

Paek Hak-chin　白학진

Paek Nak-chun　白樂濬

Paengmok chŏndoga　白木廛都家

Pak Che-ga　朴齊家

Pak Che-sun　朴齊純

Pak Chŏng-hŭi: Park Chung Hee
　朴正熙

Pak Chŏng-yang　朴定陽

Pak-ssi　朴氏

Pak Yong-hun　朴龍勳

Pak Yŏng-hyo　朴泳孝

p'ansa　判事

p'ansŏ　判書

P'ap'yŏng Yun clan　坡平尹氏

Penghu　澎湖

pich'ŏn huhak ham'ang sŏnsaeng
　鄙淺後學 咸仰先生

p'il　疋

"Piŏ"　『備禦』

"Piŏji chesip wal"　『備禦之第十日』

pisŏsŭng　秘書承

Pobedonosŭssep: Russian official　보베
　도노스쎕

podŏk　輔德

poguk　輔國

poguk sŭngnok taebu　輔國崇祿大夫

pŏl　閥

Prince Kong (Yi Xin)　恭親王 (突訢)

Prince Tang　成湯

Pua　負兒

Puak　浮嶽

Pua kijŏng　赴俄記程

puch'ongjae　副總裁

pu'gyori　副校理

puha　部下

pujang　副將

pujehak　副提學

Pukhan Mountain　北漢山

p'um　品

pun (p'un)　分

P'ungdŏkch'ŏn　豐德川

Pup'yŏng　富平

Pusan　釜山
puyun　府尹
P'yohunwŏn　表勳院
Pyŏlgigun　別技軍
P'yŏng'an　平安
Pyŏng'in yang'yo　丙寅洋擾
Pyŏngjo　兵曹
P'yŏngniwŏn　平理院
P'yŏngyang　平壤
Pyŏngnyŏng pŏppu　並令法部

Qi　齊
qian bu chang　千步銃
Qianlong　乾隆
Qiao　僑
Qin　秦
Qing　清

sadae　事大
sadaejuŭi　事大主義
saengwŏnsi (saengwŏn'gwa)　生員試
　(生員科)
Sagu sokch'o　使歐續草
Sahŏnbu　司憲府
sain　舍人
sakoku　鎖國
sallim　山林
sambang p'a　三房派
sa'min chohoeso　士民照會所
Samnye　參禮
Sangniguk　商理局
San guo ji　三國志
Sa P'a-a: Alexis de Speyer　斯婆兒
Sartaq　撒禮塔
Sa Tŏg-in: Evgenii Stein　師德仁
sayak　賜藥
Sech'ang yanghaeng (Meyer & Co.)
　世昌洋行
sedo　勢道
sei-Kan-ron　征韓論
Seja sigang'wŏn　世子侍講院
Shanghai　上海
she cang　社倉

Shenzong　神宗
Shi e cao zai　使俄草載
Shijing　詩經
Shimonoseki　下關
shu bang　屬邦
Shu jing　書經
Sich'algi　視察記
siho　諡號
Si-in: Sheen (British official)　시인
sijongmu kwan　侍從武官
sijongmu kwanjang　侍從武官長
Silla　新羅
Sim Hong-t'aek　沈弘澤
Sim Sang-hak　沈相學
Sim Sŭng-t'aek　沈承澤
Sin'gap'a: Singapore　新嘉坡
Sin Hŏn　申櫶
Sin Hyŏn-ju　申鉉ɥ
Sin Ing-nok　申益祿
Sinmi yangyo　辛未洋擾
sinsa yuramdan　紳士遊覽團
Sin Yong-jin　신용진
sirhak　實學
Sirhakp'a　實學派
"Sise"　『時勢』
"Siseji cheil wal"　『時勢之第一日』
Si shu ji　四述記
Sŏbinggo　西氷庫
Soch'a　疏箚
Sŏ Chae-p'il: Philip Jaisohn　徐載弼
Sŏdaemun　西大門
Sŏhak　西學
Sŏin (Westerner faction)　西人
sŏk　石
Sŏ Kwang-bŏm　徐光範
Sŏ Kyŏng-sun　徐庚淳
sŏlsŏ　說書
Song　宋
Sŏnggyun'gwan　成均館
Sŏng Ki-un　成岐運
Song Sang-do　宋相燾
Sŏnhyech'ŏng　宣惠廳
Son Hŭi-yŏng　孫熙榮

Sŏnjo　宣祖

sŏnmusa　宣撫使

Son Pyŏng-gyun　孫炳均

sŏŏl　庶孼

sŏri　胥吏

Sŏ Sang-u　徐相雨

Sŏ Sŭng-ik　徐승익

Sŏ Yu-gu　徐有榘

Sŏyu kyŏnmun　西遊見聞

sŏwŏn　書院

such'an　修撰

Such'ŏngsa　水淸社

Sui　隋

Sujimyŏn　水枝面

Sukchong　肅宗

sŭngji　承旨

Sŭngjŏng'wŏn　承政院

Sunhŭng An clan　順興安氏

Sunjong　純宗

suryŏng　守令

suwŏn　隨員

Tae Chosŏn konggwan　대조선공관

Tae Chosŏn Kŏnyang Yi Nyŏn　대조선 건양 이년

Taedong River　大洞江

t'aegŭkki　太極旗

taegyo　待敎

Taehan cheguk　大韓帝國

Taehan kyenyŏnsa　大韓季年史

Taehan maeil sinbo　大韓每日申報

taehunwi t'aegŭkchang　大勳位 太極章

taeryŏm　大斂

taesasŏng　大司成

taesin　大臣

Taewŏn'gun　大院君

Taiwan　臺灣

T'akchibu　度支部

t'akchibu taesin　度支部大臣

Takezoe Shinichiro　竹添進一郎

Talsŏng Sŏ clan　達城徐氏

Tang　唐

tangsanggwan　堂上官

Tang zhi　唐志

Tianjin　天津

Tianshan　天山

tŏgin kyosa　德人敎師

tojang　圖章

Tok Island　獨島

tokp'an　督辦

Tŏksugung　德壽宮

Tokugawa shogunate　德川幕府

Tokyo　東京

Tollyŏngbu　敦寧府

Tolmoru　돌모루

tongbusŭngji　同副承旨

tongdo sŏgi　東道西器

Tonghak　東學

tongmong kyogwan　童蒙敎官

T'ongnigimu amun　統理機務衙門

Tongnip chyŏngsin (chŏngsin)　독립 정신 (정신)

Tongnip hyŏphoe　獨立協會

Tongip sinmun　독립신문

tong 'wŏn pugi　東園副器

Tonnyŏngwŏn　敦寧院

Tonŭimun　敦義門

tosŭngji　都承旨

T'owŏlli　吐月里

Tsushima: Taemado　對馬島

tŭkchin'gwan　特進官

t'ŭngmyŏng chŏn'gwŏn kongsa　特命 全權公使

t'ŭngmyŏng chŏn'gwŏn taesa　特命 全權大使

tun tian　屯田

tzu-chu/zhi zhu/chaju　自主

ubin'gaek　右賓客

ŭibyŏng　義兵

ŭibyŏng undong　義兵運動

Ŭigŭmbu　義禁府

Ŭihwa, Prince　義和君

Ŭijŏngbu 議政府

ŭijŏngbu ch'amjŏng taesin 議政府
參政大臣

ŭijŏngbu ch'anjŏng 議政府贊政

ŭijŏng taesin 議政大臣

ŭiwŏn 義院

Ullŭng Island 鬱陵島

Ŭlsa ojŏk 乙巳五賊

Ŭlsa poho choyak 乙巳保護條約

ŭmyul 音律

Unbyŏlgyŏl: Russian official 운별결

ŭnggyo 應敎

Unyōkan 雲揚艦

uyŏngsa 右營使

uyun 右尹

Vladivostok 海參威

wakō: waegu 倭寇

Wang Anshi (Panshan) 王安石 (半山)

Wang Jichun 王之春

Wanhwagun 完和君

Waryongdong 와룡동

wijŏng ch'ŏksa 衛正斥邪

Wi P'ae: Karl Waeber 韋貝

wŏn 元

wŏnim taesin 原任大臣

Wŏnsan 元山

Wŏnsubu 元帥府

Xi 肸

Xiamen 廈門

Xian 西安

Xie Rengui 薛仁貴

Xiongnu 匈奴

xiu shi 秀士

Yamagata Aritomo 山縣有朋

yang 兩

yangban 兩班

Yangtze River 揚子江

Yantai (Chefoo) 烟臺

Yaso: Jesus 耶蘇

yedang (yejo tangsang) 禮堂 (禮曹
堂上)

Yejo 禮曹

Yemun'gwan 藝文館

yen 元

Yesig'wŏn 禮式院

Yesig'wŏnjang 禮式院長

yi cang 義倉

Yi Chae-gŭk 李載克

Yi Chae-jŏng 李在正

Yi Chi-yong 李址鎔

Yi Ch'oe-ŭng 李最應

Yi Chŏng-gun 李정군

Yi Han-ŭng 李漢應

Yi Ha-ŭng: Taewŏn'gun 李昰應

Yi Ha-yŏng 李夏榮

Yi Hŭi: Kojong 李熙

Yi Hun-jin 李훈진

Yi I 李珥

Yi jing 易經

Yi Ki 李琦

Yi Ki-p'yo 이기표

Yi Ki-yang 李基讓

Yi Kŭn-t'aek 李根澤

Yi Kwang-nin 李光麟

Yi Kwang-su 李光洙

Yi Kyŏng-ho 李경호

Yi Kyu-gyŏng 李圭景

Yi Kyu-hwan 李圭煥

Yi Mok 李牧

Yi Myŏng-bok: Kojong 李明福

Yi Pŏm-jin 李範晋

Yi Sang-ch'ŏl 李相哲

Yi Sŏn-jik 李선직

Yi Sŭng-man: Syngman Rhee 李承晩

Yi To-hŭng 李도흥

Yi U-myŏn 李愚冕

Yi Wan-sik 李完植

Yi Wan-yong 李完用

Yi yan 易言

Yi Yong-ik 李容翊

Yi Yun-yong　李允用

Yŏhŭng　驪興

Yŏhŭng Min clan　驪興閔氏

Yŏhŭng Min-ssi chokpo　驪興閔氏族譜

Yŏhŭng Min-ssi sambangp'a segye　驪興閔氏三房派世系

Yokohama　横濱

Yŏnch'usa　連秋社

Yongin County　龍仁郡

yŏngsa　營使

yŏngsang　靈床

Yŏnmu kongwŏn　鍊武公院

Yuan Shikai　袁世凱

Yubulguk: Malaya　柔佛國

Yug'yŏng kongwŏn　育英公院

Yu Kil-chun　俞吉濬

Yulgok　栗谷

Yuminwŏn (Suminwŏn)　綏民院

Yun Ch'i-ho　尹致昊

Yun Ch'i-ho ilgi　尹致昊日記

Yun Pyŏng-gu　尹炳求

Yun Ung-yŏl　尹雄烈

Yu Pyŏng-san　유병산

yusŏ　遺書

yusu　留守

Yu yan si tiao　論語四條

"yu zhe qian lu bi you yi de"　『愚者千慮必有一得』

zao shi　造土

Zhang Yinhuan　張蔭桓

Zhangyuan　張園

Zhang Zaichu　張在初

Zhao Cho　鼂錯

Zhao Chongguo　趙充國

Zhao Lie (Liu Bei)　昭烈

Zhaoxian ce lyue　朝鮮策略

Zhaoxian da ju lun　朝鮮大局論

Zhao xian guan　招賢舘

Zhejiang　浙江

Zheng　鄭

Zheng Chenggong　鄭成功

Zheng Guanying　鄭權應

Zhili　直隷

Zhou　周

Zhu Xi　朱熹

zhu za Zhaoxian zong li jiao she tong sang shi yi　駐箚朝鮮總理交涉通商事宜

Bibliography

Allen, Horace N. *Things Korean: A Collection of Sketches and Anecdotes Missionary and Diplomatic.* New York: Fleming H. Revell, 1908. Reprint, Seoul: Royal Asiatic Society, Korea Branch, 1975.

Baedeker, Karl. *London und Umgebungen: Handbuch für Reisende von K. Baedeker.* Leipzig: Verlag von Karl Baedeker, 1901.

Baker, Donald. "Sirhak Medicine: Measles, Smallpox, and Chŏng Tasan." *Korean Studies* 14 (1990): 135–166.

Ban, Byung-yool. "Korean Emigration to the Russian Far East, 1860s-1910s." *Seoul Journal of Korean Studies* 9 (1996): 115–143.

Basic Glossary of Korean Studies. Comp. Song Ki Joong et al. Seoul: Korea Foundation, 1993.

Bishop, Isabella Bird. *Korea and Her Neighbours: A Narrative of Travel with an Account of the Recent Vicissitudes and Present Position of the Country.* 2 vols. London: John Murray, 1898. Reprint, Seoul: Yonsei University Press, 1970.

Bunker, Annie Ellers. "My First Visit to Her Majesty, the Queen." *Korean Repository* 11 (1895): 374. Reprint, New York: Paragon Books, 1964.

Burnett, Scott S. *Korean-American Relations: Documents Pertaining to the Far Eastern Diplomacy of the United States.* Vol. 3: *The Period of Diminishing Influence, 1896–1905.* Honolulu: University of Hawai'i Press, 1989.

Carles, W. R. *Life in Corea.* London: Macmillan, 1888.

Cavendish, Alfred Edward J. *Korea and the Sacred White Mountain with an Account of an Ascent of the White Mountain by H. E. Gould-Adams.* London: G. Philip and Son, 1894.

Chandra, Vipan. *Imperialism, Resistance, and Reform in Late Nineteenth-Century Korea: Enlightenment and the Independence Club.* Berkeley: Institute of East Asian Studies, University of California, 1988.

———. "The Korean Enlightenment: A Re-examination." *Korea Journal* 22:5 (May 1982): 14–20.

Chay, Jongsuk. *Diplomacy of Asymmetry: Korean American Relations to 1910.* Honolulu: University of Hawai'i Press, 1990.

Cho Ki-jun. "Yi Yong-ik." In *Han'guk minjok munhwa taebaekkwa sajŏn* [Encyclopedia of the culture of the Korean people]. Vol. 18. Sŏngnam: Han'guk chŏngsin munhwa yŏn'guwŏn, 1991.

Cho Yong-man. *Aegukcha Min Ch'ung jŏnggong* [Patriot Min Yŏng-hwan]. Seoul: Kukche munhwa hyŏphoe, 1947.

Choe, Ching Young. *The Rule of the Taewŏn'gun, 1864–1873: Restoration in Yi Korea.* Cambridge: Harvard University Press, 1972.

Choi, Kyung Ju. "Korea: The Politics of Survival, 1894–1905." Ph.D. diss., University of Pennsylvania, 1978.

Chong, Chin-Sok. *The Korean Problem in Anglo-Japanese Relations 1904–1910: Ernest Thomas Bethell and His Newspapers: The* Daehan Maeil Sinbo *and the* Korea Daily News. Seoul: Nanam, 1987.

Chŏng Kyo. *Taehan kyenyŏnsa* [History of the last years of the Yi dynasty]. Hanguk-saryo ch'ongsŏ [Korean historical materials series], no. 5. Seoul: Kuksa p'yŏnch'an wiwŏnhoe, 1955.

Chun, Hae-jong. "Sino-Korean Tributary Relations in the Ch'ing Period." In *The Chinese World Order,* ed. John K. Fairbank, 90–111. Cambridge: Harvard University Press, 1968.

Conroy, Hilary. *The Japanese Seizure of Korea, 1868–1910: A Study of Realism and Idealism in International Relations.* Philadelphia: University of Pennsylvania Press, 1960.

Cook, Harold F. *Korea's 1884 Incident: Its Background and Kim Ok-kyun's Elusive Dream.* Seoul: Seoul Computer Press for the Royal Asiatic Society, Korea Branch, 1972.

Deuchler, Martina. *Confucian Gentlemen and Barbarian Envoys: The Opening of Korea, 1875–1885.* Seattle: University of Washington Press, 1977.

————. *The Confucian Transformation of Korea: A Study of Society and Ideology.* Harvard-Yenching Institute monograph series, 36. Cambridge: Harvard University Press, 1992.

Dennett, Tyler. "Roosevelt's Secret Pact with Japan." *Current History Magazine* 21 (October 1924): 15–21.

Dickins, Frederick V., and Stanley Lane-Poole. *The Life of Sir Harry Parkes.* 2 vols. London: Macmillan, 1894.

Duus, Peter. *The Abacus and the Sword: The Japanese Penetration of Korea, 1895–1910.* Berkeley: University of California Press, 1995.

Eckert, Carter J., et al. *Korea Old and New: A History.* Seoul: Ilchokak, 1990.

Fairbank, John K. *China: A New History.* Cambridge: Belknap Press of Harvard University Press, 1992.

————, ed. *The Chinese World Order: Traditional China's Foreign Relations.* Cambridge: Harvard University Press, 1968.

Fendler, Karoly. "Deutsche diplomatische Dokumente zur Gültigkeit des Protektoratsvertrags von 1905 zwischen Korea und Japan." *Koreana* 25 (1993): 8–13.

Finch, Michael. "German Diplomatic Documents on the 1905 Japan-Korea Protectorate Treaty." *Korean Studies* 20 (1996): 51–63.

————. "Min Yŏng-hwan: A Political Biography." Ph.D. diss., University of Oxford, 1998.

————. "The Role of Min Yŏng-hwan in Korea's Protest against the Ŭlsa Treaty of Protection (1905)." *Papers of the British Association of Korean Studies* 7 (2000): 61–73.

Gale, James S. *Korean Sketches.* New York: Fleming H. Revell, 1898. Reprint, Seoul: Royal Asiatic Society, Korea Branch, 1975.

Gooch, G. P., and Harold Temperley. *British Documents on the Origins of the War, 1898–1914.* Vol. 4: *The Anglo-Russian Rapprochement, 1903–1907.* London: His Majesty's Stationery Office, 1929.

Hall, Basil. *Account of a Voyage of Discovery to the West Coast of Corea and the Great Loo-Choo Island.* London: John Murray, 1818. Reprint, Seoul: Royal Asiatic Society, Korea Branch, 1975.

Hamel, Hendrik. *Hamel's Journal and a Description of the Kingdom of Korea, 1653–1666,* trans. Br. Jean-Paul Buys of Taizé. Seoul: Seoul Computer Press for the Royal Asiatic Society, Korea Branch, 1994.

Hamilton, Andrew W. "British Interest in Korea, 1866–1884." *Korea Journal* 22:1 (January 1982): 24–41.

————. "The Kŏmundo Affair." *Korea Journal* 22:6 (June 1982): 20–33.

Han, Woo-keun. *The History of Korea.* Trans. Lee Kyung-shik. Ed. Grafton K. Mintz. Seoul: Eul-Yoo, 1970.

————. "Tonghak and the Tonghak Revolt." In *Introduction to Korean Studies,* ed. Yi Hŭi-sŭng. Seoul: National Academy of Sciences, 1986.

Han'guk chŏngch'i oegyosa hakhoe, ed. *Han'guk oegyosa* I [Korean diplomatic history, vol. 1]. Seoul: Chimmundang, 1993.

Han'guk inmyŏng taesajŏn [Korean biographical dictionary]. Seoul: Sin'gu munhwasa, 1967.

Han'gŭl hakhoe, ed. *Urimal k'ŭn sajŏn* [Dictionary of the Korean language]. 4 vols. Seoul: Ŏmun'gak, 1991.

Harrington, Fred Harvey. *God, Mammon, and the Japanese: Dr. Horace N. Allen and Korean-American Relations, 1884–1905.* Madison: University of Wisconsin Press, 1944, 1966.

Henderson, Gregory. "A History of the Chŏng Dong Area and the American Embassy Residence Compound." *Transactions of the Korean Branch of the Royal Asiatic Society* 35 (1959): 1–29.

————. *Korea: The Politics of the Vortex.* Cambridge: Harvard University Press, 1968.

Hwang Hyŏn. *Maech'ŏn yarok* [Unofficial records of Mae Ch'ŏn]. In Korean. Trans. Kim Chun. Seoul: Kyomunsa, 1994.

————. *Maech'ŏn yarok* [Unofficial records of Mae Ch'ŏn, 1864–1910]. Han'guk saryo ch'ongsŏ [Korean historical materials], no. 1. Seoul: Kuksa p'yŏnch'an wiwŏnhoe, 1955.

Hwang, In K. *The Korean Reform Movement of the 1880s.* Cambridge, Mass.: Schenkman, 1978.

Independent (Seoul).

Ireland, Alleyne. *The New Korea.* Seoul: Royal Asiatic Society, Korea Branch, 1926, 1975.

Jones, Francis. "Foreign Diplomacy in Korea, 1886–1894." Ph.D. diss., Harvard University, 1935.

Kang Chae-ŏn. *Han'guk ŭi kŭndae sasang* [Korea's modern thought]. Seoul: Han'gilsa, 1985.

Kang Sŏng-jo. "Kyejŏng Min Yŏng-hwan yŏn'gu" [Study on Kyejŏng Min Yŏng-hwan]. *Kwandong sahak* 2 (September 1984): 37–70.

Kim, C. I. Eugene, and Han-Kyo Kim. *Korea and the Politics of Imperialism, 1876–1910.* Berkeley: University of California Press, 1967.

Kim, Dalchoong. "Korea's Quest for Reform and Diplomacy in the 1880s: With Special Reference to Chinese Intervention and Controls." Ph.D. diss., Fletcher School of Law and Diplomacy, 1972.

Kim, Han-Kyo, ed. *Studies on Korea: A Scholar's Guide.* Honolulu: University of Hawai'i Press, 1980.

Kim, Key-Hiuk. *The Last Phase of the East Asian World Order: Korea, Japan, and the Chinese Empire, 1860–1882.* Berkeley: University of California Press, 1980.

Kim Sŏng-kyun. "Min Yŏng-hwan." *Han'guk minjok munhwa taebaekkwa sajŏn* [Encyclopedia of the culture of the Korean people]. Vol. 8. Sŏngnam: Han'guk chŏngsin munhwa yŏn'guwŏn, 1991.

Kim, Tai-jin, ed. and trans. *A Bibliographical Guide to Traditional Korean Sources.* Seoul: Asiatic Research Center, Korea University, 1976.

Kim Wŏn-mo. *Kŭndae Han-Mi kyosŏpsa* [A modern history of Korean-American relations]. Seoul: Hongsŏngsa, 1979.

Kim, Yung Chung. "Great Britain and Korea, 1883–1887." Ph.D. diss., Indiana University, 1964.

Kiro sup'il [Biographical essays]. Comp. Song Sang-do. Han'guk saryo ch'ongsŏ [Korean historical materials], no. 2. Seoul: Kuksa p'yŏnch'an wiwŏnhoe, 1955.

Ko Pyŏng-ik. "Nohwang taegwansike ŭi sahaenggwa hanno kyosŏp" [The Russo-Korean negotiations on the occasion of the coronation of Nicholas II in 1896]. *Yŏksa hakpo* [Korean historical review] 28 (1965): 41–69.

Kojong sidaesa [History of the Kojong era]. 6 vols. Seoul: Kuksa p'yŏnch'an wiwŏnhoe, 1966–1972.

Kojong sillok [The annals of King Kojong]. In *Chosŏn wangjo sillok* [Annals of the Chosŏn dynasty]. Seoul: Kuksa p'yŏnch'an wiwŏnhoe, 1955–1958.

Ku, Dae Yeol. "A Korean Diplomat in London: Yi Haneung and Anglo-Korean Relations." In *Korean-British Relations: Yesterday, Today, and Tomorrow,* ed. Chonghwa Chung and J. E. Hoare. Seoul: Korean-British Society, 1984.

Ku Han'guk oegyo munsŏ [Diplomatic documents of the late Yi dynasty]. 22 vols. Comp. Asiatic Research Center, Korea University. Seoul: Asiatic Research Center of Korea University, 1965–1970.

Kwŏn, Moo-soo. "British Policy towards Korea, 1882–1910." Ph.D. diss., University of Sheffield, 1979.

Ledyard, Gary. *The Dutch Come to Korea: An Account of the Life of the First Westerners in Korea (1653–1666)*. Seoul: Seoul Computer Press for the Royal Asiatic Society, Korean Branch, 1971.

Lee, Ki-baik. *A New History of Korea*. Trans. Edward W. Wagner with Edward J. Shultz. Seoul: Ilchokak, 1984.

Lee, Peter H. *Sourcebook of Korean Civilization*. Vol. 2: *From the Seventeenth Century to the Modern Period*. New York: Columbia University Press, 1996.

Lee, Sun-keun. "Some Lesser Known Facts about Taewongun and His Foreign Policy." *Transactions of the Korea Branch of the Royal Asiatic Society* 39 (December 1962): 23–46.

Lee, Yur-Bok. *West Goes East: Paul Georg von Möllendorff and Great Power Imperialism in Late Yi Korea*. Honolulu: University of Hawai'i Press, 1988.

Lensen, George Alexander. *Balance of Intrigue: International Rivalry in Korea and Manchuria, 1884–1899*. 2 vols. Tallahassee: University of Florida Press, 1982.

———, comp. *Russian Diplomatic and Consular Officials in East Asia: A Handbook of the Representatives of Tsarist Russia and the Provisional Government in China, Japan, and Korea from 1858 to 1924 and of Soviet Representatives in Japan from 1925 to 1968, Compiled on the Basis of Russian, Japanese, and Chinese Sources with a Historical Introduction*. Tokyo; Tallahasse, Fla.: Sophia University in cooperation with the Diplomatic Press, 1968.

Leuteritz, Karl. "Auf der Spur im politischen Archiv." *Koreana* 25 (1993): 13–16.

Lew, Young Ick. "American Advisers in Korea, 1885–1894: Anatomy of Failure." In *The United States and Korea: American-Korean Relations, 1866–1976*, ed. Andrew Nahm, pp. 64–90. Kalamazoo: Western Michigan University Press, 1979.

———. "An Analysis of the Reform Documents of the Kabo Reform Movement, 1894." *Journal of Social Sciences and Humanities* 40 (December 1974): 29–83.

———. "The Conservative Character of the 1894 Tonghak Uprising." *Journal of Korean Studies* 7 (1990): 149–180.

———. "Korean-Japanese Politics behind the Kabo-Ŭlmi Reform Movement, 1894 to 1896." *Journal of Korean Studies* 3 (1981): 39–81.

———. "The Late Yi (Chosŏn) Dynasty: 1876–1910. In *Studies on Korea: A Scholar's Guide*. Honolulu: University of Hawai'i Press, 1980.

———. "Minister Inoue Kaoru and the Japanese Reform Attempts in Korea during the Sino-Japanese War, 1894–1895." *Journal of Asiatic Studies* 27:2 (1984): 145–186.

———. "The Reform Efforts and Ideas of Pak Yŏng-hyo, 1894–1895." *Korean Studies* 1 (1976–1977): 21–61.

———. *Yi Sŭng-man ŭi samgwa kkum: The Life and Dreams of Syngman Rhee (1875–1965): Prior to His Assumption of Presidency in 1948*. Seoul: Joong Ang Ilbosa, 1996.

———. "Yu Kil-chun." In *Han'guk minjok munhwa taebaekkwa sajŏn* [Encyclopedia of the culture of the Korean people]. Vol. 16. Sŏngnam: Han'guk chŏngsin munhwa yŏn'guwŏn, 1991.

———. "Yüan Shih-k'ai's Residency and the Korean Enlightenment Movement (1885–1894)." *Journal of Korean Studies* 5 (1984): 63–107.

Lone, Stewart, and Gavan McCormack. *Korea since 1850*. Melbourne: Longman Cheshire, 1993.

Lord Kimberley's Letters, MS Eng. c. 4396. Bodleian Library, University of Oxford.

MacNamara, Dennis L. "Imperial Expansion and Nationalist Resistance: Japan in Korea, 1876–1910." Ph.D. diss., Harvard University, 1983.

Malozemoff, Andrew. *Russian Far Eastern Policy, 1881–1904: With Special Emphasis on the Causes of the Russo-Japanese War*. Berkeley: University of California Press, 1958. Reprint, New York: Octagon Books, 1977.

McCune, George M., and John A. Harrison, ed. *Korean-American Relations: Documents Pertaining to the Far Eastern Diplomacy of the United States*. Vol. 1: *The Initial Period, 1883–1886*. Berkeley and Los Angeles: University of California Press, 1951.

McGrane, George A. *Korea's Tragic Hours: The Closing Years of the Yi Dynasty*. Ed. Harold F. Cook and Alan M. MacDougall. Seoul: Taewon, 1973.

McKenzie, Frederick A. *Korea's Fight for Freedom*. New York: Fleming H. Revell, 1920. Reprint, Seoul: Yonsei University Press, 1975.

———. *The Tragedy of Korea*. London: Hodder and Stoughton, 1908.

Min Yŏng-hwan. *"Ayŏng kijŏng"* [Record of a journey to Russia and Britain]. MS. Sogang University, Seoul.

———. *Haech'ŏn ch'ubŏm* [Sea, sky, autumn voyage]. Seoul: Ŭlyu munhwasa, 1950.

———. *Min Ch'ungjŏnggong yugo* [The posthumous works of Prince Min]. Seoul: Kuksa p'yŏnch'an wiwŏnhoe, 1971.

Morrison, G. E. *The Correspondence of G. E. Morrison*, ed. Lo Hui-Min. 2 vols. Cambridge: Cambridge University Press, 1976.

Morse, Hosea B. *The International Relations of the Chinese Empire*. 3 vols. London and New York: Longmans and Green, 1910–1918.

Nahm, Andrew C. "Korea and Tsarist Russia: Russian Interests, Policy, and Involvement in Korea, 1884–1904." *Korea Journal* 22:6 (June 1982): 4–19.

———. "Reaction and Response to the Opening of Korea, 1876–1884." In *Korea's Response to the West*, ed. Yung-Hwan Jo. Kalamazoo, Mich.: Korea Research and Publications, 1971.

Nelson, M. Frederick. *Korea and the Old Orders in Eastern Asia*. Baton Rouge: Louisiana State University Press, 1945. Reprint, New York: Russell and Russell, 1967.

Oliver, Robert T. *Syngman Rhee: The Man behind the Myth*. New York: Dodd Mead, 1954.

Paik, Lak-Geoon George (Paek Nak-chun). *The History of Protestant Missions in Korea, 1832–1910*. P'yŏngyang: Union Christian College Press, 1929. Reprint, Seoul: Yonsei University Press, 1987.

Pak, M. N., with Wayne Patterson. "Russian Policy toward Korea before and during the Sino-Japanese War of 1894–1895." *Journal of Korean Studies* 5 (1984): 109–119.

Palais, James. *Politics and Policy in Traditional Korea*. Cambridge: Harvard University Press, 1975.

Palmer, Spencer J., ed. *Korean-American Relations: Documents pertaining to the Far Eastern Diplomacy of the United States*. Vol. 2: *The Period of Growing Influence, 1887–1895*. Berkeley and Los Angeles: University of California Press, 1963.

Park, Il-Keun. *Anglo-American Diplomatic Materials relating to Korea, 1866–1886*. Seoul: Shinmundang, 1982.

Patterson, Wayne. *The Korean Frontier in America: Immigration to Hawaii, 1896–1910*. Honolulu: University of Hawaiʻi Press, 1988.

Reischauer, Edwin O., and John K. Fairbank. *East Asia: The Great Tradition*. Boston: Houghton Mifflin, 1960.

Rhee, Syngman (Yi Sŭng-man). *The Spirit of Independence: A Primer of Korean Modernization and Reform,* trans. Han-Kyo Kim. Honolulu: University of Hawaiʻi Press and the Institute for Modern Korean Studies, Yonsei University, 2001.

Rockhill, William W., ed. *Treaties and Conventions with or concerning China and Korea, 1894–1904: Together with Various State Papers and Documents Affecting Foreign Interests*. Washington, D.C.: Government Printing Office, 1904.

Romanov, Boris A. *Russia in Manchuria, 1892–1906*. Trans. Susan Wilbur Jones. Ann Arbor, Mich.: Published for the American Council of Learned Societies by J. W. Edwards, 1952.

Sahoe kwahagwŏn minjok kojŏn yŏn'guso, ed. *Lijo sillok* [Annals of the Yi Chosŏn dynasty]. P'yŏngyang: Sahoe kwahak ch'ulp'ansa, 1991.

Sands, William Franklin. *Undiplomatic Memories*. New York: Whittlesey House, 1930. Reprint, Seoul: Kyung-In, 1975.

Satow, Ernest Mason, Sir. *Korea and Manchuria between Russia and Japan, 1895–1904: The Observations of Sir Ernest Satow, British Minister Plenipotentiary to Japan (1895–1900) and China (1900–1906)*. Selected and edited, with a historical introduction, by George Alexander Lensen. Tokyo; Tallahassee, Fla.: Sophia University in cooperation with the Diplomatic Press, 1966, 1968.

Setton, Mark. *Chŏng Yagyong: Korea's Challenge to Orthodox Neo-Confucianism*. Albany: State University of New York Press, 1997.

Sŏ Kŏn-ik. "Min Yŏng-hwan." In *Han'guk inmul taegye* [Korean biographical sketches]. Vol. 6: *Kŭndaeŭi inmul 1* [Modern personages], ed. Pak Sang-nyŏn. Seoul: Pak'usa, 1972.

Sohn, Pow-key. "The Opening of Korea: A Conflict of Traditions." *Transactions of the Korea Branch of the Royal Asiatic Society* 36 (April 1960): 101–128.

Son In-su. "Hŭnghwa hakkyo" [Promoting reform school]. *Han'guk minjok munhwa taebaekkwa sajŏn* [Encyclopedia of the culture of the Korean people]. Vol. 25. Sŏngnam: Han'guk chŏngsin munhwa yŏn'guwŏn, 1991.

Song Sang-do, comp. *Kiro sup'il* [Biographical essays]. Han'guk ch'ongsŏ [Korean historical materials series], no. 2. Seoul: Kuksa p'yŏnch'an wiwŏnhoe, 1955.

Story, Douglas. *To-morrow in the East*. London: Chapman and Hall, 1907.

Sunyŏl chŏngsin sŏnyanghoe, ed. *Tongguk hyŏlsa* [Biographies of Korean patriots]. Seoul: Han'guk munhwasa, 1955.

Swartout, Robert R., Jr. "Cultural Conflict and Gunboat Diplomacy: The Development of the 1871 Korean-American Incident." *Journal of Social Sciences and Humanities* 43 (June 1976): 117–169.

———. *Mandarins, Gunboats, and Power Politics: Owen Nickerson Denny and the International Rivalries in Korea.* Honolulu: University of Hawai'i Press, 1980.

Synn, Seung Kwon. "Korean-Japanese Relations, 1894–1904 (I)." *Korea Journal* 21:2 (February 1981): 12–25.

———. "Korean-Japanese Relations, 1894–1904 (II)." *Korea Journal* 21:3 (March 1981): 4–20.

———. "Russian Policy toward Korea, 1894–1895." *Korea Journal* 21:11 (November 1981): 47–57.

———. "The Russo-Korean Relations in the 1880s." *Korea Journal* 20:9 (September 1980): 26–39.

Taehan maeil sinbo (Seoul).

Times (London).

Tongnip sinmun (Seoul).

Tongnip undongsa p'yŏnch'an wiwŏnhoe [Compilation committee of the history of the independence movement], ed. *Tongnip undongsa charyojip* [Collected materials on the history of the independence movement]. Vols. 1–3. Seoul: Tongnip yugongsa saŏpkigŭm unyong wiwŏnhoe, 1971.

Underwood, Lillias Horton. *Fifteen Years among the Top-knots or Life in Korea.* Boston: American Tract Society, 1904. Reprint, Seoul: Seoul Computer Press for the Royal Asiatic Society, Korea Branch, 1987.

———. *Underwood of Korea, Being an Intimate Record of the Life and Work of the Rev. H. G. Underwood, D.D., LL.D., for Thirty-one Years a Missionary of the Presbyterian Board in Korea.* New York: Fleming H. Revell, 1918. Reprint, Seoul: Yonsei University Press, 1983.

United Kingdom. *Parliamentary Debates,* 4th ser., vol. 51 (1897).

———. Public Record Office (PRO). FO 350. Sir John Newell Jordan's correspondence with the Foreign Office.

———. PRO. FO 371. General correspondence: Political from 1906.

———. PRO. FO 405. Foreign Office Confidential Print 1897. Further correspondence respecting the Affairs of Corea, 1897.

———. PRO. FO 228. Foreign Office Embassy and Consular Archives. China, Vol. 1, 1834–1930.

United States. Department of State. Division of Historical Policy Research. *United States Policy regarding Korea, 1834–1950.* Pt. 1 (1834–1941), pt. 2 (1941–1945), pt. 3 (December 1945–June 1950). Ed. Institute of Asian Culture Studies. Ch'unch'ŏn: Hallym University Press, 1987.

Weems, Clarence N. "Reformist Thought in the Independence Program (1896–1898)." In *Korea's Response to the West,* ed. Yung-Hwan Jo. Kalamazoo, Mich.: Korea Research and Publications, 1971.

Wells, Kenneth M. *New God, New Nation: Protestants and Self-Reconstruction Nationalism in Korea, 1867–1937*. Honolulu: University of Hawai'i Press, 1990.

Witte, S. I. *The Memoirs of Count Witte*, ed. and trans. Abraham Yarmolinsky. London: Heinemann, 1921.

Yi Hyŏn-chong. *Tongyang yŏnp'yo: kaejŏng chŭngbop'an* [East Asian chronology: Revised and enlarged edition]. Seoul: T'amgudang, 1992.

Yi Ki-baek. *Han'guksa sillon* [A new history of Korea]. Seoul: Ilchogak, 1990.

Yi Kwang-nin. *Han'guksa kangjwa 5: k'ŭndae p'yŏn* [Korean history course, vol. 5: Modern period]. Seoul: Ilchogak, 1981.

Yi Min-wŏn. "A'gwan p'ach'ŏn chŏnhu ŭi hanno kwangye: 1895–1898" [Korean-Russian relations around the time of Kojong's flight to the Russian legation]. Ph.D. diss., Han'guk chŏngsin munhwa yŏn'guwŏn [Academy of Korean Studies], 1993.

Yi Sang-ch'an. "1896 nyŏn ŭibyŏng undong ŭi chŏngch'ijŏk sŏnggyŏk" [The political characteristics of the "Righteous Army Movement" of 1896]. Ph.D. diss., Seoul National University, 1996.

Yi Sŏn-gŭn. *Taehan'guksa* [History of Korea]. 12 vols. Seoul: Sint'aeyangsa, 1973.

Yi T'ae-jin, ed. *Ilbon ŭi Taehan Cheguk kangjŏm: "poho choyak" esŏ "pyŏnghap choyak" kkaji* [Japan's forcible occupation of the Taehan Empire: From the "protectorate treaty" to the "annexation treaty"]. Seoul: Kkach'i, 1995.

Yu Yŏng-nyŏl. "Yun Ch'i-ho." In *Han'guk minjok munhwa taebaekkwa sajŏn* [Encyclopedia of the culture of the Korean people]. Vol. 17. Sŏngnam: Han'guk chŏngsin munhwa yŏn'guwŏn, 1991.

Yun Ch'i-ho. *Yun Ch'i-ho ilgi* [Diary of Yun Ch'i-ho]. 6 vols. Seoul: Kuksa p'yŏnch'an wiwŏnhoe, 1973–1976.

Index

About the Author

Educated at the University of Cambridge and Yonsei University, Michael Finch received his D.Phil. in Korean history from the University of Oxford in 1999. A former visiting professor of Korean history at Humboldt University of Berlin, he is currently visiting assistant professor of Korean studies at Keimyung University and associate editor of *Acta Koreana*. He has been a contributing translator for the Academy of Korean Studies' *Encyclopedia of Korean Culture* and anthologies of modern Korean literature sponsored by Cornell and Harvard universities. He has also published several articles on modern Korean history.